David Mitchell is a comedian, actor, writer and the polysyllabic member of Mitchell and Webb. He won BAFTAs for *Peep Show* and *That Mitchell and Webb Look*, and has also starred in *Jam and Jerusalem*, *The Bleak Old Shop of Stuff* and *Ambassadors*. He writes for the *Observer*, chairs *The Unbelievable Truth*, co-hosts *10 O'Clock Live*, is a team captain on *Would I Lie To You?* and has been in two films, neither of which made a profit.

DAVID MITCHELL

THINKING ABOUT IT ONLY MAKES IT WORSE

AND OTHER LESSONS FROM MODERN LIFE

First published in 2014
by Guardian Books, Kings Place, 90 York Way, London, N1 9GU
and Faber & Faber Ltd, Bloomsbury House,
74–77 Great Russell Street, London, WC1B 3DA

Typeset by seagulls.net
Printed in the UK by CPI Group (UK) Ltd, Croydon, CR0 4YY

A CIP record for this book
is available from the British Library

ISBN 978-1-783-35069-8

To Mum and Dad

CONTENTS

*With less money around, people have to make their own
entertainment these days, which has been a boon for those who
enjoy the sensation of righteous anger.*

*Go on! Enjoy it while it lasts! After all, websites are only really
entertaining when you're supposed to be working. And just look at
the wonders of the old media's Jurassic ecosystem: from daytime TV
to* Downton Abbey, *from* Harry Potter *to* Homer Simpson, *from*
Lewis *to* Endeavour, *there's never been more to doze off in front of.*

*To my mind, corporations are like giant robots which have
been programmed to make money at all costs. So they're quite
dangerous to live around, but at the same time there's no more
point in getting cross with them than there is in blaming a satnav
for never changing the oil.*

4 Saying You Want to Make a Difference Makes No Difference

Politicians will go to unreasonable lengths in order to seem reasonable. It's almost enough to make you thirst for a refreshing tyrant. Warning: this section contains an eye-wateringly inaccurate prediction of the outcome of the 2010 general election.

5 It's Not Just Poets That Need Abstract Nouns

Rates of religious observance may be falling, but that doesn't mean that our society is any less reliant on strange and intangible concepts than the most obsessive ghost-, chicken entrail- or tree spirit-worshipping tribe. What do raising capital and raising awareness have in common? You don't need a forklift truck to do either.

6 What You Don't Know Can't Hurt You

In depressed moments, I often console myself with the thought that I WILL NEVER HAVE TO GO BACK TO SCHOOL. I wonder what thoughts teachers turn to for comfort in such moments? This section discusses many of the crazy educational theories that the majority of us who delight in never having to set foot in a classroom again are free to enjoy.

7 A Sorry State is Nothing to Apologise For

An update on the condition of the British Empire. I fear it may have peaked.

INTRODUCTION

When I started writing regularly for the *Observer* in 2008, a new world era began. It was a coincidence, I hasten to add. Despite patches of enthusiasm on Twitter and, on one occasion, a mention on Andrew Marr's TV show, my weekly attempt at a public moan with jokes hasn't quite ushered in a new age. It sometimes comes quite high up the "Most Viewed" list on Comment Is Free (when people have hated it, that is – not so much when they haven't), but in historical terms it's no fall of Constantinople.

But, looking back now, with the tiny amount of hindsight that remaining alive for six more years generates, I'm pretty sure that 2008 marked the end of, and the beginning of, an era.

You've always got to have an era on the go, you see. Once one era ends, another begins automatically. In fact, the first one probably ends because the second one has begun and totally stolen its thunder. But it's very much a "The King is dead – long live the King" kind of set-up. You're absolutely not allowed a calm era-less interregnum of unremarkable pottering – a couple of years when the global situation is "between projects", like an ageing celebrity who can pick and choose thanks to sky-high credibility and accumulated property equity.

With history, the moment the Twenties stop roaring, the Depression starts slumping and then the Nazis start rising and then the world starts warring and then the instant, the very *instant*, the war ends, it's post-war. Can you believe it? Not a millisecond

1

that isn't either the war or the post-war era. It's fucking relentless (to paraphrase Herodotus) but it's the only system we've got.

Of course, some era changeovers are harder to pinpoint than the end of a war. The one I'm talking about was like that. No new toothy smiling suit had been swept to office, no nationally beloved beauty had been chased to death by photographers, no building had been blown up or completed, no new technology suddenly launched or discredited, no disease gone pandemic or been cured. But, as when a premiership football team runs on in front of an away crowd, and opposition fans reach vindictively for their 2ps, change was palpably in the air.

In fact, this change was all about money. Money may not bring you happiness but, if there's one thing the credit crunch of 2008 showed, no money brings a hell of a lot of grief. And that's what we were at risk of experiencing that autumn: no money. Anywhere. At all. The sudden absence of money – its collapse as a human construct.

Money isn't really anything, after all. Humans don't need money – we need food and shelter. Living the sophisticated life of the westerner, it appears that you need money in order to obtain food and shelter. But that's not actually, fundamentally, true. Food and shelter come from farming and building. The fact that the products of those activities are swappable for money is just a convention. There's nothing about the money itself that anyone actually requires.

Even when it was backed by gold or, before that, made of gold, it still didn't have intrinsic value. No one needs gold (I know it's in microchips but that's a side issue – King Midas didn't go all funny in the hope of reinvigorating the Lydian tech sector). It's just shiny and it doesn't rust, so it was convenient to develop the convention whereby little roundels of it were exchangeable for items of value. The subsequent convention that numbers on a computer screen were equally exchangeable for such items was even more convenient, but also even more dependent on everyone's confidence in and adherence to the convention.

What started in the mists of early history as a useful aid to barter had become, by 2008, a vital element of the world as we knew it. So vital that many people who worked in the financial sector seemed to have completely forgotten that money, and credit, were just a convention – and had begun to believe that they were something solid: an actual, tangible, useful thing. Something invulnerable, something which undeniably exists.

And so the piss-taking began.

And, by "piss-taking", I mean casino banking: the buying and selling of the intrinsically worthless. The immoral exploitation of the market in denial of its fundamental purpose – which was supposed to be to facilitate trade, to bring resources to enterprise, not to pass round empty financial concepts before anyone realises that they have no actual value, just a transitory and astronomical price. A system of money-making which involves no real wealth-creation at all – nothing made, no useful service provided, nothing done which remotely conforms to the ancient and fundamental laws of "what you should get paid for".

And by "began", I mean "intensified". I may be a pitifully naive financial analyst but I'm not quite a shit enough historian to think that any of this market immorality was unprecedented. Dishonest but somehow legal bucks have probably been made since a microsecond after the invention of the buck. I know none of this was new – but the scale of the activity certainly was. As was the terrifying computer-driven speed at which it was practised.

And I assume it's obvious what I mean by "And so the".

The result of all this, as we know, was the collapse of many financial institutions and, subsequently, economies, coupled with expensive efforts to prop others up using taxpayers' – ie ordinary people's – money. The climax of the crisis, for Britain at least, was a weekend in October 2008 when, had the Royal Bank of

Scotland not been bailed out by the government, its cashpoints wouldn't have been working on Monday morning. And not for the usual reasons of being smashed in and/or covered in sick because of all the stag dos we indulge in to sustain turnover in our hospitality sector. This time it would be because the bank had run out of money, and also of people to call to borrow money. That terrifying eventuality would have led to a run on other, healthier banks – and no bank in history, however prudent, has ever been able to return all of its investors' money at once.

That was the moment when money nearly broke. It became clear that all the numbers on screens didn't add up any more. Suddenly the value that these institutions were claiming to represent had to be found, and they didn't have it. So we, the normal people, would have to – and I shudder at the injustice of the phrase – *give it to them*.

Never has the weirdness of what really money is – what a service economy is, how distant we've become from our basic survival needs, and yet how pervasive those needs remain – been more evident. "Why can't we just pretend the money is still there?" we thought. "Send the number from the screen to the electricity people to increase the number on their screen and they'll give us the power to keep the screen on, won't they?"

Sadly, it turned out that's what had already been happening for quite a while. The global fiscal Wile E. Coyote had long since run off the edge of the cliff and had been scampering ineffectually in mid-air for some time. But now the period during which he has yet to start falling, because he still hasn't noticed the absence of solid ground beneath him, was ending. We'd collectively looked down. We were caught in the beat of stillness, the panicked look to camera, that precedes the plummet.

Money didn't collapse. Credit became terrifyingly scarce – institutions which a month earlier were betting billions on three-legged horses were suddenly withdrawing loans from solvent businesses – but the basic convention of currency just about held. That was probably for the best.

But the eye-watering injustice of the bailout – the disconnect between guilt and punishment – soured the national mood. We were angry. But we were also frightened. We were struck simultaneously by sudden and severe national poverty, after a decade of unthinking prosperity, and with something beyond poverty: a deep and deracinating sense that our previous wealth had been an illusion. The expensive frothy coffees of the early 2000s retrospectively turned to ashes in our mouths.

And, while the economic downturn brought on by the crisis was felt all over the world, it did not hurt everyone equally. Of course, that's always the case, but the nature of that inequality had changed. Britain remained among the richest nations on Earth but, for the first time anyone could remember, countries like ours didn't get off lightest. True, there were still plenty of people unimaginably less fortunate than ourselves. But now there was also the unsettling emergence of people who might be, or come to be, *more* fortunate.

The fast-growing economies of countries such as India, Brazil and, most unnerving of all, China, barely suffered a blip, while ours dropped off a cliff, still pointlessly clutching its Acme Giant Credit Magnet. For the first time since the cold war, the west, the world's dominant politico-economic force for 500 years, seemed fallible and fragile. The frailty of money and the financial services industry having been laid bare, we were forced to contemplate where real wealth comes from: making stuff and selling it. And, reality TV and artisanal cheese aside, more and more of that manufacturing was being done by the Chinese.

The Blair-era dream of remaining rich and becoming richer, of driving our economy purely by providing services and dining out regularly, with maybe a bit of web design and party planning thrown in to keep us honest, was suddenly revealed as foolish. We felt at once deeply stupid and deeply resentful. We despised one another, and of course the government, for the mistakes that had been made, but were also nostalgic for the prosperous feeling we'd had while it was happening.

I realise the shine had been taken off New Labour long before 2008. That war in Iraq went down like a cup of cold piss, for a start. But I'm not sure that really upset Britain as much as we're apt to think. The war made Britons shake their heads, but the credit crunch had us banging them against walls.

You only have to look at Blair and Brown's relative electoral fortunes: Blair won a general election after getting the country involved in an unpopular and unsuccessful war, a war of which he remained unashamedly in favour; yet Brown lost one after a global economic downturn which he admittedly failed to avert, but for which he certainly wasn't primarily responsible.

It turns out that it's not the morality or otherwise of our foreign policy that predominantly affects the national mood, it's money. We might not have thought we were money-obsessed, but then we probably don't think we're oxygen-obsessed. But you certainly get to thinking about it if someone takes it away.

The horrible shock of 2008, much more than any horrible shocks we allowed our military to impose abroad, changed our national personality. It's as if Britain was a sprightly and twinkly pensioner who then, in the autumn of 2008, had a serious fall. It survived but has never been quite the same – it's more timorous and judgmental, envious and angry. As a nation, we've lost confidence and creativity, and we're readier to blame each other and slower to laugh at ourselves.

This is the glum conclusion I've come to from looking back over all the columns I've written. I didn't think any of this when I started writing them six years ago. I was just glad things were going wrong because that makes it easier to write jokes – utopia is a living hell for satirical columnists. I probably fretted about what it would be like if there was a fiscal apocalypse and we were reduced to growing our own food – satirical columnists also have a rough ride in subsistence economies. But I only thought about it in economic terms: how bad and how long would the crisis be?

I thought about it a lot. Most people thought about it a lot. And thinking was what had precipitated the crisis in the first place. It wasn't foolish and feverish speculative investments that caused the crash – it was thinking about those investments. It was realising they were foolish and ultimately valueless. As with Wile E., it was the realisation, not gravity, that made us plummet.

It had to happen at some point, I suppose. The realisation was inevitable, and so the plunge was too; it could have happened later and been worse. But it's hard not to blame all that thinking, just as we blame, rather than thank, the surveyor who finds dry rot.

And having sparked the whole thing off with thinking, we couldn't get out of the habit. "What does this crisis mean? How unfair is it? Where does this leave Britain now? Is anything certain any more?" We thought and thought and thought. We locked ourselves into the mindset of emergency. It became like Queen Victoria's mourning: unhelpful, self-indulgent, but very difficult to argue against or snap out of.

"I hope you know there's a lot of massive shit going down!" became the country's perpetual Facebook status. Being cheerful or optimistic just allowed others to say you didn't realise how bad things were – and to imply that therefore you, as one who'd got off lightly, were part of the problem, that you were on the wrong side of the casino-banker/thankless-nurse national divide.

As a result, this new era has been enormously and relentlessly recriminatory and angry. What started off as righteous fury at the investment banker community for their incompetence and amorality has spread to almost every aspect of public life. First, Russell Brand and Jonathan Ross's misjudged Radio 2 broadcast invoked a storm of rage, directed not just at them but against all broadcasters and celebrities. Then MPs were pilloried for fiddling their expenses in a way that didn't just lead us to tweak how parliamentarians were financed, but to dispute the honesty of our entire political class. That group subsequently had its revenge on the pesky scrutinising newspapers when the illegal hacking of Milly Dowler's mobile phone provided the opportunity to question the whole basis of a free press. Newspapers, politicians, the BBC and celebrities have all regularly been put through the mill. It's as if the whole culture is screaming: "Everything feels all wrong!"

How much of this is justified by current circumstances? How much of it is justified by the unsatisfactory nature of the human condition? How much is self-perpetuating and self-indulgent? When the current coalition government took office, it did so stating explicitly that the Conservatives and Liberal Democrats had come together in statesmanlike response to the emergency the country was facing. This is one of the few of that administration's assertions to be left largely unquestioned. We miserably and crossly accepted the premise that everything was deeply and unprecedentedly screwed. By then, that feeling had already dominated our contemplations for the best part of two years.

I think this pervading fury and sense of crisis has reached crisis levels. Which is ironic, if you think about it (which I don't recommend). I reckon there actually is a good reason to be angry and deeply concerned, and that's the pervasiveness of anger and deep concern about everything else. I think it imperative that everyone calm down. I think a loud emergency "Chill out!" alarm should screech from every rooftop till everyone relaxes. I told you thinking didn't help.

If we could just let our angrily folded arms drop to our sides for one minute, we'd feel so much better. Most of us, anyway – to some, it would feel like failure or defeat.

I was particularly savagely slated on the *Guardian* website and Twitter for a column I wrote in March 2012 (it's not included here because there weren't enough jokes in it – but that wasn't what got people's goat) in which I argued against trade unionist Len McCluskey's assertion that "The idea the world should arrive in London and have these wonderful Olympic Games as though everything is nice and rosy in the garden is unthinkable." I reckoned that, despite the country's problems, we weren't undergoing a calamity sufficiently grave to call off the world's premier sporting event, something that had previously been cancelled only during world wars. I wasn't saying things were fine; I was saying they were less serious than in 1940.

I stand by that. However, many online commenters considered it a disgraceful underestimation of the problems facing the NHS/ retail sector/disabled/homeless/donkey sanctuaries – that any reference to our current problems in less than utterly superlative terms was a disgrace. That exemplified, for me, a pervading and angry loss of perspective.

Saying that things could be worse, and that they have been worse for the overwhelming majority of humans throughout the overwhelming majority of history, is not the same as being complacent. It is stating an undeniable fact. It is retaining a sane sense of proportion. It should be reassuring, but at the moment many people hate to hear it.

This wilful loss of perspective – this self-importance about our own times – means that we could do dangerous things. Our disdain for the bathwater is making the baby give us anxious looks. We're thinking hard, casting around for solutions: a privatised NHS, an independent Scotland, pulling out of the EU, a mansion tax, getting rid of the licence fee, greater press regulation, more Tasers, a German water cannon. We're not ruling anything out – except being careful we don't destroy something precious, except resisting the urge to act hastily and in anger, except a period of tranquil reflection. We desperately need a break from this era. But you know the rules: as soon as it ends, another one will only start.

1

Taking Offence, Demanding Apologies, Making People Do Things and Stopping People Doing Things: A Guide to Modern Hobbies

So, in the spirit of the age, let's kick off not only with a fucking football metaphor, but also by tetchily discussing self-righteous bad temper. Which really annoys me. It puts me in a self-righteous bad temper. And I'm sure some of the things I've written as a result have put other people in self-righteous bad tempers. It's all very infectious, this cross, bossy, suspicious, aggressive state of mind – and this section is full of it.

It touches on the mockery of Hitler, the electrocution of the blind, the hysterical enforcement of respect and the pompous hauteur of French chefs. People's irritation at piss, palm crosses, photography, Radio 4's Any Questions, *glitter, Louis Walsh's use of language and Robert De Niro's witticisms are all explored. It's infuriating.*

If you're ever going to throw a book at a wall, it'll be during the next few pages.

* * *

When I heard that *Piss Christ* had been vandalised, I instantly thought of *Cock Jesus*. More of *Cock Jesus* later. In case, like me, you hadn't heard of *Piss Christ*, let me explain that it's an artwork: a photograph, taken by artist Andres Serrano, of a plastic crucifix submerged in his own quite orange urine – maybe he'd just had a Berocca. On the weekend before Easter, some devout Christians attacked *Piss Christ* with a hammer.

I say that's just a continuation of the artistic process. By creating a new work, *Shards Piss Christ*, these extremist Catholics made a profound artistic statement about *Piss Christ*'s desecration of holy imagery by themselves violating the sanctity of the gallery. It's a devotional work worthy of comparison to the Sistine Chapel.

I hope the process continues. *Shards Piss Christ* could, say, be pelted with excrement, making *Shit Shards Piss Christ*. That could be shoved in a bin bag, making *Bin Bag Shit Shards Piss Christ*. Someone might be sick on that, creating *Vomit Bin Bag Shit Shards Piss Christ*.

It need never end. This captivating dialogue between the most provocative elements of the contemporary art scene and the hooligan wing of the Church of Rome, this great clash between two such fundamentally annoying groups, could one day result in the eclipse of the *Mona Lisa* and *Hamlet* by *Explosion Threshing-machine Pig's-alimentary-canal Toilet-bowl Inhaled-then-sneezed-out Set-on-fire Vomit Bin Bag Shit Shards Piss Christ*, mankind's most provocative masterpiece.

Which brings me to *Cock Jesus*. Roughly 2,000 years after the birth of Christ, Robert Webb and I wrote a sketch based on the daytime TV show *Watercolour Challenge*, in which the peace of the sleepy contestants, staring at hillsides and dabbing at easels, is shattered by the presence of a "shocking" modern artist. To his consternation, the programme's presenter refuses to be provoked, reacting to even his most horrific blood-, death- and swastika-strewn imagery with a patronising: "Well done, that's very pretty!"

In the first draft of the sketch, *Cock Jesus* was his final attempt to shock (it never appeared in the broadcast version for reasons of budget, taste and decency). It's a statue of Jesus, he explains, "made out of the amputated cocks of dead Anglican vicars whose bodies I've been illegally exhuming for the last six weeks!" "Ooh,

I do love angry art," coos the presenter as she moves on to the next contestant to advise on a quick way of doing clouds.

Cock Jesus and *Piss Christ* have more in common than penises and the Son of God. Their artists, real and fictional, both craved conflict, and only in the fictional case was the craving left unsated. In real life, someone, unlike the indulgent presenter in the sketch, always reacts. But I don't think those who protested against *Piss Christ*, who insulted the artist, sent hate mail to the dealer, protested outside the gallery or finally attacked the work itself, were duped. I think they succeeded in their aims as much as Serrano. It's the rest of us who are the mugs for dignifying these squabbles with our attention.

I've come to a similar conclusion about the case of Colin Atkinson, the electrician whose employers have told him to stop displaying a palm cross in the van he drives for them. For a while I got sucked into trying to work out the rights and wrongs. Is the heavy-handedly pro-Atkinson line taken by the newspaper reporting the story correct? Is it genuinely "political correctness gone mad", as George Carey was tempted out of retirement to say (there's a phrase that might catch on – he's got the gift of the gab, that guy), and "one rule for Christians and another rule for followers of any other religion", as Ann Widdecombe broke off from dance rehearsals to add? Or has the employer got a point? Or maybe the employer hasn't got a point and it's just my contrarian response to that newspaper which is making me look for one? After all, what harm can a little cross do?

Then I thought: "Hang on, I know what might be going on here. Maybe everyone involved in this dispute is awful." It would explain a lot. Most people, if they're not very religious and see someone displaying a cross, would think anything from "Nothing wrong with that" to "Mental note: this guy's a bit of a God-botherer – don't get stuck with him at a party." It takes quite a leap of self-importance to decide: "I'm going to put a stop to that!"

Equally, when told by their boss to stop displaying a cross in their van, most people's response would be somewhere on a scale between immediately acceding to the request and complaining before giving in because it's really not such a big deal. Taking it all the way to a disciplinary procedure and talking to a national newspaper is the mark of an unusual man. But is he principled or just stubborn? Righteous or self-righteous? Would it be a better world if everyone was like him?

God, no! It would be a much better world if no one was. The only useful role for people like that is to stand up to each other. You need the unbending Churchills to save us from the mass-murdering Hitlers but, with no Hitlers around, the Churchills are annoying as hell.

The media's obsession with conflict means that we're confronted with it so relentlessly that we've stopped questioning why it's there in the first place. We ask: "Which side is right? Who do I support?" but not: "Do they really need to be arguing about this? Why is so much of our time taken up by listening to small minorities who are incensed by other small minorities, rather than to the vast majority who just want to rub along OK?"

When watching the news, it's so easy to forget what most of us are like: pleasant, polite, socially shy. We don't want rows, we want a quiet life. We feel inadequate because we don't protest and argue more – we don't stand up for ourselves. And, in feeling that, we forget that the sort of people who do stand up for themselves are cut from the same cloth as the sort of people you have to stand up to.

It's a tyranny of the argumentative, an unholy alliance of the unholy and the holy, of the extreme right and the extreme left, of Stars-and-Stripes-burners and Qur'an-burners – people who define themselves by their mutual hatred, have a jolly good time doing it and leave the acquiescent majority running around in circles trying to pick up the pieces.

Well, I'm not going to take it any more! By which I mean, I'm sure it'll work itself out.

* * *

In April 2009, like a lot of people, I was railing against broadcasting standards . . .

I was deeply offended by something on the BBC recently. It wasn't Jeremy Clarkson reading out the menu from a Chinese restaurant in a funny voice, or Frankie Boyle's 10 best jokes about the Queen's genitals, or even a repeat of Diana's funeral with an added laugh track. No, it was a new low.

It was Hazel Blears, the communities secretary, eliciting a round of applause on *Any Questions* for suggesting that Jonathan Ross and Russell Brand should pay the BBC's "Sachsgate" Ofcom fine. The rest of the panel bravely agreed with her.

"Well, you would be offended by that!" you may be thinking. "You work in television and radio. I don't suppose you like the idea of having to foot the bill if something you say appals the nation!" That's true, but we live in the era of the subjective offendee and my complaint is just as valid as those made about jokes involving dead dogs by viewers who say their dog has recently died.

As an insider, I can tell you that such opinions are deferred to by the post-Sachsgate BBC. Everything is scrutinised for potential offence by jumpy "compliance" staff who endure no professional setback if the comedy output ceases to be funny. They have the right to do this because they're ultimately responsible for what's broadcast – their organisation pays the Ofcom fine.

But it strikes me that, if I'm going to have to pay the fine, they no longer have the right to censor the content. And it's all academic anyway; if things continue as they are, TV comedies will only ever get fined for blandness.

Let me try to fake some objectivity and seriously address Blears's suggestion, which has since been reiterated by Jack Straw and Tessa Jowell. She says it's unjust that the fine comes out of the licence fee, paid for by everyone, so instead the wrongdoers should pay.

There are only four problems I can instantly think of with this. First, this idea of a net cost to the licence fee payer is nonsense; Ross was suspended for three months, saving the BBC £1.5m, and Brand resigned, saving it £200,000 a year. So the licence fee payer is well up on the deal and Ross and Brand have each taken a greater hit than the corporation will.

Second, Blears defines the wrongdoers as only Ross and Brand and gives the BBC's producers and executives no share of the blame. This is grossly unfair. The offending segment was pre-recorded. As a sick comedian myself, I genuinely understand how they could improvise something that offensive in that context. But I cannot understand why the station chose to broadcast it. So the then channel controller, among others, is at least as much at fault. But she's not as rich, so suggesting she pays a massive fine is a less applausey route for Blears to take.

Third, Blears says that regulators' fines are supposed to hurt those responsible and that, in this instance, there was "no sense they're going to be hurt". I don't know whether the fine will hurt the BBC or whether it would particularly hurt Brand and Ross if they paid it, but how can she possibly think that the fallout from the whole business hasn't hurt that institution and those men?

Barely a day goes by when the press doesn't pillory them because of it, and the announcement of this fine has given it another splendid opportunity, as have Blears's remarks. Far from the arrogant, unaccountable, elitist coterie it's portrayed as, the BBC is now a quivering shell, rattling with neurotics. The only truth in her statement is that even losing £150,000 could barely make it more miserable.

And fourth, the law requires that the BBC pay the fine rather than the individuals concerned. This is not a law that Blears, Straw or Jowell has ever queried before. But they're willing to come out against it for a short-term popularity boost for a beleaguered government – for an egg-cup sized bailer on the *Titanic*, for one round of applause.

It's never a good idea for politicians to get involved in comedy. From Margaret Thatcher's *Yes Minister* sketch to Tony Blair's "Am I Bovvered?" appearance, their attempts to associate themselves with humour have generally been awful. And the reason for this is that they don't really care what's funny.

Being funny involves taking risks, and no politician (except possibly Boris Johnson) can understand why anyone would take the slightest risk of public disapproval in order to get a laugh. They're about power – they don't understand the instinct to amuse, and that's why Vince Cable's pretty unfunny remark about Gordon Brown being transformed "from Stalin to Mr Bean" has led to his being acclaimed a great parliamentary wit. Well, it might make them fall about in the Commons but it would barely raise a smirk at Wimbledon, where even a pigeon perching on the net gets guffaws.

This spineless intervention from Blears, Straw and Jowell exemplifies modern politicians' witless, craven and opportunistic approach to communication. How long do these ministers imagine the friendships in the rabble-rousing tabloids that they're buying with this will last? And the price is high: they're supporting a campaign to associate the BBC, its comedians and producers – my whole profession – with all that is offensive, smug and self-serving; to encourage millions who are justifiably angry or afraid, who imagine a mugger in every hoodie, who fear for their jobs and houses or have lost both, to associate the causes of that fear and anger with entertainment and, of all things, the BBC.

The BBC is an institution of genius, one of the great achievements of the 20th century. It's famed for its news reporting, drama, comedy and documentaries; it provides the best radio stations and website on Earth. But there is a plot to destroy it; a plot to which Ross and Brand's childish remarks gave an unwitting but enormous boost; a plot led by people who say they support the BBC but not the licence fee, by people who find the word "fuck" more offensive than Holocaust denial. By its competitors.

The newspapers that take every opportunity to knock the corporation do so because they're in the same market and the BBC is the market leader. They can't dominate that market while the BBC exists in its current form because what they provide is so risibly inferior – the licence fee costs less than a daily tabloid newspaper. So they lobby for its destruction and whinge about the profit made by its commercial arm, BBC Worldwide, neglecting to mention how much money that saves the licence fee payer.

Without the BBC, they'd make more money, even if the whole nation would be left comparatively uneducated, unentertained and uninformed. Their argument is the moral equivalent of private hospitals campaigning against the existence of the NHS. And now three members of a Labour government have joined in.

I don't think those ministers really want to damage or destroy the BBC, but they're willing to risk it on the outside chance of saving their political skins. I, for one, find that very difficult to forgive. But then I'm easily offended.

* * *

A statement from Madame Tussauds has been causing offence. The world's most famous collection of wickless candles announced: "We proactively encourage our visitors to interact with the waxworks should they so choose." No surprise that caused a stink, you're probably thinking. It's one of the most horrible sentences ever written. Why "proactively encourage" rather than "actively encourage" or just "encourage"? And what's that "should they so choose" doing there? If the visitors have so chosen, you're not encouraging them actively, proactively or otherwise, you're just letting them. That's the opposite of proactive: antipassive, presumably.

That's not why the statement is controversial, though. It's because it defends tourists' right to stand beside a waxwork of Adolf Hitler doing Nazi salutes. An Israeli couple visiting the attraction ("attraction" is the word people use, right? Rather than "museum" or "racket". "Attraction" as in: "I really can't understand the . . .") were horrified both by the fact that there was a likeness of Hitler at all and that people were posing next to it doing fascist gestures. It was their complaint that elicited Tussauds' assault on the English language.

I'm not doubting for a moment the sincerity of the couple's distress. Well, all right, maybe just for a moment. There. It's over now and I've concluded they were properly upset. God knows, they'd just queued up to get into Madame Tussauds on a summer's day in London. They'd be tired, hot and £57.60 poorer. Of course they'll have been disgusted and horrified by what they saw inside. And then, to make matters worse, they notice people saluting next to Hitler's waxwork.

They wrote in their complaint: "We are the grandchildren of concentration camp survivors – the very people that Hitler tried to kill." Of course I can understand why they might consider tourists frolicking with his likeness to be a display of inappropriate levity. But their complaint went further than that, claiming that the Nazi gestures and cries of "Heil Hitler!" were "an unequivocal demonstration of antisemitism and bigotry".

I just don't think that's true. The couple actually photographed two young tourists heil-Hitlering next to the waxwork, and one of them is doing the moustache with her other hand. I'm pretty sure that neo-Nazis don't do the moustache. They certainly didn't do the moustache at the Nuremberg rallies. What those kids in the picture are doing, I'm willing to bet, is taking the piss out of Hitler.

That's why I think it's a shame that Tussauds' reasonable response created a stir. Having apologised for any offence caused, Tussauds continued on the subject of interacting with the waxworks: "We absolutely defend the right of our visitors to make such choices for themselves, as long as they behave themselves responsibly." The repeated "themselves" isn't great but I completely approve of the sentiment. And I was disappointed that Lord Janner, chairman of the Holocaust Educational Trust, did not. He said: "I'm appalled at Madame Tussauds' insensitive comments defending such activity, as surely they have a responsibility to ensure visitors behave appropriately and respectfully at their museum."

Respectfully of what? Hitler? Does he think the girl shouldn't have done the moustache? Or does he think Madame Tussauds should ban a specific arm gesture when people are standing next to the Hitler waxwork? Or ban it in general so they can't do it next to Margaret Thatcher, Sting or Timmy Mallett either? After all, Germany has banned it throughout the whole country. What a stereotypically German solution to a stereotypically German problem. Given the chance, they'd ban authoritarianism.

When you ban something like this, you only dignify it with significance. You spoil the harmless piss-takers' harmless fun and you justify fascists in their feelings of oppression. You take a stupid gesture out of the realm of mockery and you give it illicit cachet. Whereas, in general, freedom engenders freedom. If you let people do what they like, human decency usually prevails. Anyone doing a Nazi salute and saying "Heil Hitler" for reasons other than a joke is unlikely to garner sympathy. There are always evil, oppressive forces at work on any society but they'll be found wanting in guile if they come at us goose-stepping and shouting "Sieg Heil!" for a second time. The only thing that could make that seem attractive or worth following, even to an idiot, is if it were banned.

It appears that Lord Janner and I fundamentally disagree on the importance of solemnity where discussion of Hitler is concerned. He seems to think that, since the murder of millions isn't funny, there is nothing to laugh at about the Nazis. I think that's nonsense. One of the attributes of the British of which I am most proud is our reaction to Hitler and his regime: both during the war and subsequently, we've always found them so funny, so ridiculous.

It beggars belief, it is positively hilarious that a whole country fell so completely in thrall to a posturing little prick like Hitler, who needed no help from our propagandists to look daft. There he is in the footage, making his speeches, all weedy and sweaty and cross – and there are the thousands of people cheering him as if he's Elvis. It makes you laugh like Titania falling in love with Bottom.

It's perfectly possible – and important to our understanding of the human condition – to find that amusing, to laugh at the goose-stepping, the shouting and the pomposity, while simultaneously holding in our heads the tragic murderous consequences of Nazi power. That's what makes the joke bite and also what reminds us that the massive disaster was human.

Churchill got this. It was no accident that he insisted on mispronouncing Nazi as "nar-zee" and referred disparagingly to "Corporal Hitler". He wasn't underestimating the scale of the threat or making light of people's suffering. But he knew it was vital to remember that the evil men who were jeopardising civilisation were also risible little twerps.

Many second world war veterans were accustomed to joking about Hitler. Spike Milligan and his contemporaries founded a comic tradition of making fun of the Nazis which has given us Peter Sellers's performance in *Dr Strangelove*, "The Germans" episode of *Fawlty Towers*, *Dad's Army*, *'Allo 'Allo!*, endless YouTube resubtitlings of *Downfall*, and Prince Harry's party gear. Just because the wartime generation has largely gone, we mustn't lose our comic nerve. While we must never forget the scale and severity of Hitler's crimes, we will have lost something precious if we start taking him seriously.

* * *

In the tense presidential election campaign of 2012, feelings were running high . . .

Robert De Niro has got into trouble for telling a joke. When introducing Michelle Obama at a Democratic fundraiser, he said: "Callista Gingrich, Karen Santorum, Ann Romney. Now do you really think our country is ready for a white first lady?" It went down well at the time but the next day Newt Gingrich seemed unamused: "What De Niro said last night was inexcusable and the president should apologise for him. It was . . . beyond the pale and he should be ashamed of himself."

That's a tough response. Gingrich reckons that De Niro's remark is so offensive that he can't even apologise for it himself. The apology has to come from the head of state. Not even Russell Brand ever went so far that Her Majesty was called upon publicly to atone. So I doubt that De Niro's half-hearted attempt to say sorry will have quite slaked Newt's thirst for contrition: "My remarks, although spoken with satirical jest, were not meant to offend or embarrass anyone – especially the first lady," the actor said.

Gingrich is attempting a particularly ambitious scam here, but it comes amid a thriving apology extortion racket in public life.

Those who wish to silence others have noticed that expressions of offence and demands that people say sorry are the best way of doing it. Once you've demanded an apology, you can logically continue to demand it until you receive it. Often those called upon to apologise will do so just to silence the clamour – they can't match the complainants for bloody-mindedness.

Not even Jeremy Clarkson can. He's a man accustomed to causing offence and yet even he said sorry for a remark he made on *The One Show*, purely to silence apology-extortionists' demands. I say "purely" because, when seen in context – even a *tiny bit* of context – there was nothing offensive about what he said. On the subject of public sector strikers, he spoke the words: "I would take them outside and execute them in front of their families," but he was clearly not advocating any such thing, or even using it as an off-colour superlative of disapproval. It was a comedic dig at the BBC's requirement to represent all opinions. I'd be surprised if I agreed with Jeremy Clarkson's views on the trade union movement, but not as surprised as if I discovered that they were that strikers should be shot. He's a Tory, not a Nazi.

But we live in such lamentably literal times that those who understood the joke were shouted down by an alliance of the stupid and the opportunistic – which meant the government called for an apology, and so did the opposition; the BBC gave way and then Clarkson also caved, saying: "If the BBC and I have caused any offence, I'm quite happy to apologise for it alongside them." Like De Niro, he covered his pride by saying sorry for the offence caused rather than the remark itself – but you can feel the frustration, the shrug: "So we surrender to stupidity, do we?" Freedom of speech is sacrificed at the altar of manufactured rage.

It reminds me of being made to apologise as a child. I remember a specific occasion when my parents were furious with me for some reason. And I was furious with them. It was a standoff. They were demanding an apology or else, as I recall it, basically nothing was to be allowed in future: food, sleep, not eating all my food, not immediately going to sleep, going outside, being allowed inside, contact with the cat – all banned. It was a massive campaign of sanctions and I was livid. And so I apologised. And then my mother said: "Say it like you mean it."

"But I don't mean it!" I screamed, trying to reason with her.

"Well, it doesn't count if you don't mean it."

This was evil, I immediately felt. They might be able to force me to apologise but surely it was inhuman for them to attempt to make me mean it. It was none of their business what I meant. Was I to be punished for a thought crime? My insincere apology was the best they were going to get.

What they tried to explain was that such an apology was worthless to them. They wanted me actually to be sorry, not just to say it – to understand that I'd done something wrong. Only that sort of apology meant anything. They didn't want to humiliate me – they wanted me to learn something.

The same cannot be said for Newt Gingrich. If he were acting honourably in this case, then an extorted apology, one that he'd demanded, whether it came from De Niro or Obama, would have no value for him. If he or his wife were really hurt, or if he felt genuine concern that the joke, as he complained, "divides the country", then he should say only that. And if, in consequence, Robert De Niro felt sorry and said so, then it would mean something. Or if, bizarre though it would be, Barack Obama felt guilty that this epoch-endangering quip had been made at an event in aid of his cause and was moved to express contrition at having been so thoughtless as to allow an Oscar-winning actor to make an unvetted remark at a dinner, then that would have some power to soothe poor Newt's bruised soul.

But that's not the situation. Clearly Gingrich isn't hurt. Nor is he worried that a gag at a fundraiser will have any negative impact on American racial harmony. It would take a bigger fool than him to think any such thing. He merely sees this as an opportunity to humiliate an opponent and boost his fading chances of the Republican nomination in the process. That's how politics is played these days, both in Britain and America.

Such vindictiveness offends me and I demand an apology. Also, as a pale person, I consider Gingrich's phrase "beyond the pale" to be deeply racist. It's inexcusable, in fact. The least Newt could do is get down on his knees and pray for forgiveness – preferably to Allah. And I want Robert De Niro to say sorry too, just for being in the same sentence. And I want an autograph. Anything less would be disgraceful. I mean it. I'm as genuinely upset as Newt.

* * *

The police have been going through a rough patch. First they were implicated in the phone-hacking scandal – though they managed to escape most of the blame when we collectively came to the surprising conclusion that it was more serious for tabloid journalists to neglect the public interest than officers of the crown. But while they deflected a lot of that responsibility, their attempts to deflect it over Hillsborough have been catastrophically counterproductive. And while senior officers have been caught dining with Murdochs or maligning the dead, officers on the ground have been getting shot and called plebs. Or not called plebs, depending on whom you believe.

Meanwhile, the Police Federation's attempts to extract retribution for the disputed p-word, in the form of Andrew Mitchell's sacking, have been roundly slagged off by former Labour minister Chris Mullin, who described the organisation as "a bully", "a bunch of headbangers" and "a mighty vested interest that has seen off just about all attempts to reform the least reformed part of the public service". He didn't call them plebs, though. Then again, some police have taken to wearing "PC Pleb and Proud" sweatshirts, so perhaps the insult has lost its sting? Maybe they'll soon be sporting "Sergeant Headbanger Will See You Now" riot shields or stab vests with the slogan "You Needn't Try Stabbing *This* Mighty Vested Interest".

Another accessory which the Police Federation advocates is the Taser. It has written to the prime minister asking for the number of Tasers to be trebled so that every frontline officer can have one. "They need to have the proper equipment to do the job," says Paul Davis, secretary of the Federation's operational policing subcommittee. And officers certainly seem to be getting a lot of use out of them. While, in London, Andrew Mitchell was pondering whether he could continue as Chief Whip, or would be reduced to private self-flagellation, a policeman in Lancashire Tasered a 61-year-old blind man as part of an operation to check whether his white stick was a samurai sword. It wasn't.

Of course, anyone might get rattled by a semi-paralysed blind man slowly tapping his way with a stick towards you. Apart from anything else, it's so spooky. Those are the high-pressure moments when you need the training to kick in. According to guidelines, officers are permitted to use Tasers when they "would be facing violence or threats of violence of such severity that they would need to use force to protect the public, themselves and/or the subject", and this moment is surely eerie enough to qualify. The whole event would barely be worthy of note if it weren't for the fact that they shot him in the back. But then the gentleman is quite old and has suffered two strokes in the last few years – so the comparatively slow rate at which he was fleeing was probably taken as provocation.

Incidentally, if you do get Tasered by the police, it's advisable to watch your language. As Boris Johnson has pointed out, it's now an offence to swear at a police officer. So should you incur a public-spirited 50,000-volt warning shot – perhaps for brandishing your pension book in an aggressive manner or because a young PC has mistaken your tartan shopping trolley for a piece of field artillery – don't accidentally shout "Oh fuck!" or you might get sent to prison. Keep it to a "Dash it all, that smarts, constable!" and be on your way. As soon as you can stand.

In the case of Colin Farmer, the suspected samurai, the police have apologised and Chief Superintendent Stuart Williams said: "We have launched an urgent investigation to understand what lessons can be learned." That response demonstrates everything that's wrong with large organisations. In terms of dereliction of duty, I think it's worse than Tasering a blind pensioner. What possible good can this "investigation" do? We know what happened. A police officer, who Colin Farmer described as "an absolute thug with a licence to carry a dangerous weapon", made a brutal and stupid mistake. How can an investigation illuminate the situation further? Will DNA analysis of the stick reveal that it's a sword after all?

All of which means it feels like an inopportune moment for Keith Bristow, the director general of the new National Crime Agency, to request more police powers. He's trying to influence the new communications data bill so that he'll be able to scour Skype and social media networks for wrongdoers. But he's quick to allay the fears of those who call the bill a "snoopers' charter": "I value my privacy, I don't want to be snooped upon," he explains. "That's not what we're talking about here. We're talking about criminals who run organised crime gangs that import drugs . . . We're talking about predatory paedophiles, we're talking about dangerous people."

Oh, well that's OK then! He's only going to be snooping on criminals. Personally I don't think that's enough – I think criminals should be arrested and charged, not just snooped on. But just as long as the NCA won't accidentally be snooping on anyone who's not definitely a criminal, I can't see the harm in it.

In an ideal world, Keith Bristow would be wasting his breath. When a state law enforcement agency says "We need more powers", it should carry as little weight as when I say "I want you to read my book". Not because either statement is insincere: all writers genuinely want people to read their books and all law enforcement agencies really believe they need more powers. But when they say that, they should be completely ignored. Not criticised, not accommodated, just disregarded.

The sincerity is beguiling but it's meaningless. "Help us to do our jobs better," the police implore. "We can see the good we could do if you let us." They almost certainly can. But they can't see what it would cost society in lost freedoms. They can't know the consequences of potentially irreversible authoritarian steps.

It's a frightening state of affairs. Those who know most about law enforcement – those who actually do it – are the least qualified to advise on what its rights, powers and funding should be. We have to ignore their cries and trust our instincts. We have to balance our fears of the indefinable, nebulous worlds of crime and terrorism with the fact that, if we put Tasers in our public servants' hands, at some point they'll use them on us.

Since I wrote this in October 2012, the police and Police Federation's public image has deteriorated further. In May 2014, the home secretary rebuked the Federation's conference, calling on them to "Show the public that you get it", and issuing a threat: "The Federation was created by an act of parliament and it can be reformed by an act of parliament. If you do not change of your own accord, we will impose change on you." Meanwhile, the communications data bill, having lost Nick Clegg's support in April 2013, looks unlikely to become law.

* * *

As someone who enjoys food, I'm surprised by how irritable chefs make me. Whenever I read about a chef or chefs campaigning for, complaining about or promoting something, I can feel myself metaphorically folding my arms. And sometimes I literally fold my arms at the same time – which, if you count both real and metaphorical limbs, briefly makes me an insect. A disdainful beetle, gearing up to get cross with a chef.

"Oh, what is it now, chefs?" I sneer to myself – not out loud because chefs are famously handy: I'm thinking of Gordon Ramsay, or John Cleese in that sketch where he bursts out of the kitchen waving a cleaver. "You moaning chefs get my goat, which left to you would presumably be locally sourced, turned into a jus or a foam and piped all over a perfectly harmless starter! Why don't you shut up, you bloody chefs?"

You may be uncertain of what I'm talking about. What are all these occasions when chefs say, want or bemoan something? you may wonder. Maybe my chef-irritability is making me delusional, but to my mind it's constant. Some chef is always saying something, and it's never just: "Can you make sure that doesn't boil over? I'm popping out for a fag."

It's probably the fault of the media – most things are. When you've retyped all the news agency stuff about Syria and Ukraine, and reprinted today's cameraphone snap of a goose swimming past someone's upstairs window, what are you going to put on page two? Probably best just to ring up some chefs and find out what's bugging them.

My view of chefs as a vocal part of the community is reinforced by the fact that most television programmes are now about cookery – about 52%, according to a survey I just conducted into what would bolster my argument. I quite like cookery programmes – something I have in common with every other viewer. That's why there are so many. The future of television, according to haircuts and focus groups, is stuff that everyone quite likes, rather than stuff that anyone particularly likes. It's best just to make cookery programmes, because dramas are expensive, nature documentaries are fake and those horrible panel shows are brash and rude and have more chefs on them than women. But no one ever got annoyed by shots of a casserole.

So I already had more metaphorically folded arms than a metaphorical millipede exchanging insurance details with some chefs who'd just crashed into his car when I heard the latest from the chefs: they're annoyed by shots of a casserole. Or probably not actually a casserole – that sounds a bit 70s – more likely a reduction or a daube or a posset or a phucking pho. They're cross that customers often photograph (or pho-tograph) their food and put those images online.

These particular chefs are French, which, I must admit, doesn't allay my suspicions that they may not have quite got over themselves. So I'd completely prejudged Alexandre Gauthier (of La Grenouillère in La Madelaine-sous-Montreuil) before I heard what he had to say – which, as it turns out, was an efficient use of time.

"They used to come and take pictures of themselves and their family, their grandmother, whoever, as a souvenir," he said of his customers. "Now they take pictures of the food, they put it on Facebook or Twitter, they comment. And then the food is cold . . . I would like people to be living in the present. Tweet about the meal beforehand, tweet about it afterwards, but in between stop and eat." To this end, he printed pictures of cameras with lines through them on all the menus.

You may think he's got a point. People's urge to photograph every aspect of their lives is pretty wearing – I wish they wouldn't do it too. But my sympathy for him melts like sorbet under a flashbulb when he progresses from wishing they wouldn't to trying to stop them. They've bought the food: if they want to take a picture of it, that's their choice. Just as it's his choice to be irritated rather than flattered.

The implication that these plates of grub should be treated with reverence makes me bridle. And it's even worse because they already *are* being treated with reverence, but he's objecting to the nature of that reverence. It's too disrespectful a form of respect: he doesn't want people cooing and snapping with joy as if his masterpieces were merely a birthday Knickerbocker Glory with sparklers in it – he wants the murmured acclamation of an art gallery.

Nevertheless, Gauthier claims that he's "not banned photographs at all" (which doesn't make much sense as I don't see what else could be inferred from the signs on the menus). And neither has his fellow complainant, Gilles Goujon (inventor of the goujon?) of the Auberge du Vieux Puits – but that's only because he hasn't "yet found the right words that won't be too shocking". He hates his food to be photographed because "it takes away the surprise", "it takes away a little bit of my intellectual property" and "a photo taken on an average smartphone . . . doesn't give the best impression of our work".

I understand his feelings, but basically he needs to suck it up. If his customers have trawled strangers' Facebook pages and Twitter accounts for inexpertly photographed gourmet meal spoilers, they only have themselves to blame if their expensive dinner's appearance fails to exhilarate. And Goujon's still got whatever the food tastes like to wow them with – you can't put that on Tumblr (at time of writing). As far as the intellectual property is concerned, I feel his pain, but he should take comfort from the fact that whoever first arranged a fry-up into the shape of a smiley face almost certainly never earned a penny from it.

But what irritates me most about these chefs is that they're being so clever. They may come across as precious, but it won't make anyone think less of their cooking. On the contrary, by heavily implying that their food is beset by the greedy lenses of photographers – that it looks so good it gets papped and is forced to shun the limelight like Garbo – its deliciousness is taken as read. This is a problem, we all assume, suffered only by the best restaurants, the big chefs. At a Little Chef, it's not an issue – largely because they already provide photographs of the meals on the menus.

* * *

Have you noticed those special sparkly poppies that some people on television have taken to wearing instead of the normal ones? I don't know when they first cropped up – it feels like about two years ago, which usually means it's roughly 10. It took them a while to get on my nerves, but now they have.

I don't know why I was initially fine with them. That's not like me. Maybe it's because of the context. *The X Factor*, where I first noticed them, is such a hellish environment, such a horrendous, screaming, Klingon parliament of a space, that even those glittery whored-up symbols of remembrance seemed to have an incongruous innocent simplicity about them, rather like the original poppies which grew out of the cordite-wrecked soil of the western front.

But then Louis Walsh changed my mind. I was flicking through the channels when, like a moth drawn to the flame, like an addict returning to the needle, like an early 20th-century emperor lured into a conflict he will be able neither to control nor comprehend, I paused to watch some hopeless hopefuls forgettably finish singing a song and then line up to hear it described as unforgettable.

Walsh, his very presence a more devastating refutation of the principle of the sanctity of human life than Verdun, was repeating a platitude that had been expressed seconds earlier by someone else – only altering the word order slightly so that it didn't quite make sense. His mouth was opening and closing, his ears were waggling, his voice was straining to be heard over the screeches of audience approval which his empty praise was generating, and my eyes, drawn to the screen yet repelled by his face, lighted on the blinged-up poppy on his fucking shirt. I saw it clearly for the first time.

How dare television designers adapt this token of remembrance to blend in with their trashy aesthetic? How dare they make it twinkly? The poppy is an incredibly moving symbol. This flower somehow flourished on battlefields smashed by the world's first experience of industrialised war – a war of unprecedented carnage which became almost as terrifying to the statesmen who had let it start as it was to the millions of soldiers who were killed or wounded by it.

Such was the international shock that, even after our side had won, no one could bring themselves to remember it with anything other than unalloyed sorrow. Not with victory arches or triumphal parades, but with the plain, mournful Cenotaph and a tradition of wearing paper versions of the flowers that had grown among the dead, the petals with which nature had rebuked the murderousness of men. That's why, while I understand the point they're trying to make, I disagree with those who eschew the red poppy but wear a white one for peace. To me, the poppy is already a pacifist rather than a martial symbol – a sign that war should be rejected at almost all costs.

The poppy represents the consensus that existed after the armistice – not a military or political consensus, but an emotional one: an overwhelming sense that the indiscriminate bloodletting of total war was too terrible ever to be forgotten, that only in solemn remembrance can any sense be made of those millions of deaths. On that simple point, almost everyone was, and continues to be, agreed. And for the symbol to be powerful and meaningful, I think it needs to be uniform – as uniform as the franchise. We should all wear the same type of poppy or it's like some of us saying "I'm Spartacus" in a funny voice. By encouraging the sparkly poppy, TV producers almost literally gild the lily. And literally glamorise war.

However, this broad consensus is only powerful if it's genuine, and genuinely voluntary. So people were rightly outraged by the wrongful outrage provoked by ITV News presenter Charlene White's decision not to wear a poppy on TV. This included a fair bit of racist and misogynistic abuse, much of it emanating from rightwing extremists up in arms at the disrespect they claimed she'd shown to soldiers who'd died fighting against rightwing extremists.

In a way, Charlene White is fortunate that her detractors came mainly from organisations like the English Defence League, because it's not unknown for more respectable members of the community to have a pop at poppy-absence – and their censure is harder to shake off. The *Mirror* generated some negative publicity for the BBC out of the fact that some viewers complained about a lack of poppies on the Halloween-themed edition of *Strictly Come Dancing*, broadcast more than a week before Remembrance Sunday. And Labour MP Gerry Sutcliffe wasn't too busy to criticise Google for sporting too small a poppy on its homepage, saying: "Around Remembrance Day it is demeaning not to have something that is spectacular." Something more like the artillery barrage which started the Battle of the Somme, perhaps.

The effect of these criticisms is corrosive. It means that people on TV, and appearing in public in general, will come to wear poppies primarily to avoid disapproval – in fact, they're undoubtedly doing so already. Privately they may buy and wear poppies as an act of respect or remembrance, or they may not, but publicly they'll just wear them for a quiet life. "Lest We Forget" will be reduced to the level of remembering to check your flies are done up. That's not a meaningful consensus any more – that's just bland conformity.

If this development goes unchallenged, the next stage in the story of the poppy is inevitable: if people *have* to wear them to be deemed respectable, then gradually more people will start refusing as a gesture of rebellion against the establishment. The poppy will cease to be a symbol of the horror of war and of soldiers' sacrifice and it will become a political badge of the status quo – the Unknown Soldier will be displaced by George Osborne. The fallen will be forgotten as a direct result of the efforts of those who wish to enforce their remembrance.

It's wonderfully humane and moving if everyone wears a poppy – but only if they don't feel they have to, and wouldn't fear not to. Otherwise, we really might as well doll up our poppies with sequins, because they'll have stopped meaning anything at all.

2

Just Turn On Your Television Set and Stay In and Do Something More Boring Instead

This bit is mainly about TV, although it touches on most of the old media – by which I mean books, theatre, cinema, gardening and lasagne.

Television is the medium I grew up with. As a child, time spent watching television was time when I was winning. It was my aim. With my eyes and brain nicely distracted from focusing on anything in real life, I could relax.

I still love television, partly because of all the brilliant programmes it's generated but, to the same extent, because of all the terrible programmes and mediocre programmes and forgettable programmes. Pretty much whatever is on television, the process of reacting to it, of working out what I reckon about it, is interesting to me. Except if it's football or a soap.

TV has gone through hell in the last few years. Its existence has been threatened by a confluence of general economic gloom, consequent creative cowardice and, most of all, the bloody internet, which seems to change everything, but particularly seeks to change the way we have fun – and I'm not even talking about porn. The poor old entertainment media could really have done without the credit crunch and the internet happening at once.

* * *

It's been a ridiculously long time coming but it's here at last. What's the guy been doing? He makes Kubrick look like Barbara

Cartland. Doesn't he understand the country's in recession, the media in crisis? We need product – reliable product from an established name. He has fewer new ideas than Mel Brooks and Eric Idle put together! It's a disgrace.

And, come to think of it, it's about time we had a serious look at what some of these playwrights are earning. I reckon the cash-strapped British public have had enough of this self-appointed metropolitan artistic elite blowing Arts Council money on quills and flagons of sack. He should get himself a Dell and pay for his own booze, just like journalists. Bet he'd insist on a Mac. Wanker.

Where was I? Oh yes, William Shakespeare has at last deigned to write a new play for his adoring public, who've been so supportive through all the tabloid rumours of his being dead or not existing in the first place. The project is shrouded in secrecy – it's not even clear what it's called, being variously referred to as *Cardenio*, *Double Falsehood* and *The Distrest Lovers* (oh, please! That whole comedy spelling thing is so over, Bill!). Anyway I hope it doesn't pick up where *The Two Noble Kinsmen* left off, because I thought that was shit. I preferred that dead cat bounce in Woody Allen's form, *Vicky Cristina Barcelona* – although I did watch it on a plane, where films with any real plot just interrupt meal service.

None of the above is quite true. (Think of the money the *Sun* would save if it adopted that simple phrase.) Nevertheless, the latest research into the 18th-century play *Double Falsehood* shows it was probably based on a lost Shakespeare work, just as was unconvincingly claimed when it was first produced.

The fact that this academic re-evaluation was reported as the unearthing of a new Shakespeare play says much more about our culture's hunger for more of the same than it does about its literary heritage. The play isn't newly discovered, and if it were any good, it would get performed; even in its original production, the marketing seemed keener to claim that it was associated with genius than that it contained it. So if it's Shakespeare, it's not his best stuff. Desperate for guaranteed hits though our media are, we have to accept that William Shakespeare, even more than Woody Allen, has peaked. Why won't someone take a chance on brilliant young playwrights like David Hare?

This feels like an unprecedentedly derivative age. I know that almost all periods of history have considered themselves to be the most disastrous ever – and ours is no exception – but that's the only superlative we seem to allow ourselves. In the last few years, we've haemorrhaged confidence in our ability to make new stuff up. It's not just pretending we've found more Shakespeare instead of writing new plays, it's the "New Mini" and the "New Beetle", it's ironic relaunching of Salt'n'Shake and Monster Munch – we don't even trust ourselves to invent new sorts of starchy crap.

It infects books, cinema and television. The last few years have seen the publication of high-profile sequels to *Peter Pan*, *Winnie-the-Pooh* and the James Bond books. James Patterson has industrialised his novel-writing by employing a factory of uncredited writers dedicated to saving readers from the unsettling sensation of trying a new author.

Film studios, already notorious for liking new ideas to be pitched as "It's X meets Y", have now commuted the formula to "It's X again!" and are reflogging the Batman and Superman franchises with accelerating regularity. And television – poor beleaguered television, the medium that once, more than any other, had the power to make people sample new things simply because it was already in their living rooms – is becoming as unappetising a rehash of leftovers from happier times as a 27 December lunch.

We Are the Champions, which came back recently under the aegis of Sport Relief but is doubtless being pitched for a permanent return, is just another format from TV's glory days brought in as a substitute for anything new. And when a new programme is commissioned, it's often an adaptation of a novel that's already been adapted, or a drama recreating recent political events. Whatever their varying merits as viewing experiences, *Minder, Mastermind, Pride and Prejudice, Margaret Thatcher: The Long Walk to Finchley, Margaret, Marple, Mo, Lewis* and *Reggie Perrin* all illustrate this trend.

I find the last particularly upsetting since it's a good remake – written, performed and produced by talented professionals – but of a brilliant original. Why do we have a broadcasting environment where the skills displayed in the remake weren't channelled into a new idea, a different comic take on a middle-aged man undergoing a breakdown, rather than an attempt to recreate the unbetterable. I expect those that made and commissioned it would argue that the remake actually was a new take. Well, if so, have the confidence to give it a new name, to forget the original other than as a subliminal influence, rather than piggyback on people's fondness for it and consequently dilute their perception of its excellence.

When a very capable controller of BBC1 resigned a few years ago, he was extravagantly praised for the idea of bringing *Doctor Who* and *Strictly Come Dancing* to Saturday nights. Well, if that's an idea, it's certainly not his. But for one new word, inexplicably lifted from the title of an Australian film, that was the line-up in the 1970s. Are we now completely confusing the sensation of invention, of creativity, with that of deft emulation?

That's what advertisers do. But they're only trying to capture people's attention. Once captured, they have nothing to convey other than their clients' messages. The effect of defensive, derivative, cowardly decision-making at publishing houses, film studios and broadcasters, of no longer searching for anything new to express, is to reduce the popular art forms, which have the power to convince, move and educate, as well as entertain, to the same cheap bag of attention-grabbing tricks as the adverts that surround them.

And then, when they succeed in getting attention, just like an overdomesticated dog who one day catches up with a rabbit, they won't know what to do with it.

Since I wrote this in 2010, no other new Shakespeare plays have been discovered and the revamped We Are the Champions *seems to have got stuck in development.*

* * *

In February 2009, a different broadcasting trend was getting on my nerves . . .

Watching paint dry will presumably be among the attractions of *Saatchi's Best of British* (working title), Charles Saatchi's "nationwide search to discover the next generation of artistic talent", to be broadcast on BBC2 this autumn.

The aim is to use television to raise the profile and improve the accessibility of modern art, but it may end up using modern art to make people finally despair of television.

I'm not entirely clear what the point is. The last generation of artistic talent managed to limp to prominence without the help of an accompanying TV series. Or maybe they didn't and the real geniuses never even bought themselves an easel (or video camera, pickled sheep, lightbulb or bed) because TV never suggested it. Maybe the country will finally get the modern art it deserves. Can't wait.

These days, a television series is the must-have recruitment tool for any self-respecting profession: chefs, choirs, models, footballers, entrepreneurs, opera singers, pop stars, restaurateurs and novelty acts all get picked on TV. As the medium's power and popularity wanes, the technology is being rejigged for other uses. Just as Roman temples were bastardised for Saxon hovels and the SS Great Eastern was sent to lay telegraph cables, so the analogue bandwidth is being sold off to mobile phone companies and half the BBC's studios are being used for storage.

And it's patriotic, in the credit crunch, that the process by which the country's diminishing job vacancies are filled should itself create so much employment for people in TV. But, as physics-denying executives always say: "In broadcasting, if you're standing still, you're moving backwards."

So the country's development producers have been racking their brains to think of other careers that can be staffed using television shows. Here are just a few of the ideas currently being considered by broadcasters.

Bankers

You Can Bank on Me! is a collaboration between Channel 4 and HM Treasury. Alistair Darling has given us an unprecedented challenge: we've got just 16 weeks to run Northern Rock into the ground. We're on a quest to find the next generation of ludicrously overpaid alpha males bent on bringing down civilisation with their fecklessness!

Just when most bankers are repenting, resigning or both, we'll scour the country's estate agencies and lap-dancing clubs for their replacements.

We're looking for people with towering self-esteem and the morals of a virus but who, when the chips are down, behave like a frightened herd of sheep scampering towards a giant mincing machine because it's been painted to look like grass.

Members of the House of Lords

Keeping Up A-Peer-Ances (working title) is where constitutional innovation meets interactive TV meets youth-u-tainment. BBC3 has challenged us to sweep aside the sticky-fingered dullards of our upper house and replace them with teenagers.

Thanks to a hastily pushed-through amendment to the Parliament Act, we'll be temporarily ennobling 500 16-year-olds and letting them loose on all but the most vital legislation.

Watch the drug-addled, respect-averse cyber generation have their "wicked" way with the Lords Spiritual and Temporal's powers of amendment and delay. This show will keep the 16–25 demographic away from the advertising-dependent channels which so badly need it!

A girlfriend for Prince Harry

Slappersearch 09 is an exciting new entertainment format coming to Sky. We'll scour the country for the kind of publicity-hungry babe for whom attempting to sing a song, persuading a dog to dance or even going on *Big Brother* is a bit too much like hard work, but who doesn't mind red hair or casual racism.

Orifice Productions (makers of *Pornlocution*, the ratings-grabbing tits-and-diction strand on Bravo) want to find the next generation of feisty young lasses who dare to dream but can't be arsed to do much else.

The finale will feature footage of the winner having full sex with Prince Harry in a luxury Dubai hotel (pending Palace approval).

IT consultants

Have You Got IT? is a 43-part aspiromentary coming to BBC2 in the summer. Did you have a dream? Do you love to dance or sing or write poetry or do stand-up? Did it not work out?

We want to find the next generation of people who've just realised that they're going to have to get a proper job. We'll penetrate into the very heart of the grubby flats of dreamers blessed with neither luck nor talent and persuade them to get into IT.

We'll be there to capture on camera the moment when the spotlight our contestants imagine they're standing in is replaced by the flickering neon of a football-pitch-sized office just off the A1 crammed with humming servers.

A medium-sized part in a touring production of *Romeo and Juliet*

ITV1's *Britain's Next Top Benvolio* is an unrivalled opportunity for the Royal Touring Theatre to drum up interest in what many consider to be Shakespeare's most predictable play.

Ruth Madoc, who is also playing the nurse, will head the judging panel as we scour the country for the next generation of budding thespians who for whatever reason haven't bothered to try and become actors by any of the conventional routes.

But only one of them will get to say "We shall not 'scape a brawl!" at the Swan, High Wycombe!

Director-General of the BBC

First Rule of Holes: Stop D-Ging! is an innovative format ready to launch on BBC1 whenever Mark Thompson finally resigns. We'll scour the country for the next generation of hand-wringing functionaries willing to sizzle on the barbie of the rightwing press's hate.

"Like a king prawn, with these guys it's their very spinelessness that makes them palatable to predators," jokes Sir Michael Lyons, chairman of the judges.

In the last episode, the winner will be whoever makes the best job of explaining why an episode of *Songs of Praise* in which Frankie Boyle and John Sergeant spit-roast a nun was cleared for a repeat on CBeebies.

A four-part Charles Saatchi-fronted modern art show, retitled School of Saatchi, *was subsequently broadcast on BBC2 in November–*

December 2009. I didn't watch it. Saatchi has since found other ways of remaining in the public eye.

* * *

One of my least favourite programmes of the 1980s was *Why Don't You [Just Switch Off Your Television Set and Go Out and Do Something Less Boring Instead]?* I watched it anyway, of course. It was on.

It was presented by gangs of children with different regional accents, which I suppose was meant to make it feel more inclusive. It didn't work on me. I found the accents alienating. They made me worry that those were the sort of children who would despise me and call me a "posh twat", a jibe my parents worked hard to earn the bare minimum to qualify me for. They scrimped and saved to buy me just enough privilege to make me contemptible.

And the thing I did have in common with the presenters – that I, too, was a child – just made me think: "How'd they get that? Why can't *I* be on TV maddening *them*?" Sometimes things work out in the end.

The content of the show was the familiar series of tedious tasks that required items of stationery that I never possessed or physical activities that I was too weedy for. But my main beef with it was its title. That was the metaphorical photo of a cancerous lung on the cigarette packet of my viewing pleasure.

I was already aware that my predilection for watching hours of television every day was a terrible failing. The concerted censure of every authority figure left me in no doubt of what a betrayal of the opportunities of childhood that was. I should have been reading books or getting fresh air, bicycling around in crime-solving gangs and fishing in streams. Our bit of suburban Oxford seemed a bit short on streams or caves full of forgers, but then I'd never really looked.

Adults' sentences beginning "When I was your age . . ." never ended with "I'd have given my eye teeth to be left alone to watch *Knight Rider*, so you go for it, lad!" What I was doing was an insult to children of the past and of fiction; to *Coral Island* and evacuees and a ha'p'orth of gobstoppers. I should have been going to Cubs or training for swimming badges. But most worryingly, I was putting my imagination in jeopardy. Because, as surely as carrots help you see in the dark and that you'll regret giving up the piano when you're older, television rots the imagination.

You don't have to imagine *Star Trek* – the aliens and lasers and spaceships are all on the screen in front of you. There are no gaps for your mind to fill – the art department has already plugged them with chipboard and silver paint. So reading, running around the garden, riding a bicycle or, most terrifyingly, interacting with new people are important activities that strengthen the ideas-generating parts of the brain that otherwise atrophy under the influence of TV.

"Get used to these more gruelling and effort-requiring forms of fun and you'll build the mental equipment for a fuller life," was the argument. A bit like the principle by which we're weaned on to alcohol: "It may not taste as good as Coke now, but you wait – oh, you just wait." Sadly, the latter argument was the only one I had the imagination for.

But among the advantages of becoming an adult are that people stop admonishing you and you're allowed the illusion of vindication about your childish choices. "I spent most of the 80s watching TV and it never did me any harm," I can safely say, knowing that it's an experiment with no control. There's no other David Mitchell walking around who, having eschewed TV, has an imagination unstunted by assiduously following the plot of *Dynasty*. Unless it's that pesky novelist.

So it came as a shock when Jeremy Paxman stormed into the living room during *Doctor Who* and started hoovering under my legs and telling me to go outside. I protested that I'd finished my work, but he said it was a lovely day and that he'd give me 2p for every mare's tail I dug up.

I'm speaking metaphorically (a medical miracle, my old English teacher would say, after what all those episodes of *The A-Team* did to my brain). In a talk at the Hay Festival, Paxman called the public a "bunch of barbarians" because watching TV is our favourite leisure activity. He thinks we should go to art galleries instead.

I don't mind that he's biting the hand that feeds him. A healthy disdain for that hand is an attractive quality, I've always thought – that's probably why I'm more of a cat than a dog person. But has he considered what it signifies that it's the television personality Jeremy Paxman – a highly respected journalist, certainly, but hardly a potential Nobel Prize winner – who has the prominence to make this unreconstructed appeal on behalf of the highbrow?

It means that he's what counts as highbrow now, a high-rent newsreader who's done a few books as TV spin-offs, the most recent of which he got another writer to finish for him. The fact that the likes of him are the focus of literary festivals is an index of how completely the cause he's arguing for is lost.

I don't rejoice in that. But as someone who can't spend more than a few minutes in an art gallery without developing a desire for a cup of tea and a sit down as all-consuming as a sudden realisation of diarrhoea, and who often insists on watching episodes of *Cash in the Attic* to their three-figure-sum-generating conclusions, it would be hypocritical of me to echo his moans. And I'm a beneficiary of dumbing down, too. Regurgitate half-remembered facts from your A-level syllabus on a panel show, I've found, and you'll get lumped in with the learned.

It's unkind to kick TV at the moment. It may still be our favourite leisure activity, but new competitors are threatening its solvency. Eschewing television for reasons of arty respectability is no longer a choice that can be made with confidence that the medium will nevertheless prosper. Even the most bookish may soon wonder whether they'd be better off with the devil they know.

The barbarians are switching off, but a glance at YouTube confirms that they're not necessarily doing anything less boring instead.

* * *

Daytime television on BBC1 has a new slogan: "Make the most of your day." Is this capitulation? Is daytime TV conceding its addictive, time-killing, life-sapping effect and exhorting us to escape while we still can? Are the forces of evil finally losing heart, like Darth Vader turning on the Emperor to save his son or O'Brien repenting tragically too late of the soap-based booby trap she'd laid for her mistress? (And if you haven't watched either *Return of the Jedi* or *Downton Abbey*, then I'm bang out of cultural references that you're going to get.)

No. The BBC is actually claiming that watching daytime TV constitutes making the most of your day. The slogan is preceded by an exciting-looking montage of excerpts from shows. They went past in a blur so I'm not sure what they were, but they exuded an overwhelming sense of significance: a clip from *Doctors* where someone is diagnosed with a terminal illness; a heartbreakingly botched dormer window from *Cowboy Trap*; the rescue of a malnourished spaniel from *Animal 24:7*; a bit of *Land Girls* where someone gets cross, that sort of thing. "Don't touch that remote," it's imploring. "Don't change channel or get off your arse. No need to move because this, watching this, is making the most of your day. Do not leave the room! It's *Bargain Hunt* in a minute! This is life lived to the full."

The BBC Trust disagrees. In its review of all aspects of the corporation's output, it picked out daytime as the weakest link and pointless – and that's just a snippet from the schedule. It called for shows that are less "formulaic and derivative". It wants to put a stop to the endless footage of people buying and selling antiques and houses.

This makes me uneasy. I work from home a lot and so I'm a major user of daytime TV. I use it to waste time in a very specific way – to squander short chunks of it. I'm supposed to be working, I can't face it, I wander round the house, I put the kettle on, I turn on the TV, it engages me for a few minutes, then gradually I lose interest and return to my computer, maybe do a bit of work – writing this sentence, for example – then pop back to the kettle and/or television. I'm going there now. Back in a minute.

I'm back. A professional couple from Peterborough who are looking to relocate to somewhere with more space for the husband's motorbike collection didn't like house number two because it was too close to a noisy road. The host suggested double-glazing. I wandered away and put some toast on.

Texturally, daytime TV is a delicate and remarkable thing. The morning schedule on BBC1 is a series of programmes that, while apparently almost unbelievably bland, becomes more intriguing and varied the closer one looks, like a patchwork of a thousand different beiges, yet retains the key attribute of being too boring to watch for more than 20 minutes at a stretch. The toast has popped.

Well, that's the last of the good jam. A mother and daughter from Plymouth just sold a decanter for a £19 loss, but then it didn't have its own stopper. The next lot was a 1950s Mickey Mouse ashtray, so I went for a look at Twitter.

BBC Daytime is a groundbreaking experiment into how much people can be induced to take a passing interest in activities that don't concern them. There's a programme about a company that specialises in finding the relatives of people who have died intestate. It simply follows their working day: "Gladys died in St Thomas's nursing home in 2006, leaving £82,000 from the sale of her house. The nurses at the home say she often spoke of a half-sister, Gwen, who died of pneumonia during the three-day week. But did Gwen ever marry and have children? Investigator Peter Edwards goes to Preston records office to find out." Then they film the guy setting his satnav.

There's a programme in which people who want to move house are shown three hastily chosen properties, pick one and are then allowed to "try before they buy". This means they sit in it for part of an afternoon. They get the full experience of residence but not for quite long enough to need the loo. At the end, they're asked if they're going to buy the house, and they always – in my experience absolutely always – say no.

There's my personal favourite, *Homes Under the Hammer*, where the production company has just set up a video camera at a property auction and sent presenters to stalk the successful buyers. And there are three different antique-purveying shows: one where the antiques are bought and sold in the same show; one where an expert trawls someone's attic for valuables in order to raise them money for the scuba holiday of their dreams; and one which is basically a more mercenary version of *Antiques Roadshow* with worse antiques. The subtle distinctions between these formats would be lost on those with proper jobs but are as apparent to me as different types of snow to an Inuit.

Just made a tea and watched an RSPCA man give a woman a stern talking to for not giving her horse the right jabs. He'll be checking up again in six months.

I need programmes like these, shows during which it is completely unnecessary to think. Of course, I've got better things to watch – there's a cellophane-wrapped box set of *The Sopranos* on the shelf above my TV that's been gathering dust for three years – but they're no good to me. I need brief distractions that are easy to be distracted from. If I unwrapped a DVD, it would be like cracking open the scotch – I might as well file for bankruptcy.

I know daytime TV isn't primarily provided as brain massage for lazy comedy writers, but I wonder how many of its regular viewers are as displeased with it as the BBC Trust? My suspicion is that those trustees don't usually watch it; they're not familiar with the genre. They're comparing it to prime-time programming, which people are perfectly able to watch during the daytime instead – on DVD, cable repeat, iPlayer or Sky/Virgin/Freeview Plus. Daytime pap has never been so avoidable. If it's still getting viewers, isn't that a sign that it's not just feckless freelancers who are in the market for inconsequential television?

I still take issue with that slogan, though. I have a suggested replacement: "BBC1 Daytime. Because there's always tomorrow."

* * *

On the occasion of the launch, in August 2011, of JK Rowling's new website, Pottermore . . .

Harry Potter is like football. I'm talking about the literary, cinematic and merchandising phenomenon, not its focal fictional wizard. He isn't like football. He's like Jennings after being bitten by a radioactive conjuror. But, as with football, reports of Harry Potter-related events, products and personalities are everywhere. Like football supporters, Harry Potter fans seem to have an insatiable desire for more news, chat and retail opportunities related to their enthusiasm. They're standing in a monsoon screaming "I feel so dry!" while the rest of us are getting soaked.

It's bizarre. It has the intensity of a fad but it's been going for the best part of two decades. I think I'd find it easier to understand if I hated it. At least that would be an emotion of equivalent strength to the fans'. But, for me, it doesn't conform to the Marmite model: I've read three of the books and seen three of the films. I quite enjoyed them. I liked the third of each no less than the first two. I didn't feel the series had "gone off". It was just something that I only liked enough to consume so much of. It seemed perfectly good but I'd got the idea. I didn't mind not knowing what happened.

And then, obviously, because I am perverse, I was put off it by its ubiquity and other people's enthusiasm. Others' loss of perspective about its merits made me lose my own. Maybe I was trying to lower the average human opinion of the oeuvre closer to what it deserves by artificially forcing mine well below that level. Incidentally, this is where the parallels with my view of football end: even if that were a struggling minority sport only played by a few hundred enthusiastic amateurs, I would still consider it an overrated spectacle that lures vital funding away from snooker.

The most amazing aspect of JK Rowling's achievement and that of the Harry Potter marketing machine is that they have produced so much stuff for so long – kept the profile so high, the advertising so pervasive – and yet somehow contrived to leave a huge section of their audience still wanting more. They've given Harry the attributes of pistachio nuts and crack cocaine without the health risks (opening thousands of pistachio nuts can cause severe thumb-bruising, I can tell you from bitter experience of my life on the edge).

But, with the launch of the new Pottermore website, are they finally pushing their luck? In its opening weeks, trial access has been granted to a select group of a million fans. That's the real hardcore. Having a Harry Potter tattoo won't be enough – it has to be on your face. The site boasts material that didn't make it into the books, such as 5,000 words about which types of wood should be used to make magic wands and anecdotes about where Rowling found inspiration: why she called an unpleasant character Petunia, for example. But a fan writing in *The Times* wasn't impressed: "As a reader who has grown up with Harry over the years, the site dispels the magic of the wizarding world by removing the air of mystery behind the narrative that sparks debate among fans."

That's an attitude that strikes a chord with me and reminds me of *Star Wars*. Every generation must lose its innocence, must see the brightly painted nursery wall smashed away by the wrecking ball of betrayal to reveal a blighted landscape. For our predecessors, it was the Somme, the Great Depression, the Holocaust or Vietnam; for my generation, it was *The Phantom Menace*.

The problem isn't just that it's terrible but also that it retrospectively spoils the original films. George Lucas took the hinted-at, mythical, ancient yet futuristic realm of his first films and filled in all the detail like a tedious nerd. He ruined his own creation. It was as if Leonardo da Vinci had painted a speech bubble on the *Mona Lisa* in which she explained her state of mind. Everything that was magical, mysterious and half alluded to, Lucas now ploddingly dramatised, making it seem dull and trainspotterish. Those three prequels worked like aversion therapy for my addiction to the franchise.

I'd wanted the prequels to be made – I'm sure most fans did. We were desperately keen for Lucas to answer all the questions that the original films had posed. But he was wrong to accede to our wishes – not financially, but artistically. When it comes to art and popular culture, consumers are like children and chocolate, students and alcohol: they don't know what's good for them, they can't predict when certain behaviour will make them feel sick.

As with junk food, so with books, films and TV, the current trend is to give people what they think they want, rather than to leave them wanting more. Presumably that's the motivation behind making a new series of *Inspector Morse* featuring the character as a young man. ITV knows that fans of Morse will watch it (God knows, they watch *Lewis*). The original series brilliantly hinted at the character's troubled, melancholy past, so we'll tune in to find out the details.

It's like with a magic trick: you're desperate to know how it's done but, when you find out, the mundane truth usually disappoints and undermines your enjoyment of the illusion. Similarly, the specifics of Morse's past can't possibly live up to our imagined versions. Like a good magician, ITV and Colin Dexter would serve their audience better by resisting its curiosity. Fans don't really know what they want or they'd make up stories for themselves. (Some do, and "fan fiction" is an excellent way for them to slake their thirst for content without destroying the mystery for everyone else.) With a story, as with a well-chosen gift, we're happiest when surprised by something we didn't know we wanted.

So it annoys me that there's such pressure to provide more backstory and more information about films and TV. DVDs are packed with deleted scenes, out-takes, "making of" documentaries and explanatory commentary. The experience of making a TV show today is to be perpetually distracted from working on the actual programme by demands from the broadcaster's website for additional material that will inevitably be of a lower quality. Some of this is harmless, but a lot of it is telling people how the trick is done.

I hope the new Harry Potter website won't undermine the enjoyment of the Potterverse for those million golden-ticket holders. But it's a possibility. In the real world, chocolate isn't made in a magic factory by Oompa-Loompas. And as for Ginsters slices . . . there are some things that you just don't want to know.

* * *

"OK, this is the worst thing I'm going to say," announced outspoken chef Skye Gyngell. Ooh, what might it be? thought the interviewer. Casual homophobia? A libel against George Osborne? A final denunciation of the carrot? "If I ever have another restaurant, I pray we don't get a star." Bit of an anticlimax. But odd. Gyngell was talking about the Michelin star awarded last year to the Petersham Nurseries Cafe, from which she has just quit as head chef. "It's been a curse . . . Since we got the star we've been crammed every single day . . . And we've had lots more complaints." Not least from the head chef about the restaurant being too busy.

But I understand what she means. She was only running an informal cafe in a garden centre – a posh cafe in a posh garden centre, admittedly, but not really a restaurant. "People have certain expectations of a Michelin restaurant but we don't have cloths on the tables and our service isn't very formal," she explains. Her bare scrubbed wood tables (in 2004, when the place opened, there was only one of them) and seasonal ingredients wowed the Michelin men's jaded appetites. Sick of starch and the sommelier's bow, they found her approach refreshing. A tear was brought to the gastronomes' eyes by her honest home cooking in a leafy environment a world away from the tarnished splendour of haute cuisine's saline trickery. At its best, you can't beat home cooking. But Mum doesn't always make a roast and your favourite pudding. Sometimes it's fish fingers with a side order of yesterday's sprouts. Those attracted by the star, less tired of intricate dishes in swanky restaurants than the judges, may have thought the Suttons seeds rack and display of watering cans detracted from the ambience of their anniversary dinners.

In the end, the award robbed customers of the very feeling of serendipity that made the Michelinsters commend the cafe in the first place. They had denied others their delight in the food being much better than they'd expected. It's like a review of a farce which tells people they'll roll in the aisles. "They won't now," I always think. Nothing short of an earthquake will make an audience roll in an aisle when they've braced themselves.

Our level of expectation is crucial to our enjoyment of food, wine, holidays, plays, films and TV shows. We flatter ourselves that we're objective but our judgments are clouded by our hopes, by whether something was better or worse than we'd anticipated. The films I've most loved, as well as those I've most hated, are the ones I've known least about in advance. When I'm well briefed, my range of responses clusters more closely around the average. It's almost impossible to find a brilliant film brilliant if dozens of people have told you it's brilliant in advance. "You *have* to see it – you'll be amazed!" they say, and then I can't help expecting it to transcend the medium – to be more than just a film, even though I can't imagine how. A film with free sandwiches, perhaps, or useful tips for putting up shelves.

So it's difficult to know what to do if you think something's excellent. You want friends to discover it by chance, like you did. But you want to make sure they do. How do you push them towards it without elevating their expectations and increasing their capacity for disappointment?

This was a worry for me after seeing *The Muppets* recently. I hadn't read any reviews or spoken to anyone who'd seen it, so I watched with few expectations, other than having adored *The Muppet Show* as a child. And I loved it. I was alternately moved and amused. I laughed and, had my education not severed the link between my tear ducts and my brain's emotional centre, I would have cried. But, just by saying this, I may have Michelin-starred the shit out of any joy you might derive from it. Sorry.

A lot of my enjoyment, with the greatest respect to those who made the film, came from my nostalgia for the TV show. I'm a great one for sneering at remakes but, in this case, my reminiscence glands were aflame; I was desperate to experience again the warm hilarity which had made me love that programme three decades ago.

I can't help feeling that they don't make shows like that any more – that the 1970s was the golden age of television, certainly of children's television. The medium had come of age but not yet lost its youthful verve. A joyous psychedelic creativity was finding its outlet in programmes such as *Rainbow*, *The Magic Roundabout* and *The Muppet Show*. Crazy, brilliant things which wouldn't make sense on paper were being tried out because TV was still insufficiently organised to ruin itself.

I genuinely can't help feeling it but I doubt it's true. I suspect there are brilliant kids' shows nowadays and there was plenty of crap then. All I'm really bemoaning is my loss of innocence and childish wonder. When I first saw *The Muppet Show*, I had no expectations and I was blown away. I can't ever watch anything in that spirit again.

People say that we tend to read the books that impress or move us most before the age of 25. Not because we read less in later life but because we get too sophisticated to be so easily awestruck. Once you've read *Great Expectations*, anything you subsequently read would have to be even better than *Great Expectations* to impress you to the same extent as *Great Expectations* did – it would have to compensate for your greater expectations as a result of having read *Great Expectations*. That's asking a lot of Nick Hornby.

To make matters worse, we're living in an era when the media constantly try to manage those expectations with trailers, adverts and reviews. At the end of episodes of TV shows, they tell you what to expect next week. These packages of clips are designed to intrigue, to draw you in, to build keen anticipation which next week's show will then struggle to fulfil. We're consigned to a perpetual hype–disappointment loop.

There's no joy without peril. If you're not willing to risk massive disappointment – if you only eat at award-winning restaurants or watch films with five-star reviews – you'll experience it in a mild form all the time. And you'll never wander into a garden-centre cafe for a spot of lunch and have your modest expectations blown away by the bill.

* * *

On the subject of an arrestingly incongruous image from October 2012 . . .

There was an amusing photograph in the papers last week. It shows all the Disney theme park favourites – the human-sized but giant-headed mice, dogs and ducks – dressed up as *Star Wars* characters. Goofy is Darth Vader, Donald Duck is sporting elements of an imperial stormtrooper's uniform, Minnie Mouse is wearing a Princess Leia dress and Mickey is in full Jedi get-up, light sabre raised, giant immovable mousey grin turned perkily to the camera as he prepares to use the force to make Walt proud.

But the most entertaining figure is in the middle – a rotund, bespectacled old man, also holding a light sabre, dressed scruffily in shirt and jeans but with gleaming white trainers, a neat grey beard and hair as precisely coiffed as a Mollie Sugden perm. His facial expression is somewhere between exhaustion, sorrow and bafflement, as if some kindly carers have taken him on a day trip of which he has little understanding. Of course, in reality he fully grasps his surroundings, for this is billionaire film-maker George Lucas and the photo has been taken on the occasion of the sale of his movie empire, Lucasfilm, to Disney.

I don't understand why he agreed to the picture if he wasn't going to enter into the spirit of it and make some attempt with his comparatively tiny human features to echo the massive

Disney grins surrounding him. So maybe this snap caught him in a downbeat instant between exaggerated cheesy gurns. Or maybe he thought his glum look was more appropriate to the dignity of the great moment, like when a statesman signs an important treaty. Maybe he felt Mickey and co were lowering the tone with their gaping mouths.

The announcement caused excitement among *Star Wars* fans, not just because it adds another range of funny outfits to the Disney parade wardrobe, but because, along with the purchase of Lucasfilm's renowned high-tech production companies, the Indiana Jones franchise and the rights to manufacture cuddly mouse-eared R2-D2s, this deal allows Disney to make a new *Star Wars* film. That's something which, very recently, seemed unlikely ever to happen again. Lucas told the *New York Times* the previous January that he would never make another: "Why would I make any more when everybody yells at you all the time?" I think we can rule out his writing a column for the *Guardian* website any time soon.

The guys at Disney have promised to bring out *Star Wars* episode seven in 2015 and to follow that with episodes eight and nine. Thereafter their plan is to release a new film every two or three years pretty much indefinitely. Basically, they want *Star Wars* to go Bond.

To Disney's investors, the prospect could hardly look more appetising. The latest release from the 50-year-old 007 franchise is being showered with critical praise and box-office cash. Having seen *Skyfall*, I can't say I understand why. I mean, it's fine. It's probably an above-average Bond movie, but then it benefits from budgetary and technological possibilities that most of its predecessors lacked. It certainly isn't the "best Bond ever", as many are claiming. It is very nearly the longest Bond ever, narrowly beaten by Daniel Craig's first appearance in the role, *Casino Royale*. Maybe Craig has ambitions to be the longest-serving Bond but wants to get there in the fewest possible films.

There's a lot wrong with it. It takes itself far too seriously, and the suavity of the character is lost; the heartless charmer, the well-dressed psychopath who will unhesitatingly deploy violence to get what he wants – but who wants nothing more, due to an accident of his nature, than the furtherance of British national interests – has been replaced by a gnarled potato-headed bruiser haunted by his own past. Batman without the gear. I miss the jammy sod in the bow tie whose toast always lands butter side up. Yet, for all this self-importance, the plot is still as daft as in the campest days of Roger Moore. I won't spoil the ending for you – the writers have already done that – except to say: have courage, the film does, eventually, end.

Comparisons with the Bond franchise are bound to make hardcore *Star Wars* fans nervous. Most would balk at an open-ended series of adventures vaguely set in the *Star Wars* universe, but with the same variance of style, tone and competence that the Bond franchise has displayed. Will they have to endure different actors taking on the central characters? They've already seen Ewan McGregor struggle to fill Alec Guinness's shoes. But, as the roles of Luke Skywalker, Han Solo and Princess Leia are taken forward, the opportunities for other actors to screw them up – or rather "put their own stamp on them" – are endless.

Will they have to cope with a moody Russell Crowe interpretation of Han in middle age, complete with inexplicable and shaky geordie accent? Will Maggie Smith turn an aged Queen Leia of the Universe into a wise-cracking old gossip? Will Mark Hamill be allowed to reprise the role he created or will he have to stand in line to audition with the likes of Bill Nighy, Steve Martin and that bloke from *Breaking Bad*? Or are Disney's real intentions hiding in plain sight in that photo? Are they going to give the galaxy to the Great Mouse?

The prospect of a Disneyfied *Star Wars* would have appalled me 15 years ago. The thought of that corporate giant getting its weird three-fingered hands on the beloved space stories of my childhood would have seemed like sacrilege. Since then, of course, Jesus has desecrated his own altar and then set up as a money-changer in his own temple. And if you think that's a hyperbolic way of describing the fact that George Lucas made three disappointing sci-fi films, you need to get online more.

As a feckless writer and comedian, I spend a lot of pub time railing against all the occasions when creative control is wrested from the people who have the ideas by the people who keep the accounts. So I find the story of the Star Wars franchise unsettling. Lucas had the successful idea and maintained rigid creative control over it, doubtless fending off the advances of avaricious predators who wanted to exploit or develop it differently. And yet that idea was more comprehensively ruined than if it had been left exposed to the worst and most idiotic corporate abuse imaginable.

So what's to fear from Disney? They might make an entertaining film about a duck in space. It would be a lot edgier than Jar Jar Binks.

Disney didn't hang about, as we now know, and episode seven is currently in production, with JJ Abrams directing and most of the stars of the first film reprising their roles. Which means, sadly, that it'll be episode eight, at the earliest, before we see Russell Crowe attempt to wrestle Chewbacca, Bill Nighy get exasperated with R2-D2 or a duck feel the Force.

* * *

Laura Carmichael deserves to be congratulated. Few actors have achieved her kind of success. Her portrayal of Lady Edith in

Downton Abbey is so effective, and so affecting, that the character has started to become real. Not just to seem real to people watching television, but actually to *be*. The fact that this became clear on the occasion of her West End debut playing another role in no way diminishes the achievement.

You may not be familiar with Lady Edith, or with *Downton Abbey* at all. Even if you are, you may pretend not to be. It's not a particularly respectable show to admit to watching.

Or is that nonsense? In some ways, it's unassailably respectable: a Sunday night costume drama, oozing the cream of the British acting profession. But it's not particularly worthy or worthwhile, and yet neither is it trashy or amoral enough to be watched with irony. It falls equidistantly between the two vastly separated stools of *Our Friends in the North* and *RuPaul's Drag Race*. Watching it is nothing to be proud of, but neither is it sufficiently shaming to be conversationally interesting.

I've seen every single episode. I think it might be my favourite programme. I enjoy it enormously. I also think it's shit. Not badly acted or filmed, but appallingly scripted and structured. Utterly inept with regard to these elements of television production which I previously considered vital to a drama's success – or certainly its enjoyability. Yet I undoubtedly do enjoy *Downton Abbey*, and not "because it's so terrible". I unironically enjoy it despite how bad it is. Is that what they call cognitive dissonance? Or is it just really liking footage of a stately home?

So Laura Carmichael deserves much credit for turning the implausible words and actions in the script into a believable character. Lady Edith is the second daughter of the Earl of Grantham, who owns Downton Abbey (which is where *Downton Abbey* is set – it is not a real abbey, so he is not an abbot), and she has a very rough time. The plainer middle sibling, she lives her life like an emotional Frank Spencer, her heart always metaphorically being dragged along on roller skates behind a bus. The men she loves either die or get engaged to her sister or both; or are too old or jilt her at the altar or both. Everything Edith turns her hand to – driving, farming, journalism – is greeted with hostility and scorn. She's definitely the unluckiest of the three Crawley sisters, and one of the others has died.

So, when the press night of a new production of *Uncle Vanya* at the Vaudeville theatre, in which Carmichael plays Sonya, was interrupted in a weird and unlucky way, I thought: "Of course, that *would* happen to Lady Edith." And then I realised: Lady Edith has come to life.

This is what happened: in the closing moments of the play, Lady Edith (Sonya) was delivering a soft and moving final speech to Ken Stott (Vanya) in which she exhorts him to keep his pecker up, when Sir Peter Hall, who was in the third row of the stalls, started shouting, or at least talking. Accounts vary, but he definitely wasn't whispering. Accounts also vary as to exactly what he definitely wasn't whispering, but he definitely wasn't not-whispering "Bravo!" The *Telegraph* reckons he said: "Stop, stop, stop. It doesn't work and you don't work. It is not good enough. I could be at home watching television," while the *Guardian* thought "It's not working, it's just not working. It's just like something on television" was nearer the mark.

Theatre being what it is, the sentiments conveyed by Hall are less surprising than the fact that he chose to express them during an actual performance. Wishing productions to stop and that you could be transported back home to the TV are familiar sentiments to all regular theatregoers, but it seemed rude of Hall to shout those desires so audibly, and it clashed with his subsequent verdict on the show as "a fine production with a superb company of actors".

A couple of days later, Sir Peter provided the explanation: "I dropped off for a moment and on being woken by my wife I was briefly disorientated." Well, we've all been there. Theatres are warm, dark and quiet. The drama being played out on a slightly illuminated platform some yards away is often no more energising than a whispered midnight conversation at the nurses' station of a restful hospital ward. If I had a penny for every time I'd fallen asleep while watching a play, I'd nearly have enough for an interval drink. Genuinely.

As apologies for heckles go, "Sorry, I was asleep!" isn't ideal. It doesn't necessarily mean the production is bad or boring – and the critical consensus seems to be that this one is neither – but it's hardly a ringing endorsement. "This show sent me so soundly to sleep that, when I was shaken awake by my wife, I'd completely forgotten where I was or what was going on" is unlikely to be put up in lights outside the theatre.

But Sir Peter had to own up to being asleep or he'd seem boorish and brutal. His priority was to clarify that, as he said, "Remarks made in the resulting confusion were not in any way related to *Uncle Vanya*." I believe him because I think they were in every way related to *Downton Abbey* – and Lady Edith. Sir Peter's unconscious mutterings make it very clear that he is a regular viewer and has been utterly captivated by Carmichael's performance.

He walked into that theatre with his head full of Lady Edith's misfortunes: he was nervous for her, wishing her well, yet fearful that something would go wrong for her, as it always does. Consequently, when surprised in a half-waking, half-sleeping state, his fears Touretted out: he found himself saying the worst things his unconscious could imagine – precisely the remarks that Edith/Carmichael least wanted to hear.

Even while playing a lead role on the press night of a starry and classy West End show, which coincided with the broadcast of her massive TV hit, Laura Carmichael didn't seem successful or fortunate to Hall. She didn't seem like a rising talent, a celebrity, a household name, a winner, the centre of a maelstrom of opportunity. She remained every ounce the luckless Edith. Now that's acting.

* * *

I was recently infuriated by a study. I'm not talking about the type of room – I wasn't maddened by a den or seething at the sight of a home office. I was annoyed by a "survey", a "report", some "research". It was given all sorts of titles in the press, none of which was "pile of sanctimonious crap", which is a shame because that's what it was.

Some people at Netmums, which I'm guessing is the Pepsi to Mumsnet's Coke (irresponsible though it is of me to mention either high-sugar drink when children might be reading), had decided the world might be a better place if they found some way of slagging off *The Simpsons*. And, while they were at it, *The Flintstones* and *Peppa Pig* and *The Gruffalo* and *My Family* and *Outnumbered*. All of those enjoyable entertainments, and *My Family*, were criticised for their negative depictions of fathers. It was like the RSPCA moaning that *Tom and Jerry* is an unrepresentative depiction of the behaviour of the domestic cat or the Institute of Hospitality complaining that *Fawlty Towers* puts people off going to hotels.

It wasn't just a diatribe written by the website's staff members: 2,000 parents had been asked their opinions, although I'm not sure in what context and I refuse to find out. But they must've been caught in a whingeing mood because they seemed determined to take popular culture personally. Ninety-three per cent thought that the typical comedically bungling TV dad doesn't accurately reflect what fathers contribute to families in real life. They were not then asked whether or not that's a problem – whether it is the job of a show such as *The Simpsons* to accurately reflect family life, whether such shows have ever implied they're an accurate reflection of anything at all and whether Homer Simpson accurately reflects the number of fingers most fathers have.

Had they been asked those things, I hope they would have responded along the lines of "No, of course that's not a problem – it's just that you asked whether various characters in popular culture, which are clearly the product of comic exaggeration and in some cases surreal invention, were accurate reflections of reality, and they're obviously not, so I said they weren't." But I doubt that's how it would have gone because 46% of those surveyed thought that these characters could make children believe that all dads are "useless" and 28% felt that these depictions amounted to a "very subtle form of discrimination". So they do seem quite het up about it, which I think is stupid and depressing.

My state of mind was not improved by the remarks of Netmums' founder, Siobhan Freegard, which accompanied the report. "It's never been harder to be a father – but good dads have never been more needed by their families," she said, which seems reasonable enough until you think about it for a second and realise that she's wrong on both counts. There have been many times in human history when it's been harder to be a father – during the Black Death, for example – and also many times when families have needed fathers more – the tens of thousands of years when they were expected to hunt and kill all the family's food springs to mind. Sorry if you think I'm being petty but, if she's going to claim that loads of comedies that people enjoy are corroding our society, she oughtn't to kick off with a historically inept statement.

She wasn't finished: "So it seems perverse we are telling men to step up and be involved, while running them down in the media." Who is this "we"? Whoever wrote *The Flintstones*? The *Peppa Pig* production team? She presumably counts herself among the people who tell men to "step up and be involved" – fair enough – but is she annoyed that she can't also vet all scripts for comedies and children's programmes for deviations from that message? Does she expect the culture to speak in unison? Does she believe that Fred Flintstone saying "Yabba-dabba-doo!" amounts to an advocacy of shouting gibberish? Maybe she thinks Miranda Hart's pratfalls undermine the good work of the Health and Safety Executive.

"Some people claim 'it's just a joke'," she continued, "but there's nothing amusing about taking away good role models for young boys." Yes, there is. Once again, she's strayed into untruth. For example, when Homer Simpson says "Mmm . . . floor pie" on seeing a slice of pie on the floor, that is amusing, and yet he is not being a positive role model. The negative role models Siobhan Freegard has commissioned a report to complain about do amusing things all the time.

What there is, for practical comedy-writing purposes, "nothing amusing about" is good role models: a caring, conscientious father who doesn't get into scrapes – that's the stuff of government information films, not funny programmes. And the "useless dad" may not be a fair reflection of society but, if it was complete invention, the characters wouldn't resonate. Accident-prone Daddy Pig, or Hugh Dennis's hapless character in *Outnumbered*, may not be representative examples of modern fatherhood but they obviously strike a chord or those shows wouldn't be watched by millions.

This report is at once joyless and opportunistic. It seeks to say something headline-grabbing and preachy in order to garner positive coverage for a website, and is content to make a victim of some of the finest products of the noble human urge to amuse and entertain. There are many things wrong with humanity but I'm fairly sure that funny sitcoms and cartoons about family life aren't among them.

But when Freegard says, "The type of jokes aimed at dads would be banned if they were aimed at women, ethnic minorities or religious groups," she has got a point – just not the one she thinks she's got. Men and fathers are so favoured in our society, the world is weighted so much to their advantage, that comedy writers can safely make them the perpetual butt of jokes. The fact that Homer Simpson is the funniest, most prominent and most popular character in that show says far more about the continued male dominance of money and power in the west than his fecklessness or misfortunes say about the undervaluing of paternal effort.

Comedy is a misère bid – to be the biggest loser is to win. If a time comes when incompetent or hapless women are humorously depicted as often as their male equivalents, then the distorting fairground mirror of comedy might at last be reflecting a just world.

* * *

On the occasion of the first anniversary of the 2013 horsemeat scandal . . .

One year ago today the horsemeat scandal broke, when the Food Safety Authority of Ireland reported that horse DNA had been found in some beef burgers – or, depending on your point of view, that some horse burgers had been mislabelled. This wasn't to be an isolated incident. In the weeks that followed, a bewildering array of ground cow products tested positive for ground horse. It seemed that there was hardly a manufacturer or retailer in the British Isles that hadn't been cutting its sirloin with fetlock.

Horses had thoroughly contaminated the food chain. "What an oddly large animal to have infested so many factories," we thought. It's easy to envisage how mice, cockroaches or flies can sneak into dirty or badly maintained facilities to feed and breed – but horses? Surely they must have left traces, hoofprints in the butter? Why had no one smelt a rat? Perhaps because of the overpowering stench of horse.

The scandal climaxed with the news that some Findus lasagnes were found to contain 100% horsemeat. They were absolutely all horse. Not a scrap of beef had made it in. In a sense, this made Findus the worst offender. But, looked at from a different angle, it was cause for hope: restricting products to one type of meat was achievable, it seemed. If Findus could only repeat with beef this remarkable success with horse, then all would be well.

As a comedian, I am extremely glad that this all happened. To my mind, there is little to be regretted about this widespread equine malpractice and a great deal to be celebrated. This was extremely funny news and I am convinced it will have brought immeasurably more pleasure to many more people than all of the grotty ready meals that were recalled could ever have done had they solely contained ground-up cartilage and ligament of the advertised species rather than the macerated fragments of other, more glamorous, quadrupeds.

You may disagree with my definition of funny news. What's funny about incompetence, malpractice and dishonesty in the preparation of our food, you might ask. You might think this is simply a grim example of something going seriously wrong. Funny news, you might say, is when Boris Johnson gets his balls caught in a harness or Kanye West sues the online currency "Coinye West" for exploiting his image.

In my experience, news like that is too obviously amusing to be lastingly funny. You can't make a joke about it because the story is already a joke. You can laugh once, because it's daft, then it's over. But the horsemeat scandal kept on giving. It was proper news that deserved coverage – but no one had died and several large and unappealing corporations were left with egg on their faces. Well, they said it was egg.

Audiences love jokes about this sort of thing. It's not just a YouTube clip of a gibbon sneezing and it's not Syria. It's serious enough for the act of joking to seem slightly irreverent, but not serious enough for anyone (other than those with no intention of ever being amused by anything) actually to be offended. It's part of a nation's shared experience and laughing about it brings us together, like a family swapping anecdotes about a tipsy uncle.

I've noticed a few subjects like this over the years. Liberal-leaning Radio 4-type studio audiences absolutely never tire of derogatory references to the *Daily Mail*, for example. There need be nothing incisive or new in the joke, but you can guarantee a supportive laugh by questioning that newspaper's honesty, accuracy or goodwill, or mentioning once again its former warm regard for Hitler.

The excessive distances between the small airports sometimes used by budget airlines and the cities those airlines have advertised as their destination are also a reliable source of collective amusement. You have only to imply that Ryanair won't necessarily drop you off right in the centre of Paris and people will guffaw and crow as if a great and brand-new injustice has just been spotted for the very first time and simultaneously comprehensively dealt with.

In my view, the horsemeat thing is one of the greatest. It has obvious advantages. "Horse" is a funny word – only one syllable, and it's a corker. The idea of people having eaten something without realising it is inherently comic. The deep solemnity of some of those who rightly pointed out how worrying it is that we've so lost touch with where our food comes from that we can't even be sure of what noise it once made is apt to make people giggly. And the palpable desperation of the likes of Tesco, Iceland, Lidl and Findus that this whole thing should be forgotten makes hearing it repeatedly brought up intensely pleasurable. It will be decades before the words "Tesco" and "horse" stop getting a laugh just for being spoken in the same sentence – and that fact, and how infuriating the PR people at Tesco must find it, is itself hilarious.

British Rail used to be the acme of this sort of thing. As a nation we spent decades sharing a laugh at the inadequacies of British Rail with its lateness, dirtiness, rudeness and terrible sandwiches. The failings in our rail network were a shared collective reflection on our failings as a community. British Rail was crap because everything was crap, because we were also, individually and collectively, a bit crap – laughable and decrepit and doomed, like all humans have always been. But somehow redeemed by our capacity to self-mock.

The dissolution and sale of British Rail, transforming it into a disjointed network charging exorbitant prices for an unimproved and still taxpayer-subsidised service, darkened the joke a bit much for popular tastes. We stopped chuckling. It was like the tipsy uncle had assaulted a receptionist.

So let's cling to horsegate for as long as we can. You never know where the next bit of funny news is coming from. Although, I must say, François Hollande is doing his bit by being motorcycle-couriered to an actress's bed in the full view of the global media. I might well be celebrating that one in a year's time – because if there's one thing British audiences enjoy laughing at even more than their own failings, the rapacity of corporations or xenophobia in the *Daily Mail*, it's the French.

* * *

If I told you that extreme rightwing activists were using a googly-eyed character with a weird flapping mouth to try and build their support base, you'd probably tell me to stop being rude about Nigel Farage. Or applaud me for being rude about Nigel Farage. But for once I'm not slagging off Ukip's straight-talking bitter drinker. I'm referring to someone who, as far as we know, has never touched beer or cigarettes, which is probably a good thing as he seems to have rather an addictive personality. It's the Cookie Monster from *Sesame Street*, surely the world's most lovable personification of an eating disorder, whose image has been adopted by a group of German neo-Nazis in an attempt to recruit children.

"But how is this allowed?" you're probably asking. It isn't. Steffen Lange, who walked into a school playground in Brandenburg dressed as the Cookie Monster and started handing out neo-Nazi leaflets, has been arrested by the German police. I don't know whether the producers of *Sesame Street* are planning legal action but I imagine they'd have a case. Maybe they don't think there's much point since, as TV programmes go, *Sesame Street* is about as likely to be mistaken for being pro-Nazi as *Dad's Army*.

Then again, this wasn't an isolated incident: Cookie Monster-themed rightwing pamphlets were subsequently discovered at Lange's home, and the police have confirmed that the blue fluffy problem-eater's image is increasingly being abused by the region's far right to try and drum up support. A police spokesman speculated that it was an attempt to make neo-Nazism seem "a bit fun and a bit rebellious".

This is a fascinating strategy – and an insight into the mindset of the modern fascist. The Cookie Monster is anarchic, dynamic and madly driven by a very specific, but also totally random, aim: he wants cookies. He wants to charge around crazily smashing cookies into his mouth. He will never get enough cookies. It's unclear whether he understands this. Maybe he imagines some future stage of sated calm which he might achieve if, miraculously, he were to obtain all the cookies he desires. Or maybe he is wiser than that and knows it's all about the journey, his endless quest for biscuits.

These extremists' message is clear: that's what it's like to be a neo-Nazi. It's not mean, harsh and judgmental – not primarily, that's just a side-effect. It's wild, active and devil-may-care. And violent – but it's not about whom the violence is directed at, that's not important. It's about the sensual joy of the violence itself. It's fun, dynamic, outdoorsy and liberated. Those who get hurt are collateral damage – hence the usefulness of a rationale by which hurting them is either good or irrelevant. As long as you see Jews and Gypsies as only so many cookies to be ground up in a cloth mouth, rather than as actual people, then it's all good clean fun.

You can't say this doesn't tap into a side of humanity that has always existed. Since the dawn of time, there have been plenty of us who just love running around and smashing things and people to bits. Think of the Vikings. They sailed around, pillaging, burning and looting, for centuries. They did it out of economic necessity; they did it out of greed; they did it out of hatred for other races and religions. But many of them must also have done it for fun. Some of those great warriors – skilled seamen and fearless soldiers – must have loved that life, loved running up to a coastal village and unleashing carnage.

Don't focus on our specific unpalatable views, Herr Lange and his colleagues are saying, focus on the thrill. There's something more primal in the appeal of extremist politics than any of its ostensible beliefs or policies – and the sensation is a lot like running around shouting "Cooookiiiiieeeessss!!!!!" For so long considered monsters by the political mainstream, these rightwingers are finally coming clean: "That's exactly what we are!" they're admitting. "Cuddly mindless monsters – and it feels amazing!"

But will they take these intriguing new recruitment tactics further? How else might fascists perk up their image now they're dispensing with all the tiresome Teutonic discipline and hate-sponsored pseudo-science and returning to their berserker roots?

Music

Can you imagine the Cookie Monster listening to Wagner, a nationalistic anthem or a marching band? Of course not – he's far too fidgety. The modern neo-Nazi wants a tune that's a lot more energetic and fun: Yakety Sax, Killing in the Name or the theme from *Ski Sunday* are all perfect upbeat accompaniments to any frenzy of hate.

Hashtags

Everyone knows that extremists say horrible things on social media, but a hashtag is a great way to put even the most vile remarks into a more upbeat context. Threats of violence in particular can be leavened if made cartoonish with postscripts such as #biff, #blam, #kersplat or #everydayracism.

Dress

The black shirt and the brown shirt, those staples of the fascists' glory days, have been lost to the jazz musician and the 1978 Coventry City away strip respectively (I used the internet in the preparation of this section). And anyway, they're far too staid for the wacky fascism of the Cookie Monster Nazis. So what about Hawaiian shirts? They're fun, they're crazy, they're slightly anarchic (within blandly uninventive parameters) and, like pineapple on a pizza, they provide the sort of meaningless nod to multiculturalism that helps less committed racists salve their lacerated consciences.

Dance

How better to separate actions from any sense of their meaning than with dance? The global success of Gangnam Style has shown the way. The extreme right needs to move on from the discredited fascist salute and develop some new gesture or move which can be aped by millions on YouTube. Something like a double thumbs-up while running on the spot, David Brent's dance from *The Office* or just a spot of rhythmic mooning would be ideal.

Baking

The choice of the Cookie Monster suggests that, at a time when *The Great British Bake-Off* has both made baking trendy and aligned it with a sense of national identity, the far right wants to reclaim the fascist oven from the shadow of Auschwitz. But, unlike their mascot, modern neo-Nazis don't just like cookies – they're into cakes, pies and puddings, but not soufflés, which are homosexual. An inspiring recipe book could be the *Mein Kampf* of the 21st century, providing busy racists with the perfect high-carb treat to set them up for a night's angry shouting outside a mosque.

* * *

On reading that *Who Wants to Be a Millionaire?* has ended its final run, I was amazed to find myself caring. To my surprise, it made me sad. I didn't know I gave a damn about that show – I certainly never particularly enjoyed it – but it turns out I'd been quietly assuming that it would continue and, unbeknownst to my conscious brain, deriving comfort from that assumption. Suddenly it was gone and I missed it, like an old pot plant that you only remember is there when it dies.

Mind you, I'm glad I didn't watch it more – on the dozen or so occasions I caught an episode, I mildly regretted the time spent. It wasn't very entertaining, just moreish – the televisual equivalent of Twiglets. You grimly munched through it because, for some reason, it seemed easier than not.

You must be familiar with the feeling, unless it's all Radio 3 and the *TLS* round your place. You stick around for another couple of questions, and then a bit longer to see what the contestant will win, because it would be very slightly interesting to witness someone's avarice comprehensively slaked on camera. Real-time evidence of a deadly sin, a pre-watershed money shot. But no one ever won the million when I was tuned in. So when the credits rolled, I only had two or three uncontextualised pieces of trivia to show for the fact that I was now an hour nearer death.

Ageing is the key to this. Disposable TV shows of this kind are supposed to take our minds off the fact that we're perpetually getting older – to make the time pass pleasantly enough without reminding us that it's finite. But, as its last act, *Millionaire* has done exactly the opposite. It provided me with a stinging reminder of the elusiveness of time and it made me feel old. That's what elegiac dramas are meant to do, not quizzes.

In my head, you see, it was a recent programme – an example of the "terrible crap that's on TV these days". That's where I had it filed: as a contemporary example of media commercialism, of ITV joyously dancing on the grave of *The World at War* and the Jeremy Brett *Sherlock Holmes* adaptations. So hearing that it's been axed after a decade and a half, that it's been put out of its misery after a long decline, feels like getting news that Google has called in the receivers or Justin Bieber needs a hip replacement. I open my eyes after a short nap to see the jungle-choked ruins of the Shard being fought over by a savage tribe of super-evolved molluscs.

When *Who Wants to Be a Millionaire?* started, I was not yet working in television – though that's not what I was saying at the time. If you'd asked me then, the very last thing I would have said is: "I'm a delusional waster with a second-class degree in a humanity and an inability to take an alarm clock seriously. I've been to the Edinburgh Fringe and done a lot of amateur dramatics, but basically I work as an usher for less than what the minimum wage will be when it comes in next year." That was the inconvenient truth, but instead of telling it I would have claimed to be a comedian and pitched the various hungover scribblings that I pretended to be convinced would soon conjure up a generous living.

Well, somehow, in the midst of my bullshit, a career germinated; I got lucky and so got paid. But, in 1998, I was still terrified and resentful of the vast and impenetrable media in which I aspired to prosper. And *Who Wants to Be a Millionaire?* seemed to represent all that – it was the thick and immovable taproot of my problems.

All the cosiness of the TV I'd grown up with, all that "Well, of course it has far too much sentimental value for us to consider parting with it!" *Antiques Roadshow* propriety, seemed to have been blasted away by this huge, frightening, mercenary format. The *Blankety Blank* chequebook and pen, the his-and-hers matching wristwatches, even the star-prize speedboat had been pressure-hosed off our screens with cash. The future of TV was a series of mediocrities hungrily grasping at unimaginable sums of money by the ghoulish light of a monitor – they might as well televise a trading floor. Censorious and broke, I took a dim view.

So my younger self would probably be pleased at the programme's passing. But the demise of seemingly invincible entities of which you disapprove is not always reassuring. It can make you feel vulnerable – like nothing is safe. Of course, I can think of reasons for *Millionaire*'s downfall. Ultimately, its success depended on the suspense generated by ordinary people trying to become very rich. Someone genuinely becoming a millionaire on television is very watchable – for the first time. It's not bad the second. But, after a bit, a contestant's path to victory is like another *Jaws* sequel. We know how the story goes. The tension on which the programme relied was inevitably going to slacken over time.

The attempt to enliven the format with celebrities raising money for charities was deeply flawed. The crucial drama-generating ingredient of a member of the public trying to transform their circumstances is removed. The celebrity stands to gain nothing personally and, even if they win a million, unless they're campaigning for a fairly trivial cause, that huge amount will disappear into the bottomless pit of one or other of humanity's insoluble crises. It's not like, if they win, cancer will be cured or Africa will be fine or drugs will go away – that would have viewers on the edge of their seats. Win or lose, there's no thrill – just an opportunity for someone famous to raise awareness of something worthwhile. It's a good thing but it doesn't stop you changing channels at the break.

In essence, I'm sad because I realised, only when I heard the show was finished, that it wasn't a symbol of the terrifying new world of the media at all. Rather it was one of the last successes of the old. It was the Mallard, not the TGV. Fundamentally just a quiz show with a prize, it predates the tsunami of reality TV – all the personal journeys and public votes, the singing and crying and testicle-eating and diary-room self-justification. It started before the internet and channel proliferation forced broadcasters to fight for their very existence. Its confidence sprang from ignorance of the tribulations ahead.

3

Don't Expect Too Much of Robots

Lots of people seem to hate corporations, and I think that's unfair. Sometimes I sound like I hate them too, but I really don't. It's too emotional a response. In a complex economy, plcs are naturally occurring and they shouldn't be hated any more than bacteria, mould, weeds, rain or sunshine – or, more aptly since they were made by us rather than by whatever made everything else (God or general events, or perhaps a god called General Events), than robots. Like rain or robots, they can do good and harm. They're useful but they're to be feared. They can be great and they can be terrible. But they don't feel emotions, so we shouldn't feel emotions about them.

This section is full of our puny human dealings with them: the adverts with which they attempt to communicate with us, and our weird irrational responses; the things we unfairly expect of them; and the things we stupidly let them get away with.

* * *

I was puzzled by an advertising hoarding recently. It was for Courage beer and used their old slogan, "Take Courage". I'm tediously antiquarian enough to have been interested and slightly pleased by that: a phrase I've grown used to seeing in broken lettering on the side of failing, flat-roofed pubs given a new lease of life, the inherent punning opportunity in the beer's name proving useful once again to 21st-century advertisers.

This pun is only acceptable because the beer's name comes from the original brewer's surname. If the name Courage had been a marketing invention, the motto would be no cleverer than if it had been called Indefinable Allure ("Enjoy your Indefinable Allure"), 2BHappy ("Drink 2BHappy") or just Man Juice ("Swallow some Man Juice" – this one may be a bit niche). But the brewery's founder was called John Courage and so the fact that the same catchphrase can be taken to mean both "drink this beer" and "be brave" is serendipitous rather than corny.

Then I looked at the advert more closely. In case you didn't see it, it's a photograph of a curvy woman – not slim, but not obese – trying on a figure-hugging dress, while a man on a sofa, a can of Courage by his foot, regards her with a look of extreme apprehension. On the right is a picture of a pint of Courage, from which emerges a speech bubble containing the words: "Take Courage my friend."

I didn't get it. I stared at it for several minutes and couldn't understand what was going on. I'm afraid I eventually concluded that it meant that the man would need a drink to generate the nerve, or possibly ardour, to jump the woman. By which I mean, make a pass at her, try it on with her or make love to her, nothing more assaulty. Associations between alcohol and sexual assault are rarely made by advertisers – it's not viewed as a selling point.

I realise now that it was depicting a "Does my bum look big in this?" scenario. I considered that possibility at the time but rejected it for two reasons. First, the woman didn't look sufficiently bad in the dress to make the joke obvious. She looked a bit tarty, but she had a nice face – she was in no way "a sight". I imagine the advertisers toyed with making her the kind of image of nightmarish womanhood Bella Emberg used to play, but decided that would be sexist and they ought to go subtle – too subtle, I'm ashamed to admit, for me.

And second, I don't know why he needs courage in this situation. Saying "Yes, you look fat" is not an example of bravery but of tactlessness. Surely it isn't just fear that stops men telling women when they've made sartorial mistakes? They hold their tongues because there are some things it doesn't help people to know.

But when the Advertising Standards Authority banned the advert, I was surprised; it doesn't usually censure advertisers for muffing a joke. Then I heard the real reason. It was because the poster was deemed to be suggesting that the beer would give the man confidence. Apparently, adverts aren't allowed to imply that alcohol gives confidence (pro-drinking adverts, that is – the anti-drinking "booze gives you the illusion you're a superhero" campaign made it its central theme).

This is an advertising environment in which ambulance-chasing lawyers are allowed to imply that the main upshot of their services is useful relocation of bus shelters; in which make-up peddlers positively state that their products reverse the mythical "seven signs of ageing"; in which forms of words like "increases by up to a hundred per cent" (a phrase that has considerable overlap of meaning with "has no effect at all") abound. In this world of, to put a positive spin on it, half-truths, it's not permitted even to imply the self-evident, undeniable fact that beer gives you confidence.

There are lots of bad things to be said about alcohol. It wrecks and costs lives, often because it boosts confidence. It gives people the confidence to argue, fight and rape, as well as to chat more at parties or enjoy karaoke. It makes people dependent on the confidence it gives, to the extent that they'll poison themselves to get it. But it definitely gives you confidence – I know, I've had some.

And the Courage advert is even admitting that there may be a downside to boozy confidence. Their beer, it's telling us, is about to give the man the false confidence to say something that he shouldn't. They're not portraying it as lending confidence in a life-saving situation, like spinach for Popeye: "Let me have a quick glug of Courage and then I'll be able to save that coach-load of schoolchildren from falling into the volcano!"

God only knows the tearful, relationship-ending consequences of that man's forthcoming bout of Dutch courage. Rather than glamorising alcohol, I'd say it's a playful admission of some of its adverse effects, and rather more, in terms of candour, than the ASA has a right to expect.

Incidentally, advertising standards also forbid implying that alcohol makes you more likely to have sex. What? I know that teetotal cultures do procreate, but I've no idea how. I accept that saying that alcohol makes you more attractive is dishonest – it doesn't – but it certainly makes other people more attractive and, consequently, for better and worse, makes sex more likely.

Why, I wonder, does the ASA think people drink alcohol? The taste? I tell myself I like the taste of wine and beer, but it's impossible to separate it from the positive associations of feeling happy and confident and, very occasionally, getting off with someone at a party. Before I'd experienced any of that, I found it sour.

If the ASA believes that alcohol is so harmful that its manufacturers should be prevented from citing its demonstrable appeals, wouldn't it be fairer to ban booze adverts altogether? The current situation is like forcing car advertisers not to mention that cars get you to places quickly, only that they're a nice place to sit.

* * *

Some time in the 1950s, in a Kellogg's laboratory, some scientists eagerly gathered round a bowl.

"They're perfect!" the newest member of the team muttered. "Crispy yet indulgent, luxurious yet fun!"

"Let's just wait until we've added the milk," replied an old hand. "They could still go the way of Malticles."

The others shuddered at the recollection of the research dollars that had been squandered on those apparently delicious roundels – insanely moreish, tantalisingly frosted and loaded with B vitamins – but which, within 15 seconds of contact with lactose, set into a hard grey matter which you could only extract by smashing the bowl. The US military had briefly taken an interest before discovering that the substance – nicknamed Maltrete – was one of the many materials on Earth too hard for human consumption but too soft to repel even the most half-hearted of artillery bombardments.

"Hand me the jug," the chief designer whispered. With trembling hands, he poured. They waited.

"Our friends Snap, Crackle and Pop seem to have been somewhat smothered," quipped the head of the Flake Crispiness Retention team, who had slunk over to see what the fuss was about. No one laughed.

They watched.

And then, disaster! "The colour, it's not binding properly! It's running into the milk!" squealed a frosting risk assessor. He was right. As they watched, deep brown bled sickeningly into the pure white liquid around it. The scientists exhaled in collective despair. The head of FCR slipped tactfully away, this defeat too rich even for his blood. Funereal silence descended.

No one had noticed the head of marketing come in. "We can make this work for us," he said . . .

That's how I like to imagine that Kellogg's came up with the Coco Pops slogan: "So chocolatey it even turns the milk brown." Hiding a product's weaknesses in plain sight like that really takes balls. You've got to believe that the problem is so bad, so crucial, that your only recourse is to pretend it's deliberate. They never pushed Corn Flakes with the tagline: "So filled with health-giving corn you can sling it at a wall and it'll stick!"

This sprang to mind when my eye was caught by a billboard advertising the new series of *Britain's Next Top Model*, the TV show in which young hopefuls compete for modelling contracts. It had a picture of one of the judges, model Elle Macpherson, with the line: "It takes one to find one."

No, it doesn't. While a great violinist might be good at judging other people's violining, it doesn't follow that being pretty in a way that is perceived to make the clothes you wear look good will make you skilled at spotting someone else with that attribute; or that someone short, plump or bent-faced shouldn't be equally adept at finding the malnourished and photogenic – in fact, Oxfam photographers are probably best at that.

This slogan isn't like saying that a top chef is a good judge of a soufflé but that another soufflé is. Still, if you're making a TV show about modelling, it's good to have a famous model in it, rather than just aspirant thinifers of whom no one has ever heard. So, in the spirit of Coco Pops, they've drawn attention to the flaw and made it look like a deliberate feature – the TV format equivalent of a beauty spot.

I like this kind of advertising. The motives may be dishonest but the technique is brazen honesty – to scream "This is the catch!" so loudly at cynical consumers that they perversely ignore it. Here's a glimpse of how some products may be marketed in future, if this trend continues:

Bendicks Mints: "Nobody would buy them to eat themselves, but they're easy to wrap and pricey enough to make a respectable present."

Nestlé KitKat: "Pretend you care about babies in the third world if you want to. Just don't come moaning to us three bites into a Mars when all that caramel really starts to cloy."

Online roulette: "If you're even reading this slogan, it appeals to you slightly, which means you're bound to piss all your money away somehow, so it might as well be on this."

McDonald's: "Ever felt like putting on some elasticated jogging bottoms and really letting go? Why not today? Two years and 15 stone down the line, you can always bounce back via a fat-camp documentary on Sky."

British Airways: "No one is actually going to save the environment, so you might as well enjoy it while it lasts."

Payday loans: "If you were the sort of person who was ever going to understand compound interest, you wouldn't be in this mess. We can literally put off the shitstorm until next week. I mean, next week! It'll probably never happen!"

Cancer Research UK: "Don't think of this as chucking your money away altruistically, like with Amnesty. Face it, you're never going to go to North Korea but, with your diet, bowel cancer is a very real possibility."

The Royal Opera House: "For people so cultured they have literally lost the ability to feel bored."

Channel 5: "It can't all be 'appointment to view'. Sometimes you've just got to have something on in the background. And I bet you've still got an inkling that we might show some crafty porn come 3am."

Pimm's: "It may be unrelentingly sugary but you can drink it outdoors without looking like a tramp."

Twiglets: "OK, they're pretty unpleasant, but eat 12 and then tell me you don't want a 13th."

Petrol station coffee: "Of course you're going to have to compromise on flavour! You've been compromising your whole life! You're at Leigh Delamere at 11 o'clock on a Tuesday night, exhaustedly looking for caffeine. Why start trying to live the dream now?"

Conservative party: "Because, deep down, you know that posh people are supposed to be in charge."

Give blood: "Obviously you're not going to and this campaign is wasted on you – just don't go around thinking you're any kind of saint, that's all."

Ferrari: "Drive a Ferrari and most people will think you're a dick – but in an envious way, like they feel about Richard Branson, not a dismissive one, like with the chairman of a pressure group trying to block a wind farm development."

Pâté de foie gras: "Admit it, you always knew there was an upside to torture."

* * *

Half of humanity has received some much-needed assistance from an unexpected source. Out of the blue, the makers of Lion Bar Ice Cream have leapt to the aid of men. Like maggots in a wound, they didn't know they were helping – they thought they were just garnering some desperately needed publicity in an ice cream-unfriendly year – but they may have contributed to saving the world's males huge sums of money and an even greater expense of time and effort.

Lion Bar Ice Cream commissioned a survey into what sort of men women find attractive, presumably in the forlorn hope that "a man with his face in a Lion Bar Ice Cream" or "those hunks made ripplingly obese by an ice cream-only diet" would be among the responses.

They didn't quite get that, but more than 4,000 of the 5,000 respondents claimed to prefer a slightly scruffy fellow, with messy hair and even a beer belly, to the toned, groomed, David Beckham type, although I imagine they wouldn't kick him out of bed for eating a Lion Bar. The media spin on it is that "Women have turned against the metrosexual look", presumably because there's something very unattractive about a chap running after a tube train with a hard-on.

"Fantastic!" male readers may now be burping from their sofas. "I'll have another couple of pork pies and a Guinness. I knew I was over-washing!" And, indeed, these 5,000 women do seem very obliging: a fifth of them don't mind "a bit of body odour", 10% have no objection to man boobs and another 10% like their men to smell of beer. They like their men to smell of beer? That's an evolutionary cul-de-sac if ever I heard one: "Oh yeah, pick the paunchy, pissed one – he'll be there for you in a crisis." It's almost impossible to evade the conclusion that most of these women were on the pull.

But these accommodating physical preferences aren't why this study has helped men. After all, it hasn't really made the fat and smelly an iota more attractive than they were before. What women want is still what it's always been: either you or, more likely, not you. Citing an article in the *Daily Express* is unlikely to rescue any otherwise doomed, beery-breathed attempts at seduction.

No, the reason this study is good news for malekind is that it's being taken by the media as a blow to the previous trend, which it had itself created, towards male grooming, exercising and general body-image fretting. The results have been reported as if they contradicted what was formerly thought about women's taste, as if preening dandies were the established norm of attractiveness and more traditional "manly" attributes a weird fetish.

The media like nothing more than to be contrarian about their own manufactured consensus on which the paint is still not dry, just as a dog loves nothing more than chasing its own tail. Words spawn more words. Of course, I don't need to tell you that: you're reading a collection of a comedian's opinions about the news.

But it's daft to suggest that everyone previously thought most women were turned on by men with fastidiously toned bodies, reeking of cologne, hair made Himalayan with "product", dressed in gleaming Hugo Boss and generally showing every sign of effortful, self-absorbed vanity. That's just what style sections have been telling people they thought.

"Men are now expected to take just as much care over their appearance as women," has been the line; "Come on guys, step up!" the exhortation. Men have supposedly been liberated from the etiquette of not being openly vain, liberated into a world of moisturising, styling and plucking, of miserably spending money to fight nature, all in the name of self-respect, a world in which women have been trapped for centuries.

This was never much of a genuine trend – and the Lion Bar study shows it. The convention is still that men aren't supposed to care too much about how they look. Any effort they put into their appearance should be hidden. A beer belly is not ideal, but is far preferable to unconcealed calorie-counting. Obviously, there's vanity in this rejection of vanity but, crucially, it doesn't involve a high spend.

That's what underlies those claims that everyone now thinks it's fine for men to obsess about shoes, style their hair or have facials. Cosmetics and clothes manufacturers are giddy at the thought of doubling the vast sums they already make out of the weird and screwed-up social conventions about how women should look. They're trying to sell more worthless crap, and to do that you need to invoke fashion.

We men should be afraid. The forces of retail are ranged against us. The yoke of skimpy clothes that look sexy but leave your kidneys cold, expensive make-up, agonising shoes and youth-prolonging surgical roulette under which women labour is something we have avoided up to now, and that's a situation we would do well to prolong. But how?

Lion Bar Ice Cream has shown the way. We must fight retail with retail. We must show the merciless market that our slovenliness can be even more effectively monetised than the meticulousness it's trying to foist on us. If we promise to spend as much on beer, ice cream, hamburgers, video games and reinforced obesity furniture as we would on cologne, moisturiser, hair gunk and jewellery, then the retailers of the former will defend us from those of the latter. The Lion Bar studies will see off the style sections' trendsetting.

And those 4,000 women are on our side as well. "Save yourselves!" they're imploring. "It's too late for us, but you could still avoid this fashion and body-image hell!" They're right – it is too late for them. These customs are too ingrained: women will always be expected to shave their legs. Intellectually, I understand that it's just an annoying, pointless faff but, like most men, and even though our forefathers must have happily fancied hairy-legged women for millennia, I find it a bit gross when they don't. God forbid that most women should ever take the same view about back-waxing.

*   *   *

In the summer of 2010, there were two major nominees for the title of World's Most Hated Company: BP, for filling the Gulf of Mexico with oil, and Ryanair, just for being Ryanair. It was very clear to me at the time which one I preferred . . .

A recent newspaper advertisement for Ryanair has a big picture of Robert Mugabe shaking his fist, under the headline: "Here's EasyJet's New Head of Punctuality". This sends out a confused message. I'm no Zimbabwe expert but I'm fairly confident that the main charge levelled against Mugabe isn't one of unpunctuality. It's no more meaningful an insinuation than saying that Kim Jong-il is Virgin Atlantic's new head of catering or that Mel Gibson has been taken on by Thomas Cook to handle its IT.

And while Mugabe's an evil man, there's no reason to think that, had history panned out differently, he mightn't have made quite an effective "head of punctuality" for an airline. If what people say about Mussolini and trains is to be believed, a bit of murderous megalomania doesn't go amiss when it comes to getting transport services to pull their socks up.

But we'll never know how he'd have got on because Robert Mugabe isn't easyJet's new head of punctuality at all. It's not clear whether he even applied. Apparently he really, really wants to stay on as president of Zimbabwe. It would have been an eccentric career change – like when Alastair Campbell moved from handling the press for that unsuccessful war to doing the same for a rugby tour that went even worse. But maybe, like Campbell, Mugabe would have been glad of the comparative rest. EasyJet, for all its faults, isn't as unpopular as the government of Zimbabwe. It's not like it's Ryanair or something.

Ryanair is the unashamed villain of the corporate world. Other companies probably do worse things but Ryanair is the only one that delights in stepping into the public eye wearing an opera cloak and laughing maniacally. This horrendously unfair advert is typical. The sole basis for associating its rival with a brutal kleptocrat is a couple of quotations from newspapers both quoting the same third source claiming that easyJet's flights from Gatwick are "less punctual than Air Zimbabwe".

Michael O'Leary and Ryanair realise that this will seem underhand but they also know that their customers don't need to like them. They're running a "no frills" airline and have worked out that frequent flyers subconsciously consider civility and fairness to be frills. "These people will keep their prices low," we secretly think, "even if they have to treat us like cattle and stab their competitors in the back to do so."

This approach is unusual and refreshing. Most companies persist in trying to persuade us that they're nice and care about charitable causes, the obesity epidemic, equipment for schools or the environment. But these are publicly traded corporate entities, so they're incapable of caring – they're merely trying to make money for their shareholders and believe that this affectation of human feelings will help them to do so. Conversely, Ryanair has attracted customers canny enough to know that a public company can only have mercenary motives but who are happy to do business with it anyway.

BP has not reached this level of corporate development. In common with most other oil companies, it spends a lot of its marketing budget assuring us that it's obsessed with alternative forms of energy – that walking on to a BP forecourt and asking for petrol is like trying to buy a VHS cassette at an Apple store. "Petrol, you say? Not much call for that these days. Wouldn't you rather a quick zap from a solar panel or wind turbine?"

This strategy led the *Today* programme's John Humphrys to ask a silly question: "Isn't the reality that so long as the oil companies are as greedy for profits and nothing else as they are, this problem is not going to go away?" he said, with reference to the issue of replacing oil with renewable energy. It's silly because it only demonstrates Cynicism 1.0: he knows these corporations aren't as eco-committed as they claim because they can still make money out of oil. But he implies that a time might come when plcs aren't "greedy for profits and nothing else". Cynicism 2.0 is realising that it won't and that we can only properly harness the power and wealth of oil companies for developing sustainable energy sources by creating a business environment in which that activity is as profitable, or looks like it will become as profitable, as drilling for oil.

The continued prevalence of Cynicism 1.0 is presumably one reason BP considered it politic to remove its chief executive, Tony Hayward, in response to the Deepwater Horizon oil spill. The spill is an environmental disaster and the company still thinks it's worth trying to appear as if it genuinely cares about that, and not just about the consequent financial and reputational cost. So heads must be seen to roll, even if Hayward's was detached by a generous severance.

The generosity is because no one at BP, and few unemotional external observers, holds him particularly responsible for the disaster. At worst, he's deeply complicit in a corporate culture where such spills weren't made as unlikely as they could have been – but that's a long way short of it being directly his fault. At best, it was a very unfortunate accident and he's blameless. He made some PR gaffes and seemed a bit callous, but no one has suggested that any of that either hurt or saved a single extra seabird.

This makes the decision to axe him seem illogical. Businessmen of his seniority are incredibly well paid, and this gets justified by the claim that their acumen is so rare that they more than earn their wage. If this is true, surely BP can ill afford to lose a man who has ably run the firm since taking up his post in 2007 merely because his tenure coincided with an accident? If he was worth the money they were paying him, he will not be easily replaced.

Yet he has been, and things will be fine, says BP. Apparently it wasn't like trying to find another Andrew Flintoff or Tom Stoppard – people with amazing talents in their fields. It was more like replacing a good heart surgeon: Hayward's skills are uncommon, but not unique. He isn't, for example, the person who finds all the oil. That such executives know they're over-remunerated is implicit in their "it was nice while it lasted" willingness to step aside when their luck, rather than their competence, runs out. Deep down they know they're only human.

But I doubt Michael O'Leary would go that quietly. Neither, for that matter, has Robert Mugabe.

* * *

The private sector is amazing, isn't it? It's easily the best sector. Apart from the voluntary sector, of course, which is inspiring and humbling and should give us all pause. But, obviously, it's not really a proper sector. By which I mean it's vital – perhaps even more vital than the others – in just the same way that the Paralympics is perhaps more important than the Olympics.

But out of the two other sectors – which I'm certainly not going to call "the main two sectors" because that's, I think, a really unimaginative way of looking at the vital voluntary sector – the private one has got to be the best, right? It's like the free west, while the public sector is the Soviet Union but without the nuclear threat: all drab suits, grey offices, unattractive women and queues. You get a sense of concrete and drizzle, flares and puddles, all very 70s, whereas the private sector is dynamic and 80s. It's much more *Dynasty*, more *Howards' Way*, more using-proper-nouns-as-adjectives. It's fax machines and swimming pools, shoulder pads and telling people where to stick it, in both professional and sexual contexts.

Yes, people who work in the private sector must look at public sector workers in disbelief. "How did you end up there?" they must think. "What personality cocktail of laziness, self-loathing and intractable mediocrity would have led you to try to make your fortune (your incredibly modest fortune, albeit with overgenerous pension provision made possible only by tying the hands of enterprise) in that gloomy bureaucratic Mariana trench, far from the nourishing rays of the profit motive? How did the sorting hat of fate come to put you in life's Hufflepuff (but with a touch of Slytherin thrown in when it comes to local government contracts)?"

Those are the sort of questions that Carl Lygo, the chief executive of BPP, one of Britain's only two run-for-profit universities, must have to bite his tongue to stop himself asking when talking to other educators. And he has been talking to them: he's been discussing the possibility of running the business side of at least 10 publicly funded universities, going into "partnership" with them. They'd still make all the academic decisions, while BPP would deal with the admin. But isn't this an uneven partnership? It lacks a shared aim. One half wants to run a good university, the other wants to make money. If a marriage is a partnership, isn't this like getting hitched to a hooker?

Or maybe it's just paying for goods and services. As Lygo says: "Most universities are running at high costs and don't properly utilise their buildings. The private sector is better at procurement, because they are keener at negotiating better prices." That's the key argument in favour of outsourcing and subcontracting and other expressions for an institution giving up roles it was constituted to fulfil: the public sector is so congenitally wasteful that a private company will always be able to undercut it – that the inherent public sector inefficiency equates to more than the profit the subcontractor takes.

There are certainly many circumstances where this is true. There is little doubt that state funding changes an institution's attitude to money and can increase its propensity for waste. But I think it's a big jump from that observation to the current orthodoxy that the public sector's flabby inefficiency and the private's dynamic productivity are inevitable and universal – that the private sector possesses some kind of magic which, by dint of being paid by the state, no one in public service has access to; that the private sector is always brilliant and the public always useless.

I suspect Lygo of subscribing to this view when he says: "We have got a lot of universities in the UK and not all are in a strong financial position . . . the private provider would add expertise in the back-office functions." What expertise? Expertise in administering, say, Bristol University that the people currently administering Bristol University don't possess but a new company that's never done it before is going to be brimming with? Won't they just employ the same people to do the job but pay them less or sack a few? Is that what he means by expertise?

It's not expertise, it's ruthlessness, it's the prioritisation of profit. What Lygo is offering people running universities is the opportunity to divest themselves of many of the problems inherent in their jobs. If you don't want to take the tough decisions, he's saying, if you doubt you've got the backbone to make the efficiency savings, then we'll handle them for you. Pass your troubles on to those of us untroubled by conscience.

Not only would this be a dereliction of the universities' duty, it would also help perpetuate the myth of the private sector's omnipotence and the public's doltish money-burning idiocy.

The private sector caused the credit crunch, the financial crisis, the global recession. The public sector bailed out the banks and brought the world back from the brink of ruin. When our railways were in public hands, they were shabby, unreliable and loss-making. In private hands, they still are, but public money ends up in the hands of shareholders and the tickets cost vastly more. The NHS is the most efficient health service among its peers despite having, up till now, much less private sector involvement than they do. The armed forces remain in the public sector and people seldom have cause to criticise their efficiency or commitment.

Having said all that, Brent council is useless and the world glitters with the achievements of private enterprise: from smartphones to cappuccinos, from cheap fridges to full supermarkets, from Viagra to Vegas, the by-products of the profit drive have given hundreds of millions of us the lifestyles of emperors.

And, of course, the private sector is usually better at making money but, as that's its sole aim, it would be tragic if it weren't. The aims of public bodies are more complex, varied and, usually, worthwhile. We mustn't allow this necessary lack of single-mindedness to be mistaken for an inevitable lack of drive or focus.

So, if those universities with which BPP have been negotiating feel they could make savings by outsourcing their back-office functions (which sounds like a euphemism for getting a colostomy bag) but would be unwilling to cut costs without being able to blame a private company, maybe that's a sign that they're the wrong savings. If not, and if failing to make such cuts jeopardises those institutions, I hope they'll find the courage to reform themselves without holding hands with a profiteer.

* * *

There's something fishy about Google's motto, "Don't Be Evil." I'm not saying it's controversial but it makes you think, "Why bring that up? Why have you suddenly put the subject of being evil on the agenda?" It's suspicious in the same way as Ukip constantly pointing out how racist they're not – which my colleague Charlie Brooker said on *10 O'Clock Live* was "rather like someone who's just moved in next door saying, 'Hi, I'm Geoff, your non-dogging neighbour.'"

But we mustn't assume that the maxim was an attempt by executives to draw a line under some diabolical brainstorm in which the internet giant pulled itself back from the brink of green-lighting a scheme to grind our bones to make its bread. It could just as easily have come out of a discussion of the possibility of doing good. "Always do good", "Try to do some good" or "Be good" might have been previous drafts of the motto, before they concluded that goodness was as impractical as malevolence was distasteful and decided on "Don't Be Evil" as more realistic in a modern business environment. "Settling for one notch below altruism" is all the slogan really means.

Still, I suppose we should be grateful for small mercies. And there's no earthly reason why Google should do any good to anyone but itself – which is presumably why it pays so little tax. Although that's not how Matt Brittin, Google's head of sales in northern Europe, explained the situation to the House of Commons public accounts committee. "No one in the UK can execute transactions," he said. He wasn't bemoaning a lack of competence in British workers but proudly talking MPs through a tax dodge. Even though there are sales staff in Britain, "No money changes hands." Nudge nudge, wink wink. Since the vast majority of Google's £3.2bn of UK sales are routed through Ireland, the company paid only £6m in corporation tax. I'm not saying that's necessarily evil, but it's certainly not good.

Amazon, in contrast, has never ruled out evil as part of its business plan, aspiring only to "Work hard. Have fun. Make history." It sounds like an *Apprentice* contestant's Twitter profile. And it has emerged that, despite £4.2bn of UK sales, the company paid only £2.4m in corporation tax in 2012. In the same year it received £2.5m in government grants. Which makes it a net benefits scrounger. In terms of sheer rapacious acquisitive nerve, I'd say that has made a little bit of history.

Is there any point in my being angry about this? Everyone else already is. It feels like the interesting thing would be to come out in favour of it. After all, as the company's spokesman proudly announced: "Amazon pays all applicable taxes in every jurisdiction that it operates within." So maybe it's fine. Better than that, maybe it's crazy and interesting. It's a challenging artwork, but instead of oil paint or wood or clay or the excrement of the artist, it's constructed out of pure injustice. A huge, malevolent sculpture of unfairness, groundbreaking and thought-provoking, reminding us of the iniquities of the natural world – a corporate metaphor for the worms that will one day eat all of our corpses.

Like any really important work of art, it's bound to upset a few people. Just as Banksy causes collateral damage to the neatness of walls, so Amazon's masterpiece is a defacement of the public purse. But it's not just some hooligan's tag, like Google's artless Irish scam. This shows an impish wit and a dark insight. What elevates Amazon's activity is the fact that it applied for government grants. The elegance of that corporate choice is like the ambiguity of the Mona Lisa's smile, the ruthlessness of Mike Tyson's punch and the adaptability of the malaria virus combined. There is no point in criticising anyone or anything that can do that. They can only be admired or destroyed.

The more you think about it, the more brilliant it is. At first glance, the deftness of securing government funding, which was intended to sustain and encourage marginal businesses, is rather pleasing. The thought of the thousands of small enterprises that could have been nourished and helped to survive by the cash Amazon has swallowed in one tax-cancelling mouthful is challenging and absorbing. It's the monster that's made myriad food parcels into its canapé.

But it gets even better. If, for a second, you make the mistake of thinking that giving Amazon handouts might nevertheless help the UK – by incentivising the company to create jobs in Britain even if, for tax purposes, it exists only in Luxembourg – then think again. Because Amazon is the great job-killer. For every job it creates, more than one is destroyed on the high street. It's the great annihilator of work and yet it's been receiving a job-creation government subsidy. It doesn't just absorb money that would be better spent creating employment elsewhere, it deploys it to decimate the chances of that employment.

I understand that the changes in work and business patterns being caused by the internet are inevitable and irreversible. To try to stop them would be railing against the tide. Still, it's amazing that Amazon, in an act of dazzling contempt, has persuaded the treasury actually to pump water into the rising sea.

I don't really think that these problems can be fixed. It's the role of politicians to say that something must be done – with a sense of purpose if in power, and outrage if in opposition. But their jobs are too tenuous and short-lived, the international tax system too complex and the corporations too tenacious to stop this sort of thing happening. Loopholes will crop up by accident and, where they don't, the intense and remorseless lobbying of the already astronomically wealthy will ensure that more are created.

We can work ourselves up in impotent fury or – and this is a calmer way to live – just sit back and enjoy the majesty of a terrible thing done well. Amazon's tax and grant arrangements are the beautiful ivory candlestick outlined by the silhouettes of British taxpayers' incredulous faces. The politicians and public provide the backdrop of incompetence and rage in front of which huge companies can display their work of corporate perfection. As the mushroom cloud showed us decades ago, evil can be beautiful.

* * *

As you brushed your teeth this morning, what went through your mind? You may not be able to remember – it's a brief process. But perhaps you considered the state of your toothbrush or worried about a wobbly filling; or contemplated the weather, the economy or how, by focusing on your reflected face in the mirror, a dried-up toothpaste splat on its surface unfocuses into two images so that, if you move your head to the right place, you can align them with your reflected eyes and it looks like you've turned into a white-irised zombie. That sort of thing.

But if toothpaste company Crest is right, what many of you thought was: "God, this toothpaste is so boring! How can I endure these spirit-sapping seconds when there's nothing about this dreary cleansing aid to divert me? I'm a daredevil and I need more!" The manufacturer's response could not be more emphatic: "Daredevils, have we got a surprise for you . . ." it announces on the website for its new range. "It's a whole new world of deliciousness for toothbrushes everywhere. And it's ready to take your mouth on an exhilarating ride. Better buckle up."

What the company means by this is that it's launching a new chocolate-flavoured toothpaste. That's the extreme sport for the mouth it's referring to above: it's reaching out to daredevils who brush their teeth with chocolate. Except it's not really chocolate, it just tastes of it. It's actually a proper fluoride toothpaste, so the oral thrill-seekers the company is courting can buzz on the adrenaline rush – the peril junkie's high – that dicing with decay by brushing your teeth with chocolate would doubtless give, but without actually having to endure the dental rot. Their pearly white teeth will still gleam amid the delicious brown foam after every thrilling scrub.

Chocolate-flavour toothpaste sounds disgusting. I like chocolate but it's the sort of thing I need to believe I'm removing from my teeth when I'm brushing them. It's also, of all foods, the most visually reminiscent of shit. And, if there's one substance that I like to contemplate being in contact with my teeth while I brush them even less than chocolate, it's that wasp to chocolate's hoverfly, excrement. Associating any brown goo with tooth-brushing is perverse – it's like launching a washing powder that makes clothes smell of gravy or an air freshener that disseminates the odour of a damp dog.

Crest has addressed this, to an extent, and the toothpaste it's launching is "Mint Chocolate Trek" rather than chocolate alone. Mint is a flavour which has worked with both toothpaste and chocolate in the past and so, Crest must think, is the ideal choice to bring the two together – like Liz Hurley organising a threesome with Hugh Grant and Shane Warne.

Why they've used the word "trek" is lost on me – although the other two flavours in this new range are called "Vanilla Mint Spark" and "Lime Spearmint Zest", which may be a clue: they were looking for a monosyllabic noun and "spark" and zest" were taken. I still don't reckon that makes "trek" the obvious choice. One doesn't like to think of cleaning one's teeth as a "trek" – it sounds dull and arduous, and is a strange selection considering that this whole range was launched, according to Crest, in response to consumer feedback that toothpaste was boring. It's for customers with "an adventurous spirit or a sweet tooth". Some may even have two or three teeth.

Maybe, for such people, a trek that's chocolatey is preferable to even the briefest normal scrub. And, if you genuinely get bored while cleaning your teeth, the very oddness of doing it with something chocolate-flavoured, even if you find it repulsive, may help you through that purgatorial couple of minutes. If so, it can't end here. New flavours will be needed to maintain the novelty – "Bacon Cheese Wham", "Onion Beef Grind", "Lemongrass Paella Crash".

And that's the least of it. Having created a society in which some of us are so reliant on perpetual diversion that there needs to be something interesting even about our toothpaste, we must set to work on alleviating other boring moments. To do otherwise would be cruel. Modern life still contains dozens of potential tiny pits of mind-numbing despair which must be made more chocolatey . . .

Bleach MP4 player

Pouring bleach down a lavatory is boring. Long seconds alone, looking down a toilet bowl – you can't watch television and it's difficult to work an iPod wearing rubber gloves. It's an unacceptable moment of intense tedium, a massive drop in our quality of life. The solution? A new brand of bleach which has little disposable

MP4 players on the bottom of the bottles, activated as you pour. Bacteria die in their millions while, oblivious as a drone pilot, you're distracted by a YouTube clip.

Toast chloroform
Waiting for toast to pop up is like being imprisoned for a mini-eternity – unable to forget about the toast and get on with your life by putting some toast on or something, and unable to eat the toast. It condemns us to an invisible cage around the toaster for what might as well be forever until it ends. In this age of pharmaceutical miracles, couldn't the toaster be designed to administer a tiny dose of a knockout drug through the lever you press to put the bread down? Just enough to deliver oblivion for the stultifying toasting time, allowing us to wake and pick ourselves up off the kitchen floor at exactly the moment the toast pops.

Karaoke hoover
The tuneless drone of a vacuum cleaner could be made entertaining merely by altering that adjective. If your Dyson moaned a melody as it sucked its dust, the bored human hooverer would have something to sing along to. A microphone in the machine's handle could upload your vocals as an informal new first round of *The Voice*.

Waiting-for-someone-to-stop-talking jingles
Conversations stink. Half the time you're not even talking while someone you know is slowly saying what you knew they'd say, because you know them, but you have to wait until they stop saying it before you get to speak. It's tedious, it causes rows, and technology has rendered it unnecessary: a hearing-aid-sized MP3 player can alleviate these moments by playing stirring snatches of music unless you happen to be talking yourself. After you finish a

remark, it gives your interlocutor a few seconds to agree with you before fading in some classic beats, very much like the band at the Oscars when some lighting technician starts thanking his wife.

* * *

The name of the new version of Google's Android operating system has been announced. What an odd sentence that is. How sophisticated our civilisation has become! When one of our ancestors first paused for a moment to select a particularly sharp bit of rock with which to attempt to skin a mammoth, little did he, or she (that's saved me a letter), know where we'd all end up.

One day you're just restricting the roaming options of some goats using a bit of creeper, or working out which little bits of grit to stick in the ground for there to be cabbages in a few months' time, and then, within a cosmic twinkling of an eye, some people are earning their food and shelter by announcing the new name of the slightly altered version of a totally intangible thing.

They don't actually make the totally intangible thing. They don't even alter the totally intangible thing themselves. Neither do they themselves think of the new name for this updated abstract noun. They just announce that new name. That's where it was heading, Ancestor Ug, when you first got a fire to light. You started a chain reaction which led inexorably to PR.

I'm not really a luddite. I haven't got the commitment or the physical strength to smash anything. I'm just a whinger really, so I know that we sort of do need operating systems. They may be intangible but they're not purposeless. They're much closer kin to a hand-axe than they are to a mission statement. Or a poem, for that matter. But I'm fairly sure that they don't really need names and, if you give them names, it doesn't really matter what those names are as long as they're different from one another – as long as you don't give two different versions of an operating system the same name. I think I just had an idea for the most boring farce ever written.

What I still haven't done, I realise, is told you the name of the new version of Google's Android operating system. I'm slightly tempted not to. After all, if you're properly interested in that sort of thing, then (a) you probably already know its name, and (b) there's something wrong with you.

But I will. It's called KitKat. That's not a coincidence. It's deliberately named after the chocolate bar. Apparently Nestlé is fine with that. It's not sponsorship – it hasn't paid for the name of its product to be written on this thing you can't write on – but the company has allowed it. "This is not a money-changing-hands kind of deal," explained John Lagerling, director of Android global partnerships.

That's quite unusual. When A's label is sported by B, one of A or B is almost always charging to offset the reputational cost. The Premier League must reckon that the money Barclays pays adequately compensates it for being publicly associated with a discredited bank. Conversely, clothes designers wouldn't consent to their names being plastered all over so many of the world's most vain and stupid people unless they'd been lavishly remunerated first.

But for Google and Nestlé, there's no dowry. This genuinely seems to be a love match. Admittedly, Google's options were limited: every version of the operating system has been named after some sort of cake or sugary snack (unbranded ones up to now). The company has been moving through the alphabet, starting at "cupcake", and had got as far as "jelly bean". So it needed an edible treat beginning with K and went off its first idea: "We realised that very few people actually know the taste of a key lime pie," lamented Lagerling.

So KitKat really hit the spot. I'm familiar with the feeling. Sometimes I wonder how dastardly a third world scam Nestlé would need to pull to make me consider buying a Biscuit Boost. Still, Google's decision is surprising. It aspires to be squeaky clean. As aspirations go, it's not been looking particularly realistic of late as the corporation's tax avoidance has become more evident, but it's still a company that tries to generate a wholesome, quirky, Californian vibe. That's why it called an operating system Cupcake. That's why its offices are full of free snacks for employees. There's still a faint echo of "Don't Be Evil" in the think spaces and mood rooms, albeit with an irritating interrogative inflection.

So it's odd that it would voluntarily couple one of its products with that of a company with a shameful history of wringing money from the poorest people on Earth. To my mind, the risks involved in that association outweigh the fact that more people have heard of a KitKat than a key lime pie. I don't think the people at Google are doing anything wrong by using KitKat's name – they're not the ones peddling powdered milk in the developing world – but I don't understand why they've done it.

Then again, I don't understand much about them. These are people who equate a new operating system for a smartphone with a lovely cake. To me, that makes about as much sense as naming cancers after Beatrix Potter characters. Apple's equivalent system seems to be based on feline predators – Puma, Tiger, Leopard, etc – which makes slightly more sense because of the feelings of hostility and fear that every new stage of corporate tinkering with how a computer works evokes in me.

But if a simple numbering or lettering system is too unwacky for either corporation to countenance, might not a series of painful chronic illnesses be more appropriate? That would conjure up the endless spirit-sapping tedium of staring at a screen, and trying to make it do things, much more effectively than a pussy or a bun. Sciatica, Arthritis, Crohn's disease or – and maybe this is what the list of Android names is building up to – Type 2 diabetes.

(But why didn't they think of a new name when the second type came out?)

It remains to be seen how the Google–KitKat reputational trade-off will work out. Will association with the tedious smartphone millstones round all of our necks damage the KitKat's biscuity allure more than its parent company's immoral African marketing strategy? Will Google's cosying up to the cold Swiss giant piss the public off more or less than its deft accounting?

Is this, for Google, a public embrace of moral ambiguity? The world is harsh and complex, it's saying. Nothing is certain – except possibly death, but certainly not taxes. Evil is in the eye of the beholder. And there aren't many sweets that begin with K.

* * *

For as long as I can remember, there have been chocolate bars next to the tills at supermarkets. It was my first experience of retail guile. "Never mind that trolley full of boring stuff you need, like bleach and runner beans and bin bags, why not buy something you want?!" the displays seemed to be saying. "Come on, let go a little, relax your bottom on to the comfortable surface of this lovely slippery slope."

Those were the terms in which my parents, keen for me to grow up well grounded in cynicism, explained things to me. Sweets, chocolates and crisps were all very well, but to buy them by the checkout, on an impulse, was falling into a trap. Instead, I was taught the pleasure of watching other people fall into it and feeling smug. The fact that the sensation of smugness was more pleasurable to me than that of salt or sugar tells you all you need to know about the kind of monster who comes to prominence in modern Britain.

So I was alarmed to hear that this pleasure may soon be denied me. Jane Ellison, the public health minister, has identified the placing of delicious crap near tills as "an area for action under the Responsibility Deal" and said: "Parents have indicated that positioning of sweets at checkouts can increase pestering to purchase by their children." This contrasts strongly with the comments of her predecessor, Anna Soubry, who said: "There's nothing wrong with sweets," and "I just said no to my children." Her confrontational approach caught the prime minister's eye and she's since been moved to the Ministry of Defence.

However, when it comes to tempting checkout areas, David Cameron is in Ellison's camp. In 2006, still fresh with zeal to change the world, he condemned the disgraceful absence of fresh fruit from newsagents. "Try and buy a newspaper at the train station and, as you queue to pay, you're surrounded, you're inundated by cut-price offers for giant chocolate bars," he said. "As Britain faces an obesity crisis, why does WH Smith's promote half-price Chocolate Oranges at its checkouts instead of real oranges?"

That was ages ago, so I assume someone will have given him an answer by now. But just in case, I'll have a go. Well, you see, WH Smith is a newsagents' chain so it's really not set up to deal with fresh fruit. I don't know whether Mr Cameron imagined it diversifying into oranges alone or providing a whole fruit range, but either course presents logistical difficulties and wouldn't, in my view, provide sufficient revenue to compensate for stopping selling sweets and chocolate or hiding them at the back with the A–Zs and toner cartridges.

But what about his point regarding obesity? Well, you see, WH Smith is a newsagents' chain and has no responsibility for public health. Its management answers to shareholders who are unlikely to view a reduction in national fatness as mitigation for a collapse in confectionery sales. That's what happens with a free market – I'm surprised he's got a problem with it.

Suspicious though I am of supermarket chains, I do feel it's unreasonable of the government to expect shops not to arrange their wares to best advantage. It's like saying ice-cream vans mustn't turn up at parks on sunny days because it's unfairly tempting, and should only be allowed during thunderstorms – and only then selling to those who have thrice refused the offer of some lentil broth.

Special rules apply to tobacco and alcohol, but do we really want to extend similar exceptions to everything else that might do us harm? In moderation, almost anything is fine and, out of all moderation, absolutely nothing is – you can be crushed under a ton of vitamin tablets, ingest so much water you drown, eat so many sprouts you have to get a Corgi certificate.

How are we to categorise which are the officially unhealthy foods, the shameful merchandise that needs to be separated out like booze and fags? Carrots are definitely good and Haribo definitely isn't. Easy. Crisps bad, eggs good (they've got the good sort of cholesterol this month). Cheese – bad? But what about all the calcium? And kids don't tend to ask for some Shropshire Blue in the way they'll latch on to a Fanta. But what about cheese string?

Nuts – they're good, they can go by the tills. Then again, what about salted nuts? Let's keep them away. Then what about slightly salted nuts? As soon as the category is defined, the search will be on for the most unhealthy food that doesn't fall into it, which can then be arranged temptingly round the checkouts.

I'm being naive. It won't be done like that – this is the "big society", after all. As a Department of Health spokesman said: "We have been clear that legislation is not necessary and that the voluntary approach through the Responsibility Deal is working." So there'll be no new rules and the supermarkets will act of their own accord out of their sincere wish to do good. And by "out of their sincere wish to do good", I mean "to head off the threat of legislation while their lobbyists get to work on ministers".

The only virtue of which public limited companies are capable, in my view, is honesty. We can sometimes make them tell the truth. We can make them publish accurate accounts, use transparent employment practices and hold public shareholder meetings. When corporations cannot lie, the world is a better place. Yet, under this policy, we are requiring them to lie.

Supermarket employees and management may share Jane Ellison's concerns about public health, but the institutions themselves – these vast organisations owned by thousands of shareholders and shareholding institutions – are incorporated purely to make a profit. They therefore wish to sell as many sweets, as much of anything, as possible. They do not – they cannot – want customers to restrict their purchases to what is good for them and, by harassing these companies to say they do, we force them to lie.

The world is not safe and we don't make it safer by pretending it is. People should expect naked commercialism from retailers – we all need to get used to it and learn to resist it. It's as honest as any kind of predation. By forcing supermarkets to lie about their aims, we inhibit the development of public cynicism and, like an over-relied-upon satnav, lure people into believing that it is safe to proceed without vigilance.

4

Saying You Want to Make a Difference
Makes No Difference

*None of the problems discussed above is primarily our politicians'
fault. And that's a bigger problem. Modern politicians don't seem
to do much – everything happens despite them, not because of them,
starting with the credit crunch.*

*That crisis happened in spite of what Gordon Brown did – he
certainly wanted to avoid it. His political opponents claim that his
policies created the conditions for the crash, but few really believe
it would have been averted if a Tory or a Lib Dem had been
chancellor of the exchequer since 1997 instead. So it didn't matter
who the politicians were or, seemingly, what they did – the disaster
was inevitable. Whoever we'd voted for, it wouldn't have made any
difference.*

*But they command quite a few column inches for such an irrelevant
section of the community, probably even more than footballers and
royals. In this section, I look at their desperate attempts to say what
we want to hear, and at their transparent obsession with how they
come across.*

Part 1: Before the Election

*As Gordon Brown's government meandered towards its lacklustre
conclusion, it had plenty of feeble ideas, but I was particularly
depressed by one from June 2009, largely because the Tories were so
envious of it.*

Sir Alan Sugar, the government's new "enterprise tsar" (calling him "captain of the enterprise" would have been more fun), could lose his TV show if the Tories get their way. Jeremy Hunt, the shadow culture secretary, reckons BBC rules would be broken if Sugar continued to front *The Apprentice* while working for the government.

Apparently, presenters of BBC shows are supposed to be impartial. I'm not entirely clear what that means. It is sensible that people presenting programmes shouldn't secretly be in the pay of McDonald's, Ukip or the Pipe Smoker of the Year organisation. But presenters are allowed to appear in adverts, so it seems that some transparent partiality is OK (thank God). No one's afraid that Gary Lineker is covertly putting a cheese and oniony spin on the football results.

So if an openly held bought allegiance wouldn't stop Sir Alan being a presenter, then surely an equally open set of political opinions should be fine? Not according to Hunt, who said of Sugar: "The idea that he is politically neutral is a bit of a joke; he has written in the *Sun*, the *Mirror*, the *News of the World* criticising David Cameron and the Conservatives in a highly partisan way."

Who is "politically neutral"? Do the Tories really expect all BBC presenters, even of programmes as trivial as *The Apprentice* (we're not talking about *Newsnight* here), to hold no opinions at all? Has it not occurred to Hunt that, in expressing his anti-Conservative views, Sugar isn't revealing himself to be part of an insidious cabal, but merely saying what he thinks? He is demonstrating that he's someone who, like all of us except a few morons, holds opinions.

The fact that these opinions are to do with party politics doesn't make them invalidly "partisan". They're still his views about what is right and wrong – the same as if he'd said he regards theft and murder as immoral. And I don't imagine the

Tories would criticise him for writing an article that was openly anti-BNP – and that's a party political view, however much it's self-evident to all but a few thousand weirdos.

But as soon as the opinions become subtle enough to be of any interest, the Conservatives claim Sugar shouldn't be allowed to express them, merely because he hosts a pantomime version of a business show. It would help no one if every TV face were chosen from the tiny minority whose views are so bland that they tread a perfect median between left and right.

What is Jeremy Hunt's real fear here? Does he think that Sir Alan will start adding a quick "Vote Labour!" every time he says "You're fired!"? He can't be genuinely worried that the show will turn into a party political broadcast, because people would stop watching if it did.

No, the Tories are just desperate to rob Labour of its little publicity coup because Sir Alan Sugar comes across on TV as exactly the sort of cock who Tory voters like. His brand of "no-nonsense" nonsense and secondhand rhetoric, and his public affirmation that wealth makes what you say more important, are perfectly judged to appeal to the sort of idiot who thinks David Cameron talks a lot of sense, even though all he does is repeatedly bleat "change" like a tramp in a doorway, and his only stated policy is "to become prime minister".

I'm now sounding like exactly the kind of person who the Tories think shouldn't be allowed on the BBC. But let me assure Jeremy Hunt that it's not because I'm "biased" that I say that Cameron is a chancer who's even more woefully unfit for government than Gordon Brown. It's because I sincerely think it – just like I think that grilled tomatoes are nicer than tinned and Sean Connery was the best Bond. I honestly, unpromptedly believe it. Maybe I'm wrong. It looks like I'm going to get the chance to find out.

The real problem with Sugar's new appointment is that it's such an obvious and grim attempt at populism. Brown is either so short of ideas or so despises the electorate that he thinks the best way to demonstrate that the government is coping with the biggest business crisis in a century is to make it the responsibility of a man whose day job is telling self-regarding mediocrities that they should take off their Mexican hats before trying to put on their jumpers. A man who has made himself rich, but whose career as a tycoon has gone sufficiently quiet that he's got time to do TV.

Top-end billionaires are too busy for that – Rupert Murdoch and Richard Branson don't have their own programmes, they have their own channels. Alan Sugar is no longer primarily a businessman – he portrays one on TV. Brown might as well have given the new tsardom to the bloke who played Boycie in *Only Fools and Horses*.

What is even more depressing than Brown thinking that this might impress people is that the Tories, the only plausible alternative government, agree. That's how to survive in politics: don't focus on the country's problems, get someone shouty from the telly to talk stridently about them. And then go on *GMTV* and say you're personally concerned about Susan Boyle's health "because she's a really, really nice person".

Does Brown honestly believe that's how to get people to respect him? To make them think that, in the middle of the greatest crisis in his career, he's still taking a personal interest in the health of a random middle-aged woman he hardly knows? Does that kind of prioritisation play well with voters? What is still more depressing is that it might.

Sir Alan Sugar is perfectly suited to the job of "enterprise tsar" because it's not a job – it's an exercise in presentation, just like his role on the BBC. In less bewildered times, an ambitious opposition would welcome the opportunity to ridicule such a disastrously craven government appointment. Instead, they're meanly trying to block it because they're annoyed they didn't think of it themselves.

* * *

As the election campaign got under way, I found myself watching another bunch of entitled men tire themselves out . . .

I went to the Boat Race for the first time this year. It turned out to be an exciting one – quite close. "Not like those deathly dull processional contests of the 1990s!" everyone said. I remember watching those on TV: Cambridge would take an early lead and then gradually increase it until, after about halfway, you couldn't get both crews in the same helicopter shot. By the time the exhausted and heartbroken Oxford boat heaved itself over the line, the Cambridge rowers had already necked an aperitif and ordered their starters. In those years, it was difficult to understand how Oxford weren't better, considering how much longer they seemed to spend rowing.

I didn't find that dull – I thought it was great. I don't give a damn about the quality of the race, I just want Cambridge to win. I don't completely understand why. "Because I went to university there" doesn't seem reason enough. I suppose there's something comforting in any long-held allegiance, however arbitrary. That's why people support football clubs – it gives a sense of belonging, of shared achievements and disappointment. We allow ourselves to enjoy a victory we didn't contribute to because we know that in the event of defeat, we'd also have felt the pain.

But I can see that to people who don't have a connection with Oxford or Cambridge, it's just the close Boat Races that are diverting. Similarly, to an exhaustedly indifferent electorate, only the close elections are worth following.

1997 was an exciting election, even though it was a foregone conclusion, because the result pleased a lot of people. Everyone is saying how exciting this year's is going to be because you genuinely can't predict the result. This is a reason to engage, to enthuse, to speculate – all of which activity, like organising a wedding to breathe life into a failing relationship, disguises the awful truth that we don't much care any more.

A regime which has led us into recession, debt and open-ended war is difficult to get behind, even if some of the crises weren't primarily its fault. And the likely alternative seems almost wilfully unappealing: slick but lacking substance and desperate to avoid expressing any kind of opinion in case it puts some voters off.

I can see the wisdom of that when they've got the likes of Chris Grayling knocking around. I don't think his suggestion that B&B owners, perhaps balking at how those initials might be interpreted by gay couples, should be allowed to turn homosexuals away makes him a homophobe. It just means that he hopes homophobes will vote for him. The fact that he thought he could secure their support without repelling the rest of us shows a curious mixture of cynicism and ineptitude.

It's unfair to harp on about how posh a lot of the shadow cabinet are – there's nothing wrong with being posh. Some people have been kind enough to say that I come across as a bit posh sometimes. Eton is a good school – I see no reason why someone who went to Eton shouldn't be prime minister. That's the kind of broadminded guy I am.

But it does seem a devil of a coincidence that David Cameron – the dynamic new Tory who is going to lead his party out of the wilderness and his country into a sort of loving Thatcherism (which must be the political equivalent of S&M) – should have such a similar background to many of the old Tories whom he claims to be so unlike. It's an irony that you'd think he might have referred to amid all his talk of change.

The key Cameron claim slipped out on Tuesday when he said of the government: "Frankly, we couldn't be any worse." It's also an admission that they might be no better. "But even in that eventuality, what have you lost?" he's imploring. Meanwhile, Labour's contention is that these difficult times call, as Lord Mandelson put it, for Brown's granite rather than Cameron's plastic. (It depends if we're making an iPhone or a tomb, I suppose.) Cameron plugged this into the Central Office Witulator™, which came out with the brilliant riposte: "Well, I would say it's rust versus steel."

What awful, awful people. A few days into the campaign and I want to scream at them all to shut up. Even poor Nick Clegg, who hasn't got a chance, can't help being deeply annoying. One of his campaign launch soundbites was: "Our change is change that really does make a difference to ordinary people and families." Apart from the blandness, it's the "and families" that's maddening. Doesn't "people" cover families? Of course it does, but he's got to say "families" because some research document has suggested that that's a word that people (and families) want to hear.

The endless talk of "fairness" and "hard-working families" and "change" has become dispiritingly meaningless. Politicians are completely failing to connect, even when they're saying "Politicians are completely failing to connect." They make words worthless; they all say that they don't go in for negative campaigning while standing in the shadow of hoardings smearing their opponents. Do they think we don't notice that blatant lie? If so, how much must they despise us?

I know I'm stumbling into the cliché that politicians are all as bad as each other, but I can't remember ever feeling it more strongly. Increasingly, they, and much of the media that scrutinise them, seem to come from an insular political community, which explains so much of the razzmatazz surrounding the election: they're genuinely excited – they haven't noticed that Britain is weary and sceptical. We're supposed to be countering political apathy, and yet several TV channels devoted hours of broadcasting to Brown's car journey to and from Buckingham Palace to confirm an election date that everyone already knew. Compared to that, the state opening of parliament is like *The West Wing*.

Yet it's important. Understanding the tiny differences between one drably plausible group and another may be crucial to our future happiness. Our past failures to do so have had horrible consequences: one of the many truths that politicians will never utter is that their mediocrity is, ultimately, a reflection of our own – our failure to understand, scrutinise and care, which is then exacerbated by the disappointing people that that failure allows to come to prominence.

This election race isn't going to be close in a good way. It may be tense, but the standard won't be high. They're not rowing so much as messing about in boats – hurling abuse and trying to ram each other. Millions so despair of the fixture that we're glumly hoping for a draw.

* * *

When I first heard someone say "No publicity is bad publicity", my instant response was: "Yeah, I bet that's right!" It sounded so clever and cynical. "Life's all about grabbing people's attention and keeping it," I thought. The squeaky hinge gets the oil, the country that threatens nuclear proliferation gets the aid, the most-papped glamour model gets the book deal.

It's an old saw that seems horrible enough to be true, and whoever's running the Cambridge Union Society clearly subscribes to it: the debating society has announced that it's offering pole-dancing lessons to female students. They're to be held in the Blue Room, which, I assume, someone thinks is humorously apt – unless it was chosen over the "Boobs Library" or "Legs Akimbo Lounge and Conference Suite".

A spokeswoman said: "We are of the opinion that classes like these are a way of empowering women . . . if an intelligent, independent woman wishes to learn a particular form of dance in respectable surroundings –" I'd be very surprised? No: ". . . we see nothing degrading in that." And I suppose if some stupid or impressionable women want to join in, that's fine as well.

So far, so undergraduate. They've correctly identified that received wisdoms, such as the view that pole dancing is degrading, shouldn't be taken as read. But they've confused being contrarian with forming a reasoned opinion. Having stumbled upon the word "empowering", which can be deployed under so many circumstances – I use it about charging my phone – they've let it trick them into thinking that they've framed an argument.

I expect they're feeling a bit smug that it made the papers. When I was a student, I made up a story about a cat crapping on the script of a play I was trying to publicise. This duly appeared in the gossip column of the student newspaper and was subsequently picked up by the *Times* Diary. I thought this basically made me Matthew Freud. More people would be aware of the show, I reasoned. True. And they'd associate it with cat shit. If it made anyone buy a ticket, I don't want to meet them. But I'm sure that Juan de Francisco, the union entertainments officer who's organising the classes, thinks he's done himself and the society good by getting this mischievous idea some coverage.

He hasn't but that's all right. Being dickishly flippant is one of the joys of student life. The Union Society, in particular, is an institution where persuasively advocating things you disagree with or don't care about is all part of the game. It may be idiotic, but no more so than stealing road signs, guzzling so many Creme

Eggs that you throw up or crawling around the floor dribbling and eating from the dog's bowl. It's all part of growing up. Or, in my case, a Friday night out.

And it's understandable that if you're, say, a 20-year-old woman at Cambridge and a committee member of the Union Society, you may not think that the world is quite as sexist as people claim. It probably doesn't feel like it. So why not use your looks, surely as eternal as your intellect, to further "empower" yourself by making men ogle you as well as admire your keen grasp of tort law? That's not a policy with a shelf life, is it?

Pole dancing is grim and I don't see anything empowering about learning it. Even if you say that it's just dancing and good exercise, surely it would be more empowering to learn a dance that can be employed in contexts other than strip clubs? And if, as de Francisco claims, it's "not intended to be sexual", why is it only for women? Shouldn't men get the chance to be empowered too? I told you it was sexist!

People talk about sexism against men quite a lot. Everything from being officially excluded from MP selection shortlists to getting turned away from nightclubs is cited as if it demonstrated the utter hypocrisy of all feminist aims. The reactionary view is that it's all gone so ridiculously far – political correctness has gone so distressingly, dangerously and self-harmingly insane – that occasionally, would you believe it, things are now unfair on men! This doesn't seem to take into account that if situations weren't sometimes unfair on men too, it wouldn't be fair.

But, as this election campaign is demonstrating, when it comes to sexism, "PC gone mad" is a long way from power – it's still a minority party compared to "chauvinism gone senile". Just look at the horrible way that the leaders' wives are treated. To go with our medieval monarchy, we have politicians and news media whose attitudes to marriage are stuck in the 1950s. Those poor women should have nothing to do with this election beyond voting – they're not employees of the state or political parties and they should be getting on with their own lives.

I refuse to accept the argument that we need to know about the personal circumstances of potential leaders in order to trust them. There is no evidence that being "a good family man" is a necessary precursor to competent government or precludes incompetence and tyranny. Yet we insist they present a bland and dated image of family life, and complain when it looks affected.

Beyond that, we treat these women, who are paid nothing for their time, with an insolence we wouldn't adopt with a drunk tramp pissing in a bus shelter. There have been whole articles devoted to the apparently unacceptable condition of Sarah Brown's bare feet, which were revealed when she took her shoes off in a Hindu temple. In what way is a critique of the Labour leader's wife's toes in the public interest? It's just being incredibly, vindictively rude to someone who can't avoid the public gaze, and is unable to answer back.

Just as stupid and sad was the spectacle of the new female parliamentary candidates from the main parties all posing for a magazine shoot. I don't blame them for agreeing to it, but their male equivalents would never be asked – or only as the sort of ironic and tokenistic objectification of men currently in vogue as a gesture towards redressing sexism.

These normal-looking women, wearing their best clothes and smiling politely, never wanted to be in magazines. They're standing for parliament – they want to be empowered. I doubt they started with pole dancing.

* * *

I wrote the following article roughly two weeks before the 2010 general election. The politics nerds among you may note that my predictions weren't 100% accurate.

David Cameron's career is cursed by fate. With his privileged background, excellent education and meteoric rise, he may find it hard to believe but he'll be sensing something unpleasant by now. He may misattribute it and waste months taking allergy tests or eating bacterial yoghurts to reinvigorate his gut. There's no point changing your diet, David. What you're feeling is the hand of history – yanking your scrotum.

Such agony is familiar to the millions throughout the millennia who've found themselves in the wrong place at the wrong time: rural weavers on the eve of the Industrial Revolution, devout polytheists on the accession of the Emperor Constantine, Incas in the early 16th century, homeopaths in about six months' time (if there's any justice), most Russians at pretty much any point (there isn't).

This is the only explanation for Cameron's startling lack of success in the current election campaign. That may seem an odd remark to make about a man whose party is ahead in most opinion polls but, given how British politics has worked for most of the last 100 years, that's much worse than he should be doing.

The current government has undergone a horrendous series of crises: sudden and massive financial meltdown just as the man who was associated with the country's finances became prime minister; an expenses scandal discrediting the whole House of Commons at a time when most of its members were Labour; the war in Afghanistan becoming ever bloodier and more intractable; and finally the mass grounding of aircraft caused by an act of God that must have finally convinced Gordon Brown that there isn't one.

This last was an emergency which no governing party could have negotiated unscathed: either there are no plane crashes, so the ash was harmless and you've overreacted, or there are more than no plane crashes, which, to the non-statistically minded as well as those on board, always seems too many. These, then, were choppy waters indeed (like the stream beside the abattoir after the wrong sluice was opened) and Brown hasn't been much better at metaphorical canoeing than I imagine he would be at actual canoeing.

But I grudgingly admit that Cameron's failure to capitalise on this situation cannot be attributed to his deficiencies as a party leader. He may have refused to make more than the bare minimum of policy commitments; his rhetoric of change, optimism and social responsibility may have been as empty as Ann Widdecombe's little black book; and the fact that his core team is just a bunch of university mates with a towering sense of entitlement may have been ludicrously ill concealed; but, historically, none of these shortcomings would have stood in the way of his confidently assuming power under circumstances such as these.

"You're sick of the government, aren't you? So vote for me!" is how British opposition leaders have always addressed the electorate. It's usually enough. "Why commit to policies in advance when I can win just by not being Gordon Brown?" Cameron must have thought. It doesn't exactly make him a statesman, but it doesn't mean he's an idiot either. He analysed his strategic objective and, in time-honoured fashion, organised a perfectly competent cavalry charge. It had always worked in the past. And then history opened up on him with a machine gun.

It feels like something may be changing, and this could be real change rather than the mere alternative that Cameron offers. The apathy and disillusionment of the electorate may be turning into something more constructive than moaning about politicians being the same, not bothering to vote or telling ourselves that Ukip isn't racist. Instead, people are beginning seriously to question the two-party system. That's why Cameron's strategy, to everyone's surprise, isn't working.

The public's reasoning may have gone like this: "The Tories represent change, in that electing them would result in a change of government. But somehow I'm not sure they'd be a better government, just a different one. And, in fact, there's something eerily familiar about them. Big business seems to back them. Does that mean they're nice? Hmm.

"Oh, it doesn't make any difference who you vote for, does it? They all use the same platitudes. I wish they could all lose. I suppose that means I want a hung parliament? People seem to think that could happen. And everyone says Nick Clegg won the first leadership debate. I only saw a bit of it myself, but I'm quite glad – he was the underdog. Maybe I'll vote for him? That might give the Lib Dems a bit more influence if there's a hung parliament. Also, it might keep the Labour/Tory [delete as applicable] candidate out in my constituency.

"Actually, wait a minute! I feel quite good about Nick Clegg now! Nick Clegg and a hung parliament! And the Lib Dems want proportional representation, which would mean there'd always be a hung parliament. Would that matter? It seems interesting."

I hope people have been thinking along those lines because I believe that that's the sort of typically British, ponderous and cynical reasoning that could bring about proper reform. Historically, we don't change things out of ideological zeal, we change them when enough is enough. We're sick of a system where all a party leader needs to do to win power is convince us that he's not as bad as his rival. In a proportionally representative hung parliament, politicians may have to win arguments and talk about all their policies, not just scaremonger about the taxes or cuts that they claim their opponents are planning.

I'm speaking too soon but all this makes me optimistic. The savage and irresponsible response from the Tories and the rightwing press to Clegg's popularity boost reinforces my belief that something might be happening. Otherwise the Tory papers wouldn't be using words like "Nazi" and even more damaging ones like "donations". And senior Conservatives wouldn't imply that a hung parliament would usher in a sort of governmental apocalypse.

The truth is, for them it might. No party has done better under the old system than the Conservatives – they've enjoyed decades in office. But a hung parliament resulting in electoral reform could mean they never form a majority government again. They're feeling the hand of history where it hurts.

Like I said, it didn't really work out that way.

Part 2: After the Election

Nick Clegg gets a lot of stick these days. I've certainly slagged him off several times, and I feel guilty. It says a lot more about me than it does about him – I'm just cross with myself for voting for his party. If I hadn't, I probably wouldn't mind him at all. But when you vote Lib Dem, the last thing you expect is to end up complicit in what a government is doing. You expect to be merrily carping on the sidelines at the thoughtlessness of those corrupted by power. It's an almost monastic act, a renunciation of worldly power in the name of self-righteousness.

When you're trying to wash your hands of politics, it's disconcerting to discover you've just rinsed them in the blood of your countrymen, to have to explain yourself to Labour-voting friends: "I'm sorry, I got overexcited about electoral reform"; "I became intimidated by the size of Gordon Brown's head"; "It was annoying not to be able to feel smug about Iraq." You can't say: "Well, I never expected them to get into office – that was the key to their appeal." At worst, they were supposed to mitigate New Labour, not connive with the Tories.

If it's been a nasty shock for me, how much worse must it have been for Clegg? A member of the Lib Dems said to me in early

2010 that a hung parliament would be a disastrous election result for them. I didn't really understand. To me, it seemed like their best realistic outcome. I now realise we were both right. Clegg must have had a horrible time under a barrage of abuse and, as the anniversary of the election approached, it started to show. He began to look jowly and sad. One thought of him sitting through cabinet meetings, shaking his head and glumly eating crisps.

Well, there's only so much criticism a man can take before he's forced to react, and it seems Clegg has finally snapped. But instead of resigning and returning to his manifesto pledges, he's just got himself a rowing machine. Obviously he didn't mind people calling him a hypocrite nearly as much as them saying he had a paunch. To be fair, he's only going along with our whole society's priorities there.

Apparently the machine allows Clegg to work out between, and sometimes even during, meetings. Presumably this way he can intimidate advisers with his physicality: panting and dripping with perspiration, he can draw them into his circle of trust, closer to the heart of power, like the noblemen privileged to witness Louis XIV's levee. Or indeed like Winston Churchill, who often conducted business from his bed or the bath, a glass of champagne in one hand and a cigar in the other. I can't really imagine Churchill heaving away at an exercise machine, though – getting out of breath while Halifax burbled on about appeasement. The blood, toil, tears and sweat he offered members of his government were largely metaphorical.

There'll be no victory cigar for Clegg because he's given up smoking. This is a shame as it was one of the few things I still liked about him. I'm not saying it's good to smoke, but it was an engaging reminder of his humanity, his frailty – it helped me believe that he was acting more out of weakness than malice. Although an aide said that Clegg "hasn't needed gum or hypnosis or anything like that. Willpower alone has done the trick." A fine time to suddenly find some of that.

The main reason I'm disappointed by Clegg's health drive is that it means he'll stay looking exactly like all our other neat, slightly boyish politicians: Cameron, Osborne, several Milibands, Andy Burnham. Brown hair, black suit, white face, plausible smile – that's what you've got to look like, conventional wisdom tells us, if you aspire to the front rank of power. Forgettable, identical, cast in the image of Blair. Clegg's ageing and broadening features had begun to make him look like a recognisably different person – not quite as noticeable as Eric Pickles, but it was something. But now, with exercise and a diet, he's squeezing himself back into the mould.

Well, I think it's about time someone broke it. People are always claiming that a bald man can never be prime minister in the television age. But what about John Major? I know, technically, he had a full head of hair but, if they're saying that baldness makes you seem ineffectual, then Major was metaphorically worthy of a coot simile. He exuded the air of the loser, the underdog, the submissive, and yet no prime minister's government, in all of British history, has polled more votes than Major's did in 1992. Maybe it was because the country, after a decade's cruelty at the hands of a savage dominatrix, wanted to get fucked normally for a bit. But still, it's a sign that our leaders don't necessarily all have to look the same.

Not many of our top politicians from any of the main parties would declare themselves fans of Blair, but imitation is the sincerest form of flattery. It would have been difficult to believe postwar Germany's rejection of fascism if its leaders had taken to growing little moustaches. It's depressing that Blair's rise to power is the only sort our politicians have the imagination to believe possible. Surely the electorate must be sick of that style of politics?

In television, for all that people talk of creativity, the percentage game is in being deftly derivative. Don't have the big, risky, original idea, be the first to copy it. The steady money is in remakes, reworkings, shows you can signal to an audience as being similar to something they've enjoyed before. These programmes don't change the world, but they pay the rent.

It seems that politics is the same: everyone's still aping Blair. But the world is changing fast (just because people always say that doesn't mean it isn't currently true). Our next important leader is unlikely to obey the same rules as the last. Maybe the time has come for someone bald, or old, or obese, or disabled – or just less slick. It never looked likely that it would be Nick Clegg. Now he's dutifully pumping iron to make sure.

* * *

When did rebranding start? Pretty shortly after branding, I imagine. It must have been an uncomfortable feeling for those early cattle, still smarting from having the first mark seared into their hides, to notice the iron-age farmer firing up the furnace again on the advice of a trendy neighbour:

"Two straight lines is all very well, man, but I think if you added another one and a squiggle, you'd be projecting a much more powerful image."

"Would people think my cattle were more modern?"

"Totally."

"I like that bone you've got through your nose."

"Thanks – it's the new 'scourge of my enemies' chic. Makes you look like you've killed a chieftain, although in fact it's a badger's tibia."

I suppose there was a rebranding explosion when Europe Christianised: loads of mosaics having to be relaid, crosses nailed on to temples, altars altered. Plenty of lucrative work for artists who specialised in making Jupiter look like Jesus; and then, when the Vikings came, look like Odin; and then, when the Vikings converted, look like Jesus again. There can't have been a bigger payday for the rebranding industries until British Rail was smashed up into a dozen new made-up companies. That probably added more to the GDP through business-card printing than Brunel ever managed by building viaducts.

The first rebranding I was aware of was when Marathon became Snickers. It was a profoundly unsettling moment. The manufacturers were trying to mess with something inside our heads: the noise we associated with a certain object.

It's like when you start worrying that blue looks yellow to everyone else and that when they say "blue", they're thinking of yellow, and vice versa. How can you check? How do you describe blue? The mournful one? Aqua-brown? Red's old sparring partner? Ultimately it's just "the same colour as all the other things that are blue" – which, as I say, might look yellow to everyone else. When Marathon became Snickers, blue became yellow and words suddenly looked as flimsy as capital in the credit crunch. We're only two confidence tricks away from grunting and barter.

So I'm suspicious of rebranding. The recent abolition of antisocial behaviour orders, asbos, and their replacement with, among other things, criminal behaviour orders was dismissed by Bob Reitemeier, chief executive of the Children's Society, as "more of a rebranding exercise than anything else". Well, unusually, it's a rebranding exercise I'm in favour of because, unlike Jif becoming Cif, it actually means something.

Antisocial behaviour is not necessarily illegal. There are no laws against farting in a lift, smoking at an asthmatic's housewarming, browsing ringtones while travelling on public transport or picking your nose over dinner, and nor should there be. Taking crack is illegal; neglecting to offer some to other people when taking it in company – an act as antisocial, I'd have thought, as failing to get your round in – is not. "Antisocial" is a word for the general public to use when making informal judgments about each other. It should be outside the province of lawyers, politicians and police.

So I welcome the removal of the name "asbo" and all its rhetorical implications. To me, it always suggested that the authorities were punishing behaviour of which they disapproved, when disapproval is an entirely inappropriate, indeed insolent, emotion for public servants, acting in their professional capacity, to feel. If people break the law, the authorities must dispassionately intervene. Otherwise, the less they opine, the better.

That's why I hugely prefer the term "criminal behaviour orders", even if it comes to refer to the same ineffectual fudge (now Kraft fudge, I think). Criminal behaviour is within the state's area of legitimate concern. CBOs, unlike asbos, don't suggest that we're one step away from the introduction of Get-Your-Hands-Out-of-Your-Pockets-and-Stand-Up-Straight Orders.

I can't remember the last time I approved of a politically motivated rebranding. Throughout the New Labour years, I was maddened by the frequent renaming of government departments. What was once the Department of Education and Science, for example, has changed its name five times since the early 1990s. It's been the Department for Education twice (both at time of writing and from 1992–5), but has also at various times been "for" Employment, Skills, Children, Schools and Families. Every change cost us money and gained us nothing.

It makes me want to scream: "Listen, you're in government. Shut up and get on with it. We'll listen to the opposition because words are all they've got. You get to be judged on what you do!" Being "for" education, rather than "of" it; proclaiming your belief in a "big society" of kindly volunteers; and indeed, as has been mooted, moving the May Day bank holiday to October to become a "UK Day" on which we can all preen about how great our country is (which, in my view, is the kind of vulgar thing foreigners do) – this is all window dressing. It's a waste of everyone's time and we should be firm in making it clear to our elected leaders that we consider it outside their brief.

I'm not against a society with shared values, "truths we hold to be self-evident" etc, but I hate it when politicians try to determine what those values are. It's not a job we can trust them to do because they will instinctively use it to appeal for votes. Our elected representatives are there to decide how much money the government should collect, where it should collect it from, and how it should be spent. Their chances of re-election should be determined solely on how effectively, and equitably, they perform those roles. Politicians should make laws and ensure their enforcement by funding and protecting the independence of our judiciary. They absolutely should not sit in crowd-pleasing judgment themselves.

What our values are, what our civilisation stands for, what it means to be British – these are issues on which they are less qualified than the average citizen to take a view, because they have too big an incentive to be dishonest. We can't trust them, when discussing such subjects, not to descend to self-serving demagogy.

Renaming is a great tool for the demagogue or propagandist. I approve of the asbo/CBO rebrand because the new name is plainer and more accurate. But, in general, we should avoid changing the names of aspects of the state or government because politicians' tendency will always be to make the new names more emotive, more like adverts. And the government has nothing to sell us that we don't already own.

* * *

A senior member of the judiciary has got himself into terrible trouble for not being sufficiently judgmental. When sentencing a burglar, Judge Peter Bowers said that burglary took "a huge amount of courage". "I wouldn't have the nerve," he added, before letting the guy off with a suspended sentence.

As a result of these remarks, Bowers was formally reprimanded by the Office for Judicial Complaints, which must have come as a relief to him because, at the time he made them, he expressed concern that he "might be pilloried". If he thought that, he should probably go on a refresher course before he sends some poor hoodie down for a keelhauling instead of community service. Maybe he feared that if he didn't let the burglar off, the guy would get hanged. Or maybe that's what he wanted – maybe he thought that's what "suspended sentence" means.

The judge's comments drew complaints from all sides – and by "all sides" I mean the prime minister, the chairman of the National Victims' Association (don't miss their Christmas party if you like a passive-aggressive ambience) and LBC's Nick Ferrari. David Cameron said that burglars weren't brave at all but were "cowards". I don't know how he knows that but it's a good job because presumably, if they were braver, they'd break into loads more places. "Thank the Lord for the comparative cowardice of these dishonest people," he must be saying.

He isn't, of course. He just wants to slag burglars off, and so is associating them with the negative end of the bravery–cowardice spectrum without really thinking about what those words mean. He may as well have countered that burglars weren't handsome but ugly, not tall but short, not symmetrical but wonky and not fragrant but stinky. Having established that burglary is a bad thing, he thinks linking it or its practitioners with any positive attributes, however incidental, is an idea too sophisticated for the British public to grasp.

I don't mean to blame David Cameron: this culture in which any concepts more complicated than good and bad are too nuanced to bother trying to express is not of his making. And he's never seemed particularly keen to change things, either for better or worse. He just wants to make his way to a fireside in a cosy House of Lords bar, the words "prime minister" indisputably inked on to his CV, with the least possible fuss. He makes Macmillan look like Thatcher.

But obviously Judge Bowers is correct. In many cases, doing a burglary is going to require considerable courage. In order to break into a house and steal stuff you have to be brave, show a bit of gumption. In order to go and get someone else's property, you literally have to be a go-getter. Now, I'm not saying that the judge chose the best time to point out these evident truths. It would have been more appropriate and, more importantly, diplomatic to have emphasised some of the less praiseworthy attributes that burglary requires: dishonesty, unkindness, selfishness, thoughtlessness, disdain for the integrity of a window, raging narcotic withdrawal. I can understand those who dislike what he said. Not all truths need to be spoken. But that doesn't make what he said untrue.

Personally, I like it. I find the way it has annoyed people extremely satisfying. I'm attracted to its inappropriateness. It sticks out, it's noticeable, which is refreshing in the current era of public discourse, when all prominent figures seem at pains to be blandly appropriate: to show the expected level of respect, rage, shock, support, joy or grief. I like the judge for having taken the trouble to find something odd to say – something interesting and off-message.

It's a rare skill. PC Gary Archer of the British Transport Police doesn't seem to possess it. He described a series of thefts of dog-shaped charity collection boxes from station platforms in Oxfordshire as "simply unacceptable". I don't disagree but he didn't grab my attention as much as the grainy CCTV snap of a youth tiptoeing off with a large plastic labrador. It would probably hurt the policeman's career if he described the crimes as "funny" or "refreshing". "More fun than a stabbing in a nightclub." "Makes a nice change from inveigling your way into an old lady's house by pretending to read the meter." "Not what you'd ideally have people doing, but it shows a bit of enterprise." Some might say that was belittling a crime; I reckon it's looking on the bright side.

At the risk of sounding like those people who go on about how the Nazis had nice uniforms, it's worth remembering that bad things often have good aspects to them: burglars show bravery, smoking looks cool, Jeffrey Archer was quite good at athletics, the theme tune to *Casualty* is catchy. The good aspects don't stop the things being bad. It's vital to our understanding of a complex world, and to our intellectual dexterity, to be able to hold two different concepts in our heads at once without assuming that they're mutually exclusive.

This is particularly important in the arena of justice, so I like Judge Bowers's style. As anyone who has a friend keen on amateur dramatics will know, it's possible to think of something good to say about anything. Perhaps judges should have to do this by convention. Every time they sentence a criminal, they should be required to find something positive to say about the crime – not as an excuse, not even in mitigation, just as an acknowledgment that the world is always more complicated, baffling and contradictory than it seems.

So a murder could be described as cunning, an assault as physically dexterous, a fraud as punctual, an extortion racket as ambitious, an act of road rage as demonstrating spontaneity, an intense period of obsessive stalking as "daring to dream". The convicted criminal's judicial compliment could become as strong a tradition as a condemned prisoner's last meal.

Of course it would annoy the hell out of some people. But mainly those who enjoy the sensation.

* * *

We often change how we express ourselves depending on whom we're talking to. Or who we're talking to. I might say "who" or "whom" depending on who, or to whom, I'm talking (to). Meanwhile, my mum, who's Welsh but has lost the accent, unconsciously puts it on again when talking to Welsh people on the phone. I think it sounds like she's taking the piss.

Which raises the question: to whom the hell was *Newsnight* editor Ian Katz talking when he tweeted: "Tnks . . . except for boring snoring rachel reeves . . . playout was fun tho, wasn't it? telly MUCH netter [sic] than snooooozepapers innit." I put a "[sic]" after the "netter" because that was probably a typo, but there's an argument for putting one after almost every word. I was puzzled: I've looked him up on Wikipedia and he's well over 40. Why's he expressing himself like that? It's like halfway between Molesworth and Ali G. He's wearing his literacy so lightly we can see his balls.

We definitely know he had a specific recipient in mind because, as he said when subsequently apologising, it was meant to be a confidential "direct message" but he'd clicked the wrong button (as I say, he's well over 40). The rest of his Twitter feed seems to be written in normal English, but then maybe that's just for show? Maybe when he's off duty, he's all elongated vowels and superfluous use of "innit"? Maybe everyone is except me? Maybe I'm the only one left using this ancient ceremonial form of the language in daily life, like a Japanese emperor or the last Latin-speaking cardinal? Maybe there's more to sounding contemporary than remembering not to say "thou"?

None of that was why he got shit for the tweet. Innit. It was because he'd publicly called a member of the shadow cabinet boring, which is a silly thing to do if you're the editor of *Newsnight* and rely on a steady stream of politicians being willing to turn up and endure combative questions until such time as BBC2 can respectably put on a repeat. It's a very ungrateful response to the trouble Reeves took. After all, most of us can't even be bothered to *watch* the programme, so I can barely imagine the superhuman effort it must take to be bothered actually to go on it.

That doesn't mean she's not boring, of course. So I watched that section of the show and I'm afraid Katz is right: it is boring and she is boring in it. Mind you, her cause wasn't helped by Jeremy Paxman who, in his efforts to appear disinterested, seems to be moving with the adjective's shifting definition. It's hard to scintillate in the face of his resolute ennui. And, at the end, she was about to slag off George Osborne and he stopped her! He can hardly blame her for droning on about public sector pay if, as soon as she tries to inject some controversy, he interrupts.

But she did manage to say the government was "out of touch", which should please everyone in Ed Miliband's team. They seem firmly of the opinion that saying "out of touch" is all TV's good for. Or radio, for that matter – or lecterns, microphones and dispatch boxes. Just say "out of touch" as often and as loudly as you can and you'll win the next general election – that's their view. It's like that Dick and Dom game, Bogies, but with higher stakes and a much more banal thing to shout.

I don't really think it works. I don't like the government but I wouldn't say it was specifically "out of touch". Ministers are forever at press conferences, or giving speeches, or lamely launching crowd-pleasing initiatives in front of displeased crowds. I know they're on average quite rich and posh – and probably acting in the interests of their class or supporters rather than the wider public – but the evident realities of modern government necessitate their being "in touch" all the time. I think "out of touch" is the wrong slur – it conjures up an absentee emperor, a Tiberius on Capri, rather than energetic tweeters in suits feathering their political nests.

Conversely, "out of touch" is how I feel because I hardly ever watch *Newsnight*. With or without Rachel Reeves, I've always found it quite boring – not in a way I blame it for, but in a way I blame myself for. Being bored by *Newsnight*, I was brought up to believe, is an index of my own failings. One of the clearest signs of virtue, I've always known, is an ability to endure the stultifying. Not just current affairs, but art galleries and ballet and opera.

I once went to an opera. I think it was *La Bohème* but I'm genuinely not sure. It was staged in a Kilburn pub in a clever "promenade" way. I thought it was very accomplished but nevertheless, by the end, let's just say I was ready for it to finish. It did not leave me wanting more. For me, the last half-hour was an all-consuming contemplation of posterior discomfort and the weird elastic nature of time. But I was proud to have got through it.

Yet some of the group I'd gone with were crying by the end. That's how uncomfortable the seats were. No, it was because of the opera – the music, the story, the acting. They were moved to tears by the hours and hours of musical pretending. It was a level of emotional engagement that so baffled me, I found myself claiming to share it for fear of being lynched as a philistine.

Ian Katz knows where I'm coming from. He understands the need to tailor current affairs to people like me by involving professional performers. Who are also people like me, I suppose. Is that dumbing down – or interesting up? Is there any difference? Or is it just that if the TV is going to broadcast someone banging on platitudinously about the economy, they might as well also be able to make amusing remarks about the difference between cats and dogs?

But, ultimately, Reeves wasn't boring because of her presentational failings, because she lacks Churchill's or Bevan's or Russell Brand's charisma; it was because nothing she says seems to matter. Nothing any politician says on TV nowadays seems surprising or important, unless it's a gaffe. However dull the speaker, an audience will sit up and listen if what's being discussed might change their lives. But if the words are old and much repeated, even beautiful singing can be less interesting than a hard chair.

* * *

They say that nothing is more evocative of times past than a smell. For most of history, it's the smell of excrement. Though people are quicker to mention wisteria blossom and their mum's apple pie.

But, to my mind, nothing rolls back the years like the names of reports, commissions and inquiries. Those surnames that are constantly in the papers, on TV, overheard in conversations – muttered more often than the chorus of a boy band's number one, and then gone as suddenly: Calman, Taylor, Hutton, Butler and already Leveson, names kept warm for months in the mouths of newsreaders and then abandoned, cold and salivary. They take me back as vividly as a Tardis that plays 80s hits and is powered by the aroma of home cooking.

So it caught my attention recently when Nick Clegg said the words "Chilcot inquiry". It rang a peal of nostalgic bells for the death throes of New Labour – not an event that delighted me in itself, but I was younger when it happened so I remember it warmly. Similarly, I have difficulty enthusing about any world-improving developments predicted for the future, as they're likely to coincide with my decrepitude and/or demise. I think this is why people find it hard to get behind HS2.

The Chilcot inquiry probably makes Clegg nostalgic, too. It conjures up the Iraq war, which brings back happy memories for Nick. Those were his glory days of being right about stuff and ignored, before he moved into the treacherous arena of being wrong about stuff and obeyed.

I don't mean to pre-empt the inquiry's findings. Then again, I don't really have an option because the Chilcot inquiry, set up back in 2009 by Gordon Brown (remember him? Just think of the Arctic Monkeys or Henmania if you're having trouble conjuring him up), has still not published its report, which makes it more of a magnet for pre-emption than the Second Coming of Christ.

Clegg was merrily pre-empting away, saying the Iraq war was "one of the most catastrophic decisions in British foreign policy – I would say the most catastrophic decision – since Suez". I hope he hasn't pre-empted some ongoing royal commission on the Suez crisis. He'd have egg on his face if they rushed out their long-awaited exoneration of Eden.

Nick's point is that it's about time Chilcot reported and can't everyone get on with it. He's not blaming Sir John Chilcot himself, but the arguments about whether "25 notes from Mr Blair to President Bush" and "some 200 cabinet-level discussions" can be made public, which, he implied, various individuals are deliberately stringing out. "I do hope now that everybody involved, including those who know they will be subject to renewed scrutiny within the Chilcot report . . . will now accept that it is time to get this report published," he said. That's a forlorn hope. Those who are likely to get slagged off in it will never tire of waiting. That would be like queue-jumping on death row.

Clegg didn't specifically mention Tony Blair, but Tony Blair clearly thought it was all about him (a feeling I suspect he finds familiar) because he issued a riposte. It would be beneath the dignity of the great potentate to respond to a mere British deputy prime minister personally, but a spokesman said: "If Nick Clegg is implying Tony Blair is the reason for the delay, that is completely wrong. Tony Blair has as much reason as anyone for wanting the report published." Well, the second sentence is definitely a lie.

It feels ridiculous that this report still hasn't appeared – there must have been several histories of the Iraq war published by now – and apparently the earliest it'll be released, because of various inexplicable reasons, is next year, 12 years after the invasion of Iraq. This massively reduces the point of it, since everyone will have long since made their minds up about the subject by then. It'll barely be out in time for us to learn the wrong lessons from it going into the next war.

Everything seems to take too long. Maybe it's because I'm getting older – although it's precisely the opposite of what I was told getting older was like – but every public inquiry, internal investigation or official report seems, as a matter of course, to be scheduled to take a minimum of several months. At least Chilcot is investigating a whole war; the various and lengthy Plebgate inquiries are studying one bad-tempered conversation and its immediate aftermath. What is there to look at, or ask about, that takes so long? In all the reporting surrounding Maria Miller's resignation from the government, I noticed a fleeting reference to the 14-month investigation into her expenses. Why the hell should that take 14 months? This is one woman's bank accounts and property arrangements, not a full posthumous audit of Lehman Brothers – it shouldn't take longer than a week.

This is the moaning of a layman. Just because I can't understand why some things take so long doesn't mean there isn't a reason (although it doesn't mean there is). But the underlying principle to these processes seems to be that if something's really important, it should be allowed to take as long as it takes. That's flawed reasoning. If you say it doesn't matter how long something takes, then you're not saying it's important, you're saying the opposite. Important things need to be done by a certain time. If there's no particular time by which something needs to be completed, then the logical inference is that it never needs to be done at all.

Inexplicable waiting hangs heavy. My friend Toby Davies once wrote a TV sketch set in a shoe shop: the customer's requirements having been determined, the assistant disappears into that mysterious back room, while the customer waits, as we all do, wondering when the assistant will return, what he or she is doing, whether our weird foot shape or style choice has necessitated a management conference. In Toby's sketch, the shop's staff are perpetually enjoying a boozy and garrulous feast in the stock room. The assistant joins them for several minutes' wassailing before randomly picking a shoe box from the pile and staggering front of house with it.

I'm sure Sir John Chilcot will emerge at some point with the shoes. But the implication of this long disappearance is that nobody much cares how long we stand out here in our socks.

* * *

What ungodly things must David Silvester think Ukip has done to deserve this ceaseless media shitstorm? Silvester is the party's Henley-on-Thames councillor, whom it suspended for repeatedly asserting that the extreme winter weather is a punishment from God for legalising gay marriage. So what biblically prohibited acts must he think Nigel Farage has perpetrated that he is constantly tossed in a tempest of mockery and disdain? What sins has he committed to deserve such relentless tossing? What unholy transgression must Nigel have been guilty of to bring down these plagues of ridicule upon the organisation he's attempting to lead out of the wilderness?

Did Silvester feel the hand of the Lord upon him as he wrote his nutty letter? Did he descend like an avenging angel into the BBC Radio Berkshire studio to reiterate his point? Was it God's work that Andrew Scott was doing when he attacked Farage with a placard bearing the words "Nasty Little Nigel"? Was Godfrey

Bloom's assaulting a journalist with a brochure an example of the Lord moving in a mysterious way? Is Ukip, in fact, damned?

The Tories must be hoping so as Farage's party, in spite of these gaffes, seems likely to steal a significant chunk of their vote. Is "in spite of" the right phrase? Perhaps it should be "because of". After all, David Silvester used to be a Tory councillor. Conservative business minister Michael Fallon attempted to capitalise on Ukip embarrassment over Silvester's remarks by saying that "there clearly are one or two fruitcakes still around there". Fair point, but he's forgetting that many of these people used to be Tory fruitcakes. The Conservatives are losing the fruitcake vote.

Not that Ukip seems to value it. Like David Cameron, Farage is keen to shake off the "nasty party" image. For every Silvester or Bloom incident, he releases a compensating news story about how Ukip is becoming more credible and politically balanced. For example, he suddenly abandoned the party's entire 2010 manifesto in a TV interview and seeded in the media the concept of "New Ukip", in which all prospective candidates have to pass a day-long media skills and public-speaking course. One of those who passed and is to be a by-election candidate, Ukip proudly announced, is a *former Labour supporter*! How normal does that sound?!

Ukip claims it's starting to attract women voters and the young. "Women are owning the show in Ukip right now," said a female activist. "The 'blokey men's club' perception of Ukip is incorrect." Lisa Duffy, the party director, said they're "attracting more of the student vote . . . When we come . . . they may not be Ukip supporters, but by the time we leave that changes." And Farage has even spoken in favour of Britain taking in Syrian refugees.

So Ukip is following where Blair and Cameron have gone before: it's making a play for the middle ground. It's saying: "We're just decent normal people who represent the values of other decent normal people." "Hard-working families", "alarm-clock Britain", "the squeezed middle" – like Satan, they have many names, and all politicians want to appeal to them. "We're for you, you noble, struggling, put-upon, good-hearted societal contributors! Vote for us, we've got your back!" say all the parties.

Which raises the question: who is there for the nasty to vote for? If the Tories aren't the nasty party any more, and now Ukip isn't either; and if Labour is no longer the party of benefit cheats and power-hungry trade unions, but is dedicated to helping ordinary working families, whom the Tories are also dedicated to helping rather than fat-cat bankers and landed aristocrats; and if Ukip is no friend of racists, homophobes, sexists and Christian fundamentalists but welcomes women, students and Syrians; and everyone had forgotten the BNP even existed till Nick Griffin went bankrupt to give us a New Year laugh – then who will benefit electorally from the nasty demographic?

It's not as if there aren't plenty of nasty people in Britain, or that they can't vote. I suppose some are in prison – and you'd hope that the percentage of prisoners who are nasty was higher than that of the overall population. But there are still millions of law-abiding enfranchised unpleasant citizens to whom the political mainstream and Ukip are pointedly not reaching out.

One of the problems facing the nasty is that they don't agree about anything – which is probably why Ukip has proved so ungovernable. Some are rich and believe they should pay no tax, others fiddle their benefits. Some hate foreigners, some hate black people, some hate white people, some hate gay people, some hate women, some hate men. They're all out there, bickering about what's horrible, motivated to exercise the franchise, but no politicians want to know. As Tory Treasury minister Nicky Morgan put it: "If we talk about what we hate all the time, we're not talking about what we like." But that's not true: what if what we like is hatred? There's a significant bile-spouting section of the community – just look online.

I almost admired our political class for ignoring those with reprehensible views until I asked myself "Who will those who agree with what David Silvester says about gay people vote for now?" and realised the answer is almost certainly Ukip. Even though Ukip has disassociated itself from that opinion, the very fact that it had to do so suggests it's a party that homophobes are drawn to.

Similarly, benefit cheats tend to vote Labour. Ed Miliband has worked hard to distance Labour from the "something for nothing" culture, but more significant is the fact that he felt the need to do so – a Tory leader wouldn't. But most tax-avoiders will vote Conservative, despite government rhetoric. You can detect a party's unsavoury hinterland not from the people it courts but from the ones it disowns – whose votes it will probably still get.

So, in light of Ukip's rise, it may not be entirely good news for the Tories that Aidan Burley is stepping down at the next election. He's the once hotly tipped Conservative MP who organised a stag do in France at which the groom, Mark Fournier, was wearing an SS uniform (which it later transpired Burley had hired) and a "Nazi-themed" toast was drunk. Fournier was fined €1,500 by a French court for "wearing a uniform or insignia of an organisation guilty of crimes against humanity".

No party wants to be seen to appeal to the sort of person to whom that sort of thing appeals. But the central office buffet is running low on fruitcake.

*　*　*

What do the British want from their politicians? That must be a question the aides of all the party leaders agonise over. It's what they're trying to answer as they slave over the latest soundbite or policy initiative, before sending their leaders out into a hostile media environment to chorus "I am not a phoney like the others! I am my own man slash woman!"

The Russians have their answer: bare-chested aggression is what floats their boat. The merciless sturgeon-eyed tyrant. The Russians don't want to vote for the kind of sap who wouldn't rig the election if they didn't. After centuries of dysfunctional relationships with their leaders, they've given up resisting: the fact is they're attracted to a strong man, even when he slaps them about a bit.

The British are fussier. Of late, the closest we've come to electing a genocidal maniac was probably Tony Blair. And, as psychopaths go, he was pretty low-key – he kept all the killing abroad, the sound principle on which the British empire was founded. Very much your iron-hand-in-a-velvet-glove type, rather than the kind of guy who likes to be photographed swimming amid bear carcasses. I like to think of him slipping silently into hotel rooms by night, dressed in black, seeing by the light of his teeth, to leave poisoned boxes of chocolates by opinion-formers' bedsides.

Blair was also the last prime minister for whom the country felt anything approaching a consensus of enthusiasm. And we'll never get him back – he's lost to us, swept up in a whirlwind of tax avoidance and yachts. Dividing his time between high-level business meetings, absurdly remunerated public speaking and marathon sessions in his bespoke sunbed-cum-confessional.

Which leaves us with the current bunch. Cameron the posh, flushed hunting pink with the effort of appearing to make an effort; Miliband the wonk, undergoing hundreds of hours of presentational-skills training so he can give impassioned speeches without audience members worrying that he'll swallow his tongue; and Clegg the promise-breaker, who disappointed so many of his supporters within days of taking office that his critics failed to notice he's also posh and a wonk.

I don't think most of us could honestly tell them what they'd need to do to gain our respect. We just don't like them and we wish they'd turn into people we do like – a wish they share, which we despise them for. Is it the public's disdain that forces them into more behaviour we dislike? It seems like they're in a vicious circle: desperate not to annoy, desperate not to seem desperate, frantic in their demands that their advisers find them something to do or say or be which will come across as unselfconscious – like a reasonable, normal, grounded man, the kind of bloke you'd have a pint with but subsequently come to obey. Someone, and they must burn their tongues as they utter the syllables, more like Nigel Farage or Boris Johnson.

But if you want to be like someone, you've got to think like them – that's why Dustin Hoffman has won more Oscars than Mike Yarwood. And mainstream politicians' whimpering eagerness to please could hardly be more alien to the attitude of big swinging Johnsons like Farage. Those guys just don't seem to care so much, which is probably because they don't actually care so much, and reverse psychology mixed with good old-fashioned human self-loathing means that voters are instinctively attracted.

There's always a chance that people will decide who to vote for according to policy – and by "people", I mean the people that matter: the indecisive minority who change which party they vote for from election to election according to whim, and consequently determine every result. But it doesn't seem likely to me that policy is what's going to swing the swingers this time – although I may only think that because the Labour party's policies are still largely secret. I suspect everyone's going to be cutting budgets while having rhetorical rows about how quickly and which sort of hard-working person is being screwed least assiduously. And Europe, I suppose – that's actually a thing, although I don't think many of us can see past our knee-jerk isolationism or internationalism to honestly know what the best course of action is.

I don't think Cameron and Miliband believe policies are going to clinch it either, or they might be keener to discuss them. But they'd rather keep it platitudinous. After doing some running for Sport Relief, the prime minister said: "I am delighted to have taken part in such a fantastic event that is bringing people across the UK together to get active, raise money and change lives." It's so inoffensive that, for me, it pushed through the other side and was on a par with Holocaust denial. "Change lives" is the real kicker – it's actually from the Sport Relief press release. Nobody talks like that. Changing lives isn't a good thing anyway, unless you're changing them for the better. Changing lives is what Dan Aykroyd and Eddie Murphy did in *Trading Places*. It's what Ed Miliband wants to happen to him and David Cameron.

I found it hard to admire that aspiration of Ed's when he said, on the subject of Grant Shapps's twatty advert boasting about the Tory tax cut on bingo: "Have you seen a more condescending, patronising, arrogant, haughty, out-of-touch, misconceived piece of nonsense?" I didn't like the advert either, until I heard Miliband's hyperbolic gloating. His crowing glee at the sight of a passing bandwagon, the intense joy because his opponents have messed up, and so he's closer to his aims without having to do anything good, made me want to puke. And every time a Labour politician says "out of touch", I want to scream, which is difficult to do if you're already puking. I can't shake the feeling that someone in Miliband's team thinks it's unbelievably clever that they keep repeating that phrase, basically as a synonym for "Old Etonian", and I want that person's feeling of cleverness to be ripped out of them without anaesthetic.

Politicians just can't win with people like me. But then they appear to have stopped trying to win and to be willing to settle for losing least – which, as David Cameron can attest, brings with it the same job title. Is it fair to blame them? They get maligned for who they are and, when they try to conceal that, they get vilified for "not being themselves". They must feel terribly bullied. And, unfortunately for them, public opinion is not the sort of bully you can stand up to – unless you're Vladimir Putin.

* * *

"But, Miss Marple, it's all an absolute mystery!"

"What is, my dear?"

"Politics, Miss Marple! The economy! Welfare, taxation, big government, small government, justice, injustice, the NHS, the City – all of it! It's all so complex and grubby and dark and depressing. Help us, Miss Marple!"

"Well, yes, of course I understand that you'd think so, dear. But it all rather reminds me of Mr Byrne, the boys' football coach from Chalfont St Peter." The old lady paused to reflect. "Yes, a charming village over in Buckinghamshire, but not far from St Mary Mead really. Our organist arranged a tour of their crypt one very wet Michaelmas, I remember."

"She's rambling!" interjected Inspector Pleb impatiently. "What can a village football coach possibly have to do with this mystery of generally everything that the police are trying to solve?! You really must stop wasting our time, Miss Marple." He stormed out.

Later on, I asked Miss Marple to explain, and she told me more about Justin Byrne, the 42-year-old company director who used to coach the under-10s in the Buckinghamshire village, until December 2013, when he was suddenly sacked.

"He sent out rather an imprudent email – oh dear me, yes," recalled Miss Marple. "And so they fired him. He was ruthlessly dismissed for ruthlessness, in a manner of speaking."

Miss Marple looked at her knitting. "Knitting," she said.

"Yes, that is knitting," I replied uncertainly.

"No. Mr Byrne. He mentioned knitting. He said people thought sport was about knitting. That's what he told the *Daily Mail*. That his critics were 'weaker-minded' and they thought sport was about knitting. A curious man."

"But what was in the email?"

"Oh, you'll have to find out for yourself, dear. I'm far too tired."

I soon discovered that Miss Marple's recollections were completely accurate. Mr Byrne had been coaching the under-10s for over two years when he dispatched a circular email:

"I am only interested in winning," he wrote. "I don't care about equal play time or any other communist view of sport. Those that are not as good need to work harder or demonstrate more during training, or change sports. As someone who spends a huge amount of time working with graduates trying to find their first job I can safely say you are not doing your son any favours by suggesting the world is fair or non-competitive. Everything they are likely to do in life will be competitive so my view is get them used to it."

And that was the last time anyone asked him to play Father Christmas.

I showed the email to the inspector. "Quite right too!" said Pleb. "It's a horrible world. In the long run, kids won't thank you for being nice to them."

"Why not?" I asked.

"Got no manners these days."

I could understand Byrne and the inspector's point of view. Why shield the young from the harsh realities of the world? Better to get them used to the grim truths of victory and defeat, or acceptance and rejection, at a young age. Let them develop the calluses on their little souls which will protect them from life's abrasions. Then they will approach adulthood hardened and invulnerable. It worked for Sparta.

I put this to Miss Marple. "Quite so. But I wonder what you think Mr Byrne's garden is like, dear."

"His garden?"

"A mess, I shouldn't wonder. Unless he's guilty of the same weak-mindedness of which he accuses others."

"How does that follow?"

Miss Marple put down her knitting. "Well, he wouldn't see the point in keeping it tidy or pleasant, would he? He would have no appetite for the Sisyphean task of nurture, cultivation, weeding, watering, mowing, replanting. He'd see them as a denial of nature's realities. If something cannot grow and prosper amid such wildness, then it must rightly perish. He must perceive a truer beauty in all-conquering bramble and convolvulus, or count himself a hypocrite."

"But, Miss Marple, he *is* a hypocrite!" I exclaimed. "By his own admission. He confessed that he'd keep his own son in the team, whether or not he was good enough. 'The only reason I am coaching is for him to be able to play,' he said."

"And you think that makes him a hypocrite?"

"Of course."

"Because he protects his own son?"

"Exactly."

"Well, I'm only an old lady but it seems to me that you could just as easily argue that, by his own reasoning, he is sacrificing his son for the greater good. Denying his child the vital hardening effect of a merciless under-10 footballing environment purely in order to expose the others to the sort of unashamed nepotism they'll have to confront in later life."

"So he's an unfit parent?"

"Quite possibly but, by his own standards, an exemplary coach. No, it is to his garden you must look to prove him hypocritical. And to his outrageous association of communism with knitting, for which I find it impossible to forgive the man."

"But what I don't understand, Miss Marple, is how any of this helps with the mystery of politics."

"Oh yes, of course – I'm so sorry, you must think me terribly opaque. Well, what was said, after he was dismissed?"

Steve Fowler, a spokesman for the club, had said: "This is a friendly village football club that just wants to get as many children playing football as possible, and make sure they have fun doing it."

"There speaks a gardener," said Miss Marple.

I was just about to call a nurse when I thought I'd ask one last time for Miss Marple to explain.

"Yes, I may be using too many metaphors – they've got me on new tablets," she confided. "But what I'm trying to say is that all politics is contained within this. It's like the child in the third world that you sponsor in order to give charitable donations a comprehensible human scale. Well, in a similar way, this football club gives the conflict between the left and right wing a comprehensible human scale.

"Do you believe that the world is cruel and unchangeable and that we must defer to and prepare for that, as Byrne does? Or do you think, like Mr Fowler, that we can remake the world as we would like it to be – that everyone can play football together? That's the only real question, dear. When you have answered it, you will have solved the mystery."

5

It's Not Just Poets That Need Abstract Nouns

Credit, collateral, equity, market confidence, economic growth, sovereign debt – these are all weird, intangible concepts that we've become obsessed with. There have genuinely been days when I've gone online and looked up the price of the euro, or the rise and fall of the FTSE, just in the hope of calming myself down about the possibility of global financial collapse. It doesn't always work. These are statistics I don't understand and can't affect, but have nevertheless come to care about and follow obsessively, like a gloomy but weirdly addictive soap opera in a foreign language.

In a time of want, we all become interested in where the remaining money is going, and who's doing well amid the ruins. This wealth-fixated chapter explores anger at a highly paid teacher, the justification for stratospherically paid executives, how a little cash goes a long way in politics, a plutocrat banker's embarrassment at conspicuous consumption, and some unhealthy ideas for having fun on a budget. Save thinking about those less fortune than yourself for Christmas. The rest of the year is devoted to the livid contemplation of the arseholes who've got the cream (to quote the caption from an anal sex video screengrab).

* * *

Not everyone is screwed by the credit crunch. Every cloud has a silver lining, every repossession requires the employment of several bailiffs, suicide attempts keep nurses in work and on each pile of rotting, bloated corpses is a swarm of plump rats.

153

Or, to put it another way: "When life gives you lemons, make lemonade!" Well, as any drinks manufacturer will tell you, you don't need lemons to make lemonade. Neither do you need meat to make a doner-kebab-flavour Pot Noodle. Apparently this new addition to the Pot Noodle range is practically vegan.

Excellent! At last, vegans are being extended the same opportunities to get hooked on cheap junk food as the rest of society. But lemon-free lemonade and meat-flavoured starchy string are exactly the sort of products that are selling at the moment. Everyone is blowing what little spare money they have on crap treats. McDonald's sales are rising; Pontins is expanding; people are looking for the sensation of wasting money, on a budget.

Why piss away a fiver on a latte and an almond croissant when you'll get a similar buzz from a can of Tizer and a battered sausage and have change from two quid? Plus the taste of your treat is nostalgically reawakened every time you burp for the next 36 hours.

Budget foods are flying off supermarket shelves (that's genetically modified chicken for you), bookmakers are prospering – presumably because lots of unemployed bankers are trying to keep their hands in – and the number of people doing the pools has risen for the first time since the launch of the National Lottery, for which ticket sales have also increased. So we can expect brand new opera houses and art galleries to spring up everywhere, which is nice because they'll be somewhere for all the homeless to sleep.

There are green shoots all over the place, though most of them are green because they died so long ago they've gone mouldy. So, in that spirit of optimism, here are some of the businesses that have managed to buck the downward trend.

Homeless Security plc

With factories closing, hundreds of disused sites need guarding around the clock. But while all this property is falling into disuse, thousands are being made homeless. "We just took those two wrongs and made a right!" says Homeless Security's managing director. "The simple fact is that if there's already a gang of homeless sleeping in a disused factory, another gang isn't going to move in. So, on behalf of the administrators called in to wind up failed companies, we source a bunch of relatively tidy tramps to keep the place occupied. They're as dependable as guard dogs and cheaper, since the cider we pay them with costs less than Pedigree Chum."

Ice Cold Alex Ltd

"If I had to sum up my product in five words," says their chief executive who doesn't, "it would be 'Brandy Alexander in a can'. It's sophisticated, it's sugary and, if you use reconstituted pig lard instead of dairy fat, it's incredibly cheap to make. We're living through difficult times – people are hungry, stressed, they want to forget. Drinking five or six Ice Cold Alexes on the trot may not be what a doctor would advise, but my God it gets you through the day." And investors all want a piece of it. An investment analyst explains why: "Everybody knows that alcoholism is a problem, everybody knows that obesity is a problem, but this company is unique in having fully monetised both phenomena. I suppose everyone else must have been too fat or drunk to think of it."

Bee-in-Bonnet Media

Formerly the BBC complaints department, this was outsourced and is now a thriving independent company. They're proud of what they've achieved: "The whole complaints procedure needed streamlining. The rigmarole of getting feedback, reading it, evaluating its content and then responding was ridiculous in this day and age. Clearly we needed to get from tabloid-induced complaint frenzy to abject backtracking apology in a matter of minutes, if not seconds. That's what the licence-fee payer has a right to expect.

"We're building great relationships with our media partners, whereby newspaper editors can let us know in advance what they're going to tell people to be appalled by, with an estimate of the number of complaints that will generate, and then we just email the appropriate WESWEE [media slang for a 'We're Sorry We Even Exist' statement] to the DG's BlackBerry."

Belt and Braces Ltd

The collapse in TV and newspaper advertising has created a boom in the public-safety-campaign industry. "Suddenly all this advertising space is going cheap, and we've secured the government contract to provide the content," explains their head creative, who, pre-crunch, pulled down a six-figure salary inventing the names of friendly bacteria. "The days of 'Look out for motorcyclists when turning right' are behind us. It's got to be edgy, sexy: 'Taking drugs is like six different versions of you pissing each other off'; 'A stroke is a fire in your brain'; or 'If you break the speed limit you will hallucinate dead ginger children.' This is the Green Cross Code for the *Skins* generation. At the moment, we're working on an anti-gambling campaign which implies that it turns your head into a roulette wheel, meaning that, given time, your brain stem snaps. It uses a lot of CGI. We also do photos of corpses for fag packets."

Cats and Dogs Ltd

Founded five months ago, the company already has four small factories turning domestic cats, which people can no longer afford to keep, into hot-dog sausages. "Animal rights loonies have claimed that we put the cats into the grinder live. I utterly reject that allegation – they're given a lethal flavourising injection first," asserts their head of PR. "I just love the irony. People talk about 'eating a dog' when in fact it's cat!"

And looking to the future? "We're hoping to throw some gerbils and goldfish into the mix – as soon as we can get the calibration right on the mincer. The last thing anyone wants is a whole eye coming through."

* * *

"Don't mention the crunch!" hissed the manic hotelier behind the backs of the party of diners from Goldman Sachs. "I mentioned it just now but I think I got away with it!"

That's the sort of thing senior bank employees might have to endure in the coming decades. Top bankers are the new Germans. And the sooner we get to the point where we're making jokes about the outrages committed in their name, the better. We haven't got there yet.

There's a fascinating podcast from the US public radio show *This American Life* about the causes of the credit crunch. It points out that what everyone in the banking sector always says about the financial crisis is that no one saw it coming. As Ira Glass, the host of the programme, puts it: "The recent collapse of the financial system has been described as a 100-year flood, a perfect storm, a force of nature. And it is so frustrating to hear it described that way – as something that happened to Wall Street instead of something that Wall Street brought on itself."

The show then tells the story of a hedge fund called Magnetar whose business plan is as villainous as its name. The people who ran it realised that the US property bubble was going to burst and found a way both of inflating it further and betting that it would pop. Consequently, they made a fortune when it did.

They were aided and abetted by various bankers who, while nominally employed to represent the best interests of customers and shareholders, were actually rewarded for the number of deals they struck rather than their ultimate soundness.

It's a lamentable tale of the sort that the US Senate grilled Goldman Sachs executives about. I think most of us suspected that this kind of thing was going on, but hearing the details is riveting and maddening. Whether or not these business practices were strictly legal, wrong has been done here. Bankers personally took home vast sums of money – sums they still have – exacerbating a problem that has cost the world's taxpayers trillions to try to fix.

That money has effectively been stolen from us by people who, if Goldman Sachs and Magnetar are anything to go by, show very few signs of being sorry. It is, of course, fruitless to expect corporations to be moral – they are dumbly, amorally acquisitive – but the people who work for them are morally culpable. In these cases, they weren't even working in the interests of the banks that employed them, but stacking up bonuses for themselves by selling dodgy financial instruments while concealing from their customers that operators like Magnetar had induced the creation of these instruments purely to bet on their eventual worthlessness.

We're all living with the consequences of these actions – that's why bankers are like the Germans 60 years ago: they are collectively blamed for bringing disaster on the world. The analogy, like all historical analogies, is imperfect – the financial crisis has not had a comparable human cost to the two world wars – but it works in several ways. Like the Germans, not all the bankers knew what was going on. Others opposed it or went along with it grudgingly because they were in an environment where they felt they had no alternative. But others were the bad guys. They did terrible things – things that have hurt millions of people – for personal gain.

Europe's recovery after the second world war – its ability to forgive and rebuild the country that had done so much harm – relied on the fact that the vast majority of Germans were genuinely contrite. The American taxpayer poured money into West Germany to put it on its feet, just as taxpayers have done with the banking sector. It was the right thing to do in both cases, but only in the former was it received with the heartfelt apologies and thanks necessary to offset future resentment.

It's vitally important that the banking sector fully acknowledges its wrongdoing. It's not enough for it to say: "Sorry we didn't see the crash coming, but no one did." That's not a real apology and it's a lie; some people did see it coming, but used that knowledge to worsen and profit from it. The fact that the banking profession was so ethically detached from the rest of society that this behaviour seemed reasonable needs to be addressed, because the creation of a culture in which evil acts appear normal is what happened under the Nazis.

I don't hate capitalism – it broadly works. But it only works, and society only functions, because humans are basically moral creatures. When we do wrong, we believe in remorse and forgiveness – in that order. Our politicians have failed to extract this remorse from bankers because they've been too busy blaming each other for the handling of the crisis. But that's like Chamberlain squabbling with Halifax over who was more responsible for the second world war; at worst, the politicians are accessories.

Unless the bankers are penitent, the German parallels are uncomfortably closer to 1919 than 1945. Like the financial crisis, the first world war didn't have clearcut goodies and baddies. All the countries involved must take some of the blame for the wholesale slaughter, just as feckless borrowers and shortsighted finance ministers contributed to the crunch. But Germany wanted that war and conspired to ignite it, just as Magnetar did the sub-prime mortgage crisis. It was more Germany's fault than any other country's.

In the muddle and fudge of Versailles, the victorious allies forgot to win that argument. And tragically, as a result of an armistice being declared rather than the war fought to an unconditional surrender, many Germans were left with the illusion – one that Hitler exploited – that they hadn't been defeated in the war but betrayed from within. This wasn't true. The German army was thoroughly beaten.

We mustn't let the bailout of the banks be the equivalent of that armistice. The fact that banks still exist, bankers must realise, is despite rather than because of their actions. They failed utterly – morally and economically – and their continued employment is by our collective grace. Its continuance should be conditional on their taking the blame for what they did. Otherwise, the economic recovery could be as uncertain and transitory as the inter-war peace.

* * *

"Who's the richest person in the world?" That's a question I often asked as a small child. Do children ask that because so many of the stories they get read involve gold? Maybe it's peculiar to my generation, which was learning its times tables as Thatcher came to power. Or maybe I was an unusually mercenary little shit. I don't think so, though. In the good times, we admire people with money; in the bad, we resent them, but they're always interesting.

I wanted the richest person in the world to be the Queen. It suited my juvenile sense of fairytale hierarchy. To a child's mind, a world where a nerdy American in a jumper and glasses or a podgy Saudi in a sheet can outspend the posh lady in the big gold coach wearing the big gold hat is a world gone mad.

Similarly, small children might expect the answer to the question "Who gets paid the most?" to be "The prime minister." The prime minister is in charge, so it might seem logical that "the prime minister's salary" means the same as "the most amount of money imaginable", and that anyone being paid more than that is an evil usurper of the Queen's treasure. In stories, such villains, grand viziers and the like, get punished. They're humiliated and made to give the money back. A child might even contemplate, in moments of post-sugar binge viciousness, chopping their heads off.

But small children are idiots. As each human foetus sloshes into the world, wailing and weeing, unable to walk, crawl, speak or even sit – a helpless lump of ignorant self-interest – society takes a deep breath because, in just 18 years' time, that blob will be allowed to vote. The professionals whose job it is to get them up to speed are called teachers and, according to newspaper reports, one of them is paid more than the prime minister.

It's a credit to the children and parents at Mark Elms's school that they still don't want to chop his head off. In general, they seem to think that he's very good at his job and deserves the money. You don't expect primary-school headmasters to be paid that much, but he's brilliant and, to borrow a phrase from the private sector, you get what you pay for. But that's not everyone's view. Many are disgusted by the news that, contrary to our expectations, at least one teacher has a high salary.

How deeply depressing. This isn't some risibly job-titled council functionary – a "deputy manager of procurement services", a "bureaucracy maximisation taskforce co-chair" or a "litter tsar", one of those people responsible for all the "waste" we're asked to believe that the previous administration encouraged in direct defiance of its own interests. This guy runs a primary school in a grim area that was as crap as you'd expect when he took it over and has got vastly better under his leadership, to the immense benefit of his hundreds of pupils and their families. Why can't we treat him like the high-flyer his CV proclaims him to be?

I think most people are comfortable with the idea that if you're a brilliant doctor, surgeon or barrister, you'll get quite rich – nearly as rich as a second-rate management consultant or an inept banker. But the fact that we react so differently to a teacher's pay approaching that level gives the lie to our vociferous assertions that we think teaching is an important job. We don't think it's important, we think it's badly paid. And when we discover an instance where it isn't, it makes us angry, not glad.

It even makes the unions representing other teachers angry because, apparently despairing of ever seriously improving their own members' pay, they've focused on dragging headteachers down into the same under-remunerated swamp. One example is cited of a teacher's career that has involved success, fulfilment and money – a beacon of hope to talented graduates with a vocation to teach but who fear it would leave them absurdly less well-off than their peers in other jobs – and the very unions representing that profession want it snuffed out, so that teaching remains the preserve of the self-sacrificing or the mediocre.

The government agrees because this is the public sector which, according to Tory orthodoxy, is inevitably inefficient. The country must live within its means and so can't pay public sector wastrels at the same rate as their private sector equivalents, even though the main cause of those means becoming so straitened was the credit-crisis-induced recession, a disaster brought on by monumental private sector inefficiency – if the word "inefficiency" is sufficient to cover that thoughtless spiral of hedonistic incompetence.

Nevertheless, to this government the private sector is automatically better. To suggest otherwise is heresy. That's why they're restructuring the NHS in a way that will encourage more private enterprise, despite the fact that, in June 2010, the Commonwealth Fund declared it the most efficient health service out of the seven it had studied – that's ahead of Germany, Australia, the Netherlands, New Zealand, Canada and the United States, all systems with more private sector involvement. The NHS might well be, in terms of the results it delivers with the money it gets, the most efficient health service on Earth. And yet the Tories are convinced that hasty and sweeping organisational reforms will make it even more so.

Meanwhile, paying higher salaries to get more able employees is, in their view, a technique that only works in the private sector. They've arbitrarily decided that it's a scandal if any public servant is paid more than the prime minister. But the prime minister's salary has always been incredibly low considering the importance of the job. To most prime ministers, the pay is irrelevant; they don't have much time to spend it and they know they can rake it in with a book deal and a lecture tour as soon as they resign.

I don't know if the country can afford to pay hard-working and well-motivated primary-school headteachers, who also work in the community to help other schools, £180,000 a year (which is roughly what he got after backpay for the previous year and employers' pension contributions are taken away). But I hope so, and I'm pleased that Mark Elms has been well paid for doing a good job. The fact that so many felt otherwise is a sign of how hysterical with envy some people, and a lot of news reporting, have become.

* * *

Occasionally, just for a moment, I think it might be a good thing if money ceased to exist, if the eurozone sovereign debt crisis spiralled so hopelessly out of control that there was an international bank run of catastrophic proportions, and so all of the numbers – and, in millions of cases, negative numbers – next to our names on screens became academic because the screen-owning institutions had run out of the pieces of paper that the numbers were supposed to represent – and indeed weren't even sure for how much longer they'd receive the electricity to run the computers that stored these now notional numbers.

Maybe, I catch myself thinking, such a great levelling would remind us of the fundamental truth that we're just a few billion humans clinging to a rock spinning in space, with certain requirements and problems, and certain resources and skills with which to address them. The bottom line is not the proverbial bottom line. Our obsession with money has even infected our idioms; it's made us believe that cash is something concrete. (The builders got to that one before the accountants, which makes a bit more sense.) When you think about things in this way, you're harder to sway when people argue that the British economy depends on a vibrant financial services sector or that environmental campaigners don't understand the real world.

The reason I try to romanticise this potential cataclysm is that I'm depressed by how money always latches on to power – how affluent people and institutions aggressively and unashamedly lobby to sustain and advance themselves. With money gone, this couldn't happen. Admittedly, the chequebook's demise as a sign of power would mean a return of the mace. Might would be right again, which is hardly a fairer system – but at least it encourages people to take exercise.

For now, money remains sovereign. Chris Huhne's girlfriend, Carina Trimingham, has made the papers for sending a "Nod nod, wink wink, I know lots of cabinet ministers" email to a lobbying company in the hope of getting a job. Meanwhile, we had cross-party cross parties in response to Sir Christopher Kelly's proposed reforms of their funding. He wanted a cap of £10,000 on money given by individual donors so that people are primarily giving to support rather than influence a political cause; state funding would make up the shortfall.

The Trimingham email isn't much of a scandal; it's just another own goal by the Lib Dems. I doubt they've got the organisational skills to be properly corrupt. Like the priests at St Paul's when Occupy moved in, they've just been flustered by the unaccustomed limelight into briefly abandoning all their principles. And, while there's a thriving market for governmental influence, Trimingham doesn't strike me as a major stallholder. I doubt that the networking overtures of the younger woman your colleague just left his wife for seem any more inviting in political circles than they do anywhere else. She's just another hapless jobseeker, a victim of history: a hundred years ago, a woman having an affair with a cabinet minister would have been set up in her own flat on a generous allowance. Chris Huhne would probably think that was sexist. He's very much a new man who was always happy to let his wife drive, for example.

The rejection of reform to how political parties are financed is more troubling. Clearly, the parties fear that a £10,000 cap would open up a massive funding gap. This would partly be caused by genuine, generous supporters being forced to give less. But some of it would definitely be a result of those who wish to buy influence being unable to. From trade unions to Lord Ashcroft, many institutions and individuals give money to political parties because they want, at the very least, to be listened to more intently than those who haven't donated. They want to get round the pesky one-person-one-vote principle that democracies anachronistically cling to in the face of economic reality.

This is money that, in an ideal world, honourable political parties wouldn't want. But this isn't an ideal world and politicians probably tell themselves, sometimes accurately, that they can take the money, nod and smile at the donor's weird views, and then use it in pursuit of legitimate political goals. And while this grubbiness sometimes brings bad PR, it's less hassle than asking for public money at a time of hysterical state parsimony.

But this approach is not in the taxpayer's or the people's interests. The money Sir Christopher Kelly wants political parties to get would be a pittance, in terms of the national budget, and it could save us so much. In allowing political parties to be so broke they're prey to cynical donors and politicians to be so underpaid they grub around for directorships, we risk spoiling the ship of state for a ha'p'orth of tar.

The link between money and power may never be broken but, in a well-run democracy, the overall wealth of the many can be brought to bear. Collectively, the electorate is much more financially powerful than any corporation. Big business wants our wealth, our custom and preferential trading conditions in our realm. We, as customers and taxpayers, can make or break them; they know it and will pay to subvert that power. This causes immense waste and injustice, much of which would be obviated if our political system enjoyed the comparatively modest state funding that would protect it from lobbyists' cash.

* * *

By December 2011, over three years after the collapse of Lehman Brothers, the country still felt like shit . . .

Sometimes it's down to the director-general of the British Retail Consortium to sum up the national mood. "Non-food is having a thoroughly miserable and difficult time," he said. He's so right – it really is. And, of all the non-foods, the humans are particularly depressed, with more than 2.64 million of us now out of work. But I like his note of optimism. We remain non-foods. We haven't started to eat one another. While we've not yet been reduced to carrion or prey, there are still grounds for hope.

We're in the grip of a historically significant slump, possibly as notable as the Great Depression. Our current trials will definitely be on the A-level history syllabuses of the decades to come. Any more disastrous developments and we may even make GCSE.

The question the kids of the future will be trying to answer is: "What caused all that suffering?" As a former lazy history student myself, I know that the trick here is to look for the point in the debate where someone says, "It's a bit more complicated than that," and then go back to the previous assertion. The things that historical events are a bit more complicated than are, in my experience, also the things that they basically are.

Proper controversy is when one historian says "This is caused by Thing A," and another says "Shut up, you! It was caused by Thing B." But when one is saying "It was Thing A," and the other says "It's more complicated than that," I reckon we pretty much have an answer. Some say it's Thing A, others say it's partly Thing A – that's as close to a consensus as naturally argumentative people are ever likely to come to.

In the case of our current troubles, the thing that it's a bit more complicated than, but also basically is, is "all the bankers' fault". I know my saying that will annoy some people, but that's OK because they're the very people I take most pleasure in annoying. So if you're thinking about getting annoyed, you might want to consider not giving me the satisfaction and agree with me instead.

The Financial Services Authority has finally offered its considered opinion that the collapse of RBS in 2008 was caused by "underlying deficiencies in RBS management, governance and culture, which made it prone to make poor decisions". It's easy to take the piss out of this because it's a bland statement of such a self-evident fact; but it's like when a miss-hit at Wimbledon flies off into the crowd – a linesman still has to call "Out!" when it finally hits the ground.

So it's clear that, while other factors must be borne in mind, such as feckless midwestern property developers, consumers spending beyond their means, Greek fiscal imprudence, George Osborne's point that it was the snow and George Osborne, we'd be in shallower shit now if more bankers had got theirs together. This is why I'm worried about Bob Diamond.

Barclays' new boss first came to my attention in January, when he told MPs that the "period of remorse and apology for banks . . . needs to be over". I didn't like that, partly because I hadn't really noticed any period of remorse and apology, unless you count "I'm sorry our various scams didn't work" as an apology; and partly because it's not for him to say. If you're really sorry for something, you should just keep being sorry. It's for others to decide when you can be let off the hook. If you're the first to be asking whether you've apologised enough, then you haven't.

More recently, he's changed tack in a way that makes his judgment seem even more questionable. In an interview with *The Times*, he said he'd introduced a "no-jerk rule" that had led to his parting company with more than 30 senior executives. "If someone can't behave with their colleagues and can't be part of the culture, it doesn't matter how good they are at what they do, they have to be asked to leave," he said.

This doesn't make sense. Since well before the crisis began, investment bankers, and indeed all top City executives, have defended their stratospheric pay deals on the basis that, in the cold light of economic reality, they were worth it. They got the big bucks because they brought in the bigger bucks. They possessed rare profit-making skills. They had the magic touch, everyone was crying out to employ them, so being paid millions was nothing more sinister than the market functioning as it should.

But what Bob Diamond appears to be saying is that he's willing to sack the goose that lays the golden eggs for being rude to its PA. That can only mean one of two things: either Bob is an incredibly poor, albeit principled, businessman and, regrettably, Barclays probably needs to look for someone harder-nosed; or highly paid bankers aren't geese that lay golden eggs but are eminently replaceable. If so, why are they so highly paid? Is being a jerk specifically harmful to business acumen? I'm afraid I don't believe it is, even if I'm willing to accept it isn't necessarily helpful either (which I only am when I'm in a very good mood).

Diamond cites the example of six Barclays bankers who spent £44,000 on wine at a posh restaurant in 2001, saying: "to have acted that way in a public place is inexcusable". I don't understand this either. It was their money. If you want to make sure your employees don't spend tens of thousands on wine, don't pay them millions. Otherwise they'll spend it as they like, whatever the PR cost to the company. To do otherwise would imply that they were ashamed, that the money was ill-gotten, that they were bank robbers, not its employees, and were being careful not to attract suspicion.

Wayne Rooney doesn't seem like a model employee. I'm not sure he'd survive a "no-jerk rule". Conspicuous consumption is the least of his PR crimes. Yet he evades the sack because his talent is undeniably rare. What Diamond's remarks reveal is that the same cannot be said of bankers who enjoy equivalent remuneration.

If Diamond isn't bright enough to grasp that what he said, far from being canny or diplomatic, fundamentally undermines his profession's justification for existing in its current form, then it's clear that we're still in the era of overpaid mediocrities running banks.

That era, as far as Diamond was concerned, ended in July 2012, when he resigned as a result of Barclays being implicated and fined in the Libor scandal.

* * *

The recession in advertising is having an interesting side-effect. Cheaper TV and radio slots mean the government can afford to crack down on that most despised area of mortality: accidental death. No one is in favour of that form of demise, while, with any other sort, there's always someone who'll break the consensus: in murder, the murderer's pleased; in suicide, the victim is; in war, it's one up for the enemy; dying after a horrible disease can be a mercy; and death from old age ultimately needs to happen for reasons of space. I'm not saying these eventualities are exactly a picnic, but neither are they a picnic on to which a jumbo jet has accidentally fallen.

Now we can attempt to eradicate accidents entirely. A host of government campaigns telling us to be sensible has leapt into the breach left by the retreat of luxury car and holiday advertisers. And, as well-known dangers such as fire, drinking, driving, drink-driving, sparklers and playing near pylons are covered, the campaigns are getting more specific. The "Level Crossings – Don't Run the Risk" initiative is an inspiring example. Nevertheless, in 2009, there were 13 people for whom it came tragically too late – or who were no more persuaded of the momentum of an express train by TV adverts than they were by barriers and flashing lights.

The bar has been raised and a formidable safety barrier put in its place. From now on, if a pattern of events kills a dozen people annually, the full might of the media will be brought to bear against it. And not just life-threatening situations but all kinds of mishap can be prevented in what will amount to a government bailout of our whole common-sense sector. Soon we will be living in a utopia where nobody gets hurt except on purpose. Here's a taste of what's being planned:

Getting your fingers caught in a door jamb

Health professionals claim this is the most upsetting thing that can happen to you which doesn't really matter. The pain and feeling of stupidity are ludicrously out of proportion to the long-term consequences – a fact which evokes a detectable superficiality in the sympathy expressed by witnesses, which in turn leads to intensified feelings of agony and rage in the victim.

"This could be costing the country millions!" remarked the head of Aspergers Owl, the advertising company which has landed the campaign contract, although it's thought he was referring to his company's fees. A series of hard-hitting TV commercials is being planned, starring Martin Freeman as Freddie Finger and Tom Baker as the voice of the hinge.

Not taking two trips

The back strain and property damage caused by young people refusing to take two trips when moving slightly too many objects to carry safely in one go is apparently more than the economy can bear.

"There's a real problem of perception amongst the young – taking two trips just isn't cool," says Oscar-winner Danny Boyle, who's directing the new commercial. "People's parents are always saying 'Take two trips!' so trying to carry more than is sensible becomes a rite of passage, an act of rebellion. It's liberating, it's sexy – right up until you slip a disc or drop a book!"

Forgetting you're wearing a Christmas cracker hat

This is more dangerous than it sounds – although only marginally. The unpleasant atmosphere that can develop at family Christmases, as a booze-and-carb-addled dusk begins to fall, is well known. But while screaming at your loved ones, because you've landed on Mayfair with a hotel or just been told you're adopted, is an important part of making sure everyone's relieved to get back to work, doing so wearing a festive hat can cause terminal dignity damage. This campaign features a harrowing viral clip in which actor Daniel Day-Lewis roars "You've never loved me!" through a mouthful of mince pie while wearing a paper hat and a reindeer jumper.

Having that weird feeling you're still wearing a Christmas cracker hat even though you've taken it off

This phenomenon, known as "phantom hat", is usually harmless but could be an early symptom of a stroke or head lice. It can also lead to social problems in families where there's a pervasive culture of "being a sport". A companion viral for this initiative contains footage of Day-Lewis, this time hatless, being shouted at by family members not to take himself so seriously.

Worrying about carbon monoxide

Stress caused by fear of this silent killer among those far too nervous and fastidious not to have their boiler regularly serviced is costing businesses thousands of man hours. "And ironically these are the hours of some of our most conscientious men," says the head of the stress-related-statistic-generating unit at the CBI. "The problem's all about targeting our message. Monoxide warnings which just about penetrate the skulls of criminal landlords and their feckless student tenants drive the already safety-conscious into a frenzied terror of an invisible soporific assailant." So the government is launching a counterbalancing "Carbon monoxide a killer? Well, I never got food poisoning off a fart!" drive. "Of course, we'll have to be very careful that this only reaches the right people," said the minister in charge. When asked how this would be achieved, he replied: "The internet?"

Wearing the trousers of a younger man

This is not a euphemism for internet grooming but refers to the dangers incurred by men in their early 30s who affect a younger man's low-hanging trousers but lack the jealously guarded teenage technology which keeps them and an exposed eight inches of underpants from falling down despite no visible sign of support. The consequent risk of sphincteral exposure in already image-conscious men can result in lasting psychological damage. A billboard campaign is being planned with the slogan: "Don't be an arsehole at work."

Having unforeseen accidents

This is the big one. As the junior minister of the Unforeseeable and Communities points out: "99.9% of accidental deaths are unforeseen. The rest are just murders where someone gets away with it." For this campaign, they've relicensed the old Camelot slogan "It could be you!" in order to point out how much less likely you are to win the lottery than to die of tetanus because some rust particles from the Holy Grail fell into a Magna Carta-induced paper cut.

* * *

When the chairman of the Nationwide building society (whose name, like Geoffrey Howe's, is Geoffrey Howe) tried to justify its executives' pay to a restive AGM, he said several strange things. Here's one: "What would the Financial Services Authority say if our chief executive was paid just £100,000? It would shut us down. Nationwide would cease to exist."

Is that true? Is that the system? Does the Financial Services Authority reckon that anyone who gets paid £100k or less must be incompetent? That's a very cynical view to take of members of the House of Commons. But, if it is true, it certainly justifies Nationwide in keeping its chief executive Graham Beale's salary above that threshold. A full £2.16m above it, to be precise. That should make sure the FSA takes Nationwide seriously.

But the main thrust of Howe's argument was marginally less wacky: "This is a society problem, this isn't a Nationwide problem." Although, if it's a problem with society, it may well be nationwide. But not exclusive to Nationwide. He continued: "There is a huge mismatch between what pop stars earn, footballers earn, business people earn, bankers earn and what the man on the street earns. A lot of people just find it hard to understand why there is such a big differential between what the man in the street earns and what senior business people earn."

So the problem, according to Howe, is a lack of understanding. Well, the first thing to clear up is the distinction between the "man on the street" and the "man in the street". It's quite important. I don't think many people are complaining that bankers earn more than the homeless. This "society problem" can only be exacerbated by the fact that, from the plutocrat banker's vantage point, it seems, the income of someone begging on the street and that of the average passer-by are indistinguishably negligible. But I don't think that's the lack of understanding Geoffrey Howe was referring to.

It was deft of him to liken Nationwide's highly paid executives to pop stars and footballers. "Let's spread the hate," he was probably thinking. And, of course, the huge earnings of some professional sportsmen and musicians wind a lot of people up, particularly now times are hard. But being cross because some people earn more than you is different from failing to understand why. I reckon almost everyone gets why pop stars and footballers are often rich: millions of people are willing to pay significant amounts of money to watch them do their thing. It's very easy to see where that money comes from and, if you don't like Stoke City or Lady Gaga, you don't have to contribute yourself.

But, when it comes to financial services executives, I agree with Howe that this lack of understanding exists – but I don't agree that it's a problem. I think it's a good thing. I think it's the product of the wisdom of crowds. People don't understand why bank and building society executives are so highly paid simply because there is no adequate explanation. It's an anomaly which, practically speaking, could only be corrected by the very people who benefit from it. That is a key failing with the current financial system.

The Nationwide AGM was up in arms over these remuneration packages, yet only 9% of the society's members failed to approve them. Either most Nationwide investors are secretly delighted to give millions of pounds to Graham Beale or that's not a functioning democracy. It's probably because most of the voters are failing to scrutinise how their money is spent. Or they don't much care. Nationwide made £475m profit last year. In that context, the £7.9m being handed out to five senior executives doesn't seem to matter so much.

Howe argues the standard case that Nationwide must pay the going rate for high flyers or it will cease to fly high. That makes a certain amount of sense but fails to explain how this going rate was arrived at, or to allay people's suspicions that it's become artificially inflated. What is it that Graham Beale does that someone else couldn't do – someone who'd be willing to take a pittance like £100k? Despite the evidence of parliament and the early series of *The Apprentice*, it can't only be feckless attention-seekers who are willing to work for that kind of money.

When Beale moves on – probably to an even more highly paid job at a bank – his successor will be similarly highly paid. Is that because he (or she) (probably he) will be one of a tiny number of people who also have the "Beale touch", that magical ability to make an organisation hugely profitable? Or will they just be highly paid because people in jobs like that always are, and they're not going to let that situation end if they can help it? On some level, is massively overpaying executives a necessary part of engendering confidence in the whole house of cards that we now know the financial sector to be? The idea that a cut-price chief executive might do just as well is too insulting to the industry's self-image to be permitted.

If that's what's going on, then a sort of reverse market effect is in operation, where, like with designer labels, the exclusivity of costliness makes an executive seem desirable, capable, even brilliant. What a disaster for shareholders and building society members, as well as customers and social justice, if that's the case; if all of our financial institutions are being led in nude mediocrity by little emperors declaring: "If you want clothes like these, you've got to pay! Financial crisis, you say? Just think how much worse things would have been, left to the kind of chump who will work for six figures."

It's a striking contrast to how MPs talk about their pay. Chastened by the expenses scandal, they jostle to express their revulsion at any talk of a raise. They don't tend to say: "If you don't pay top dollar, you won't get the best people." Perhaps that's because it's too obvious that we don't and so we haven't.

The Independent Parliamentary Standards Authority's proposed House of Commons pay rise would apparently cost Britain, a $2.3trn economy, £4.6m a year – and the prime minister (among many others) tells us it's too much. The Nationwide building society is paying nearly twice that to five managers, and its chairman is convinced that it's barely enough. My hunch is that they're both wrong.

6

What You Don't Know Can't Hurt You

If you genuinely don't reckon you know how our schools and education system could be improved, you're a very unusual person. So unusual that your views on education might, ironically, be of great interest. But most people are full of ideas – and I'm no exception. It was only when I started to compile this book that I realised how often I've come out with something I reckon about education, based on a half-remembered experience of my own or, more often, irritation at Michael Gove (God rest his soul).

This bit contains a justification of the unfairness of exams, a celebration of aimless university research, an advocacy of teaching the fairytale version of history to give people something to talk about at parties, and a list of fun activities for pupils too obese to stand up under their own steam. But don't worry, I'm not applying to set up my own free school, so none of these ideas will ever be put into practice.

* * *

The higher education watchdog has revealed that, in 2008, it received 900 complaints from students about their universities. That's up 23% on 2007, and Diana Warwick, chief executive of Universities UK, described it as "900 complaints too many". That's taking student satisfaction pretty seriously. Quite what utopias of academic excellence and alcohol our universities would have to become to elicit zero complaints is frightening to imagine.

Now that students are paying customers, maybe they expect Club 18–30 levels of drink and sex, plus extra-soft, double-quilted PhDs to wipe their learned arses on. But, even if you provide that, you're still going to get some whingeing. I remember from my college days that not all 18- to 22-year-olds are gutsy, roll-up-their-sleeves-and-get-on-with-it troupers with overdeveloped senses of gratitude and a horror of appearing self-involved. Among Britain's 1.9 million students, I suppose there must be one or two like that, but my guess would be one rather than two. And that he's a virgin.

The other way to hit Warwick's target of zero quibbles is through tyranny. Keeping our student population in a state of terrified subjection may be a more cost-effective way of silencing their complaints than pandering to their needs. People in fear for their lives seldom write plaintive letters to their oppressors. Had there been a Pravda website in the days of Stalin, I don't suppose many snippy comments would have been posted at the bottom of the editorial pieces. God bless democracy.

But, hovering halfway between unimaginable luxury and petrified squalor, our universities are bound to get a bit of carping from their charges and for their charges. What's worrying is that most of the complaints were about exam and coursework marks, and many of these were from students seeking to improve their results by citing mitigating circumstances. There's a lot of this about. It has emerged that, in 2008, the number of GCSE and A-level students who get "marked up" rose by 10% to 330,000. There's guidance on how these mark-ups are to be worked out: up to 5% for the death of a family member and 1% for a pet; 2% for suffering hay fever but just 1% for a headache.

With the right combination of misfortunes, you could have a bright academic future. If you're an asthmatic, diabetic, hay fever sufferer who's lost a couple of grandparents and whose beloved family milk herd has been culled because of a foot and mouth outbreak, you're probably on 200% before you walk into the exam hall. The days of "the dog ate my homework" are behind us; now it's: "The dog ate my brother and consequently died. It's given me a headache."

This system is a kindly attempt to make things fair. But even if it isn't being abused, it risks rendering exams pointless. Passing an exam is supposed to represent something absolute: a certain standard being attained. "Regardless of a person's advantages or disadvantages in life," the exam certificate is saying, "they have achieved this level of knowledge or skill."

This then means something to potential employers, who may not care about the bearer's allergies or short-lived relatives. It's academic legal tender. Sterling would soon devalue if half the fivers in circulation turned out to be £4.63s that got bumped up because of cat death.

Any attempt to tinker with marks to make allowances for misfortune undermines exams. It means you'll never know what standard a candidate really attained. What if a lazy student lucks out with the death of a hated parent? Suddenly their ignorance is misinterpreted as grief.

And why is the misfortune of losing a pet seen as worthy of more consolation than the much greater one of being stupid? If it's ultimate loving fairness we're using the exams for, let's not give marks at all but join together in a heartwarming affirmation of the sanctity of human life. The country may be a happier place if we did that, although it'd be sod all use to prospective employers.

This marking up is seldom quite as arbitrary as I'm implying. It's done according to the grades teachers expected their pupils to get. But aside from the fact that league tables give schools a huge incentive to affect the highest possible expectations, if teachers can work out so accurately the grades examinees deserve, what's the point of the exams in the first place? It's probably that we think it benefits students to have to get their shit together, in a pressurised situation, in order to prove their aptitudes. That's what happens in life: people have to deal with stress, cope in weird circumstances, step up to the plate.

Universities and employers should make allowances for bright pupils with underprivileged backgrounds by being flexible about the grades they require – spotting unrealised potential is vital. But you don't do that by pretending it's been realised when it hasn't. That's just insulting to those who attained high grades properly and to the skills which that required.

It doesn't happen with driving tests, where the safety of other road users is at issue, and I hope to God it doesn't with medical degrees. It's no good saying "Physician, heal thyself" to an ailing doctor who only qualified after being marked up because he was ill. So if we think exams matter at all, the fair thing to the system, to the country, to civilisation and, ultimately, to the candidate is to give people a chance to retake, not send them out into the world bearing an accolade they haven't earned.

A qualification that means something concrete is the only help available to young people emerging into the chaotic unfairness of the job market. We do them no favours by undermining it in trying to counteract the incomparably lesser injustices of the examination hall.

After all, in the real world, luck counts. Gordon Brown became prime minister at an unlucky time. However inept the pressure made him, there's no doubt that the credit crunch and the MPs' expenses scandal are crises that could have hit earlier or later. But, in a general election, no matter how unfortunate your circumstances, you don't get marked up by a single vote.

* * *

A recent newspaper headline chilled me to the bone: "New panel to weed out 'pointless' studies," it read. Pointless studies are meat and drink to columnists like me. Not the fillet steak and vintage claret of Gordon Brown audibly farting in the Commons or Jeremy Clarkson being attacked by a miniature poodle, but a Peperami and Fanta snack that keeps the wolf from the door in the leaner times. Without a constant supply of scientific research claiming that chocolate makes you romantic, white wine enhances sarcasm or automatic transmission makes your cock go floppy, I'd have to take a lot more weeks off.

I know that there are always world events to comment on but, if you feel on shaky ground discussing North Korea, that jokes about helicopter shortages in Afghanistan might be taken amiss or that any mention of Baby P by a comedian will cause hysteria, then a lot of news is ruled out.

Strange though it may sound, politicians and celebrities don't always make dicks of themselves. As the old Lib Dem press office saying goes: "Some weeks Charles Kennedy keeps his shit together." Not all opposition statements are laughably craven, the public reaction to the weather is not always humorously irrational and not every new government policy contains a glaring logical inconsistency.

Luckily for me, this one does. The article under the terrifying headline was about the proposed new system for allocating government money for academic research, the Research Excellence Framework. It wants to weed out pointless studies by favouring research that looks like it's going to be of economic or social use.

Hooray! That won't harm the comedy studies at all! When Professor Sponsored Link of the University of Twix announces that anti-wrinkle cream gives women the confidence to have cleverer children, he's not being funded by the government but by a cosmetics manufacturer trying to grab a headline.

All the "flowers/chocolate/ice cream bringing happiness/ better orgasms/an enhanced sense of perspective" studies are entirely self-financing. They may add little to the sum of human knowledge, the fact that academics are reduced to them may show how eroded our respect for learning has become, but they're not a drain on the taxpayer – they all get paid for out of various multinationals' marketing budgets.

So what sort of pointless study is this new system going to weed out? Why, all the ones that don't have a solid social or economic goal, of course. The government isn't going to pay for clever people just to sit in universities indulging their curiosity. No, they should be allocated something useful to discover and then research as hard as they can in that direction. Nothing good ever got invented by accident, apart from some silly fun stuff like the Slinky, Post-it notes, penicillin, warfarin and X-rays.

That breakthroughs often come by accident rather than design, from a desire for knowledge rather than a gap in the market, is so well established it's a cliché – it's one of the things that every schoolboy used to know. Why don't the government's education experts? Is it linked to the fact that, under their tutelage, every schoolboy barely knows how to count to the number of A*s he's just been awarded?

The trouble is that, for a moment, it sounds perfectly sensible to demand that researchers justify their means in terms of their projected ends, but so, for a moment, does Noddy's idea of building the roof of a house first so that it keeps the rain off while you build the walls.

Academic research with a demonstrable economic goal is not the sort that most needs government help. If you'd said 20 years ago "I'd like to develop a drug that cured erectile dysfunction in men", I imagine you'd have got plenty of private-sector takers. As it happens, Viagra was also discovered by accident, when someone was trying to develop heart medicine, but you get the idea.

Research which will obviously make money if it comes off will always find private funding and so should not be prioritised for public money. In fact, it's the very place that public money should never go – it'd be like spending the Arts Council budget on profit-making pantos instead of opera, or pouring the licence fee into QVC rather than BBC Four. Public money should be made available for research that would otherwise not happen. Research of economic value is outside this category.

To be fair, the greatest factor which will determine whether research deserves funding will, thankfully, even under this new system, still be peer review. But this greater emphasis on making academics justify their work in terms that results-obsessed government bodies will understand is worrying.

And that's where the talk of research of social value comes in. It's a sop to the arts side. They're trying to find a way to quantify the usefulness of a greater insight into paintings, books or historical events because they know they're of little economic value, other than to get the odd documentary commissioned, but have a vague memory of someone saying at a dinner that they mattered. They're trying to squeeze them into a plus column in their new spreadsheet of learning. Well, if that's their only way of according knowledge worth, then they're the wrong people to be making the decisions.

What separates us from the beasts, apart from fire, laughter, depression and guilt about killing the odd beast, is our curiosity. We've advanced as a species because we've wanted to find things out, regardless of whether we thought it useful. We looked at the sky and wondered what was going on – that's why, for better or worse, we've got DVD players, ventilators, nuclear weapons, global warming, poetry and cheese string. And it's for better, by the way.

The Research Excellence Framework is starting to ask what sorts of curiosity our culture can afford, and that scares me even more than the demise of the silly survey because it strikes at the heart of what it means to be civilised, to have instincts other than survival. If academic endeavour had always been vetted in advance for practicality, we wouldn't have the aeroplane or the iPhone, just a better mammoth trap.

* * *

There's often a lot of controversy surrounding how history is taught. Maybe educationists would say I'm wrong but it seems to get discussed much more than, say, maths or geography. Politicians and hacks don't argue about how there's too much emphasis on the numbers five and seven while 11 is sadly neglected. At parties, no one moans about the modern obsession with the oxbow lake at the expense of the names of Asian capital cities.

But, when it comes to history, everyone's got a sob story: how they were taught a meaningless series of dates in an atmosphere of chalk dust and looming corporal punishment which sedated an interest in the subject that was only reawakened decades later by a visit to the Ellis Island museum. How their daughter is finding the GCSE syllabus terribly unchallenging, focusing as it does on empathising for deceased proletarians rather than learning of the triumphs of kings. How we ignore African history, or teach it to the exclusion of anything else. How we're obsessed with battles and nationalistic glory, or can't stop banging on about social history and what people's wives were doing. "Kids need to know dates!" "We mustn't bore them with dates!" everyone alternately shouts.

Professor David Abulafia of Gonville and Caius College, Cambridge, seems to be of the former opinion. In a proposed curriculum for the thinktank Politeia, he's come up with 31 events that every schoolchild should know. In a similar vein, the Department for Education has announced that it's giving £2.7m to English Heritage to compose a list of historically interesting sites to encourage schoolchildren to visit. "We have a rich island story, which can be brought to life by seeing our historical and heritage sites," said Michael Gove. Yes, a rich island story, all about a rich island.

I hate the expression "island story". People who talk about our island story are often trying to reduce history to the level of a *Pride and Prejudice* box set or a marketing strategy for scones. The things that happened on this island before what's happening now are, in many cases, interesting. But they're not a simple narrative to which we're the happy, sad or ambiguous ending – or a shaggy-dog story with the Cameron administration as the disappointing punchline. They're a confused series of events. Or rather our best guess at a confused series of events constructed from studying a random hotchpotch of surviving artefacts.

For example, we don't *absolutely* know that the Tudors didn't have CDs. I mean, obviously we completely do know that, but only because of the absence of the objects themselves or related technology dating from that period. We only know it because any other inference from the available evidence would be insane, not because there's a trustworthy place where such obvious facts are stated. We're only ever one discovery of an album of Henry VIII covers in a priest hole away from a major re-evaluation of what all the nooks and crannies in castle walls might have been used for. (Surround sound?)

But I must admit that "Some things happened but we're not sure what" is a confusing message to give schoolchildren. The emphasis on teaching the past through understanding sources has led to several generations entering adult life with a pointless grasp of 1% of the skills needed to be a professional historian but no clear idea who Richard III was. They have a right to be told that he was the hunchbacked guy who said "My kingdom for a horse". Only those doing A-level need find out that, actually, he wasn't and didn't.

Society doesn't function well unless we have shared references. When turning up at a new job, university or party, we all rely on mentioning TV characters like Spock, Bagpuss or Hitler in the confidence that others will know what we're talking about. In the last 50 years, television has supplanted history, culture and mythology as what we have in common. We're much more likely to have fond pub chats about *Blake's 7* than Gog and Magog.

Now TV channels are proliferating even faster than obscure GCSE social history modules, this cosy community of viewers is dispersing. Just as jokes about Napoleon are obscure to those who only studied the history of cutlery, or disability under the Plantagenets, so the number of TV references that we all get is being drastically reduced by the bewildering quantity of viewing options.

This gives the Gove–Abulafia approach to history a real chance of success. If everyone has learned the same 31 dates and trudged round the same 12 castles, our history (or rather, what a government-written curriculum has chosen to define as our history) could become a major national shared experience. Stand-up comedians wouldn't do jokes about *Grange Hill* any more but about the visitor centre at Sutton Hoo.

It wouldn't much matter what dates and facts were picked. Pupils, until degree level at least, would have no way of checking the importance or even veracity of what they'd been told. It would just be an exercise in learning, like Latin or remembering what objects were on a tray before a cloth was put over it: press-ups for the brain.

But this could present problems. Leaving aside the terrifying question of what right any central authority has to decide which are the most important historical dates and facts, this shared "island story" lacks generational demarcation. We feel ownership of "our" generation of kids' shows, be they *Battle of the Planets* or whatever crap you watched if you're not my age. But history is the same for the children as it was for the parents, just marginally longer. The history syllabus couldn't replace popular culture as what defines our various age groups' tribal identities unless it was deliberately changed each generation. So kids now could learn about the Jarrow crusade but, come 2020, it would need to be replaced by the suffragette movement, while the unification of Italy gets benched in favour of the war of Austrian succession.

Advertisers would love this as it would help them to reach particular demographics. If you want to appeal to the under-25s, they'd know, you could exploit their understanding of the Crimean war, while you can always touch the over-40s with Industrial Revolution-, interregnum- or Danelaw-themed stuff. Being aware of which island story each generation has been told would be the perfect complement to accessing our Google search histories. Corporations wouldn't just know what each of us wants, they'd also know what we know.

* * *

Parents' groups were shocked to discover what the Guides have been getting up to lately. That's not a set-up for an off-colour St Trinian's-style joke from an era when people took a more relaxed attitude to paedophilia. I'm talking about Girlguiding UK's officially sanctioned activities. Instead of lighting fires and tying knots, Guides are now eschewing arson and bondage in favour of giving each other makeovers and massages, and talking about celebrities. Such pastimes, with names like "Parties, Chocolate and Showtime", "Passion 4 Fashion" and "Glamorama", can even count towards badges, the Scouts' and Guides' time-honoured currency of achievement.

As the nation's womanhood polarises into anorexia and obesity – a minority miserably struggling to emulate the unattainable and bizarre bodies of catwalk models, and a majority defeatedly guzzling McFlurries in loose-fitting clothing, unable to express their aspirations other than by getting their toddlers' ears pierced – this is surely the last thing we need. Guide patrols are supposed to be fresh-air-loving paramilitary groups, not weird, self-pampering, prepubescent hen parties throwing their childhoods away learning feminine wiles. They should, as Margaret Morrissey of Parents Outloud puts it: "get dirty, look scruffy and do anything they want". As long as what they want is to get dirty, look scruffy and sing round a campfire, rather than get a facial and bitch about Adele.

What is the world coming to? First, that shooting spree in Afghanistan and now this. If we're going to put a stop to our 150-year experiment in protecting the innocence of British childhood, we'd be better off sending the kids back up chimneys and into factories rather than letting them give each other boob jobs. At least child labour contributes to the economy. All this objectification of girls only pushes up the sales of blusher and leads to more teen pregnancies. The same sort of twisted precocity once made Lancastrian cotton competitive. In China, they use it to make iPhones.

So you won't catch me questioning people's justification for getting cross. Still, you can't deny that putting on makeup is a skill most women will use more often than starting a fire without matches. I'm a sort of man and even I've needed to apply lipstick on more occasions than I've had to light an outdoor fire, tie anything more complicated than a shoelace or recognise a songbird from the colour of its shit. Isn't Girlguiding UK just responding to the realities of the modern world?

I never joined the Scouts. Growing up in 1980s suburbia, I was convinced that fresh air and the outdoors were dated concepts. *Tron* provided proof. "Soon such things will be obsolete," I thought, as I played *Frogger* on my BBC micro while simultaneously watching *Metal Mickey* – an early example of multiscreening. But had the activities on offer seemed more relevant, I might have been tempted to don a woggle and try for my dot-matrix printer maintenance badge.

Here are some other activities that the movement should encourage in order to prepare kids for a less wholesome world.

Texting while you're supposed to be talking to someone in real life

It is very rude, we can all agree, to be constantly texting when you're supposed to be socialising in "meatspace". On the other hand, when you receive a text message, it's often preferable to read it and reply immediately rather than continue listening to the droning of someone who happens to be physically present. People call this hypocrisy, when in fact it's just caring more about your own feelings than another person's; that's something we're evolved to do.

The Guides could resolve this apparent contradiction by teaching kids to text by feel. The message-sending hand could dangle covertly beneath the pub table while sympathetic eye contact is maintained with the real-world companion throughout their anecdote about builders/divorce/a friend who won't stop texting.

Stopping someone sitting next to you on a coach or train

Only a psychopath would happily stretch out over a double seat while someone else has to stand. But only a saint doesn't mind losing their own luxurious double seat before other people. Clearly, the optimal path is for the empty seat next to you to be the last to go. The trick here is to look like you might possibly be a maniac, but not to the extent of attracting wider attention. In terms of a lifetime of travelling convenience, learning these techniques has got to be a higher priority than fording streams.

Suppression of the awareness

Our society has a new scourge: awareness-raisers. We are surrounded by people, organisations, companies and charities desperate to raise our awareness of whatever they're concerned with. But if we become intensely aware of everything, comparatively speaking we're no more aware of anything. We're just hyper-aware – paranoid, terrified, our heads buzzing with issues that don't concern us directly. We need to be schooled, from an early age, in obliviousness – in being able metaphorically to stick our heads in the sand. The relevant badge could have a picture of an ostrich on it.

Always having a pen

"Be prepared!" But how is this state of preparedness to be maintained? We live in an environment of apparent pen plenty – they're given away as freebies, left lying around, found down the back of sofas. This is all designed by a malevolent God to lull us into a false sense of security that can leave us penless in a crisis. The myth that you can ever have the right amount of pens is key to this problem: in truth, you've always either got none or too many.

The trick therefore is to steal pens. Not from shops, I hasten to add, but from each other. Never use your own pen when you can borrow one and neglect to return it. In any circumstances where pens are left lying around, snaffle a fistful. Only when boxes and rooms in your house are filled with unwanted Biros can you have any confidence that you'll have a pen when you need one.

Online abuse

No young person should go out into the world without a robust schooling in both ignoring and hurling online abuse. In the fraught ecosystem of the web, the demoralising effect on your rivals of anonymous bile may give you a vital competitive edge, as may an ability to ignore their retaliatory insults. Just as Scouts of old could forage and survive in the forest, the cyber-Scouts of the future must learn to be ruthless predators in the online jungle.

* * *

Michael Gove's scheme to send a special edition of the King James Bible to every state school in the country has been saved. The plan, which was announced in 2011, was reported to have run into difficulties when it was decided that it wouldn't be appropriate for taxpayers to pay for it. Instead, the bill is to be footed by leading Tory donors. That's not to say that they're not also taxpayers. I'm sure they are. To some extent.

It's going to cost £370,000, which is a lot of money if you're a normal human. It's not quite so much if you're a leading Tory donor. That's not to say that they're not also normal humans. I'm sure they are. To some extent.

But it's not a lot of money for the government either, so it wouldn't really matter if the taxpayer had paid – apart from the principle of the thing. By which I mean all the adverse publicity. People care much more about that £370,000 than about vastly greater sums being squandered or saved less interestingly.

Just like people, some bits of money are cared about more than others. Some bits are cherished in coin collections or tax havens; others are left to fend for themselves down the back of sofas or in the budgets of lazily written action movies. In my life, the money I would otherwise spend on shampoo is very dear to me. I buy the cheapest possible shampoo. When I can steal it from hotels, I do. I use every last squirt from every bottle, eking out days' more use from each one when most people would have thrown it away. I dote on the thought of that saved money. It may amount to as much as £14 over my lifetime. Meanwhile, the money I waste because I'm perpetually on the wrong mobile phone tariff is sent out into the world neglected and unloved.

But this Bible distribution money is not just loved, it's famous. It's not part of the anonymous billions that go into servicing the national debt, or the hardworking billions that pay for doctors and nurses, or the parasitic billions that are spent on bureaucracy. It's a celebrity, always in the papers, hobnobbing at parties with what the logo for the London Olympics cost and the price of that duck island.

The fuss over who should pay for this scheme has, rather sadly in my view, overshadowed its goals. Which are stupid and loathsome in equal measure. First of all, the whole idea, practically speaking, is pointless. Many, if not most, of the schools to which Gove is arbitrarily sending a King James Bible will already have at least one. For those that do not, the acquisition of one copy of a book is useless for teaching purposes. And the entire King James Bible is available online anyway.

Second, it is self-aggrandising. Every copy of Gove's specially printed Bible has "presented by the secretary of state for education" written on it. In gold. On the spine. Not inside in small letters, but on the outside in shiny ones. That's rude to God. And, if you don't think God exists, it's rude to King James, who definitely did. This grandiose sending out of a single book is not going to be of any educational use. It's just going to annoy teachers because it's so high-handed.

Third, this very high-handedness is, I suspect, what appeals about the scheme to many of its fans. It's clearly a dog whistle to a reactionary constituency who, in a lazy and uninformed way, are suspicious of the teaching profession, which they consider decadent and liberal, and of society's general multicultural direction. "That'll knock some sense into all those socialists and Muslims – send them a big old British Jacobean book and see how they like that!" they think.

This allows Gove to perpetuate in the public's minds a view of our education system in which he's not really responsible for it. He sends out Bibles, makes speeches about how scandalous it is that private schools are so much better, moans that kids don't learn Latin or read Shakespeare enough, argues for performance-related pay and generally makes all the right old-fashioned noises – and then everyone assumes the inadequacies of our schools must be despite, rather than because of, his efforts. In short, by this dispatching of a book, Gove is clearly implying that he's not really on the schools' side. He's not asked them if they want one and made it available to those who do. He's not bothered to check which schools already have a copy of it. He's not trying to find out what other books they might want or be short of. He's just dispensing the Word of Gove from on high.

Transport minister Norman Baker would probably advocate doing it remotely. No need to drag Moses all the way up the mountain when you can just tell him what's what over Skype. Responding to the Whitehall plan to "cut or change" 50% of civil servants' journeys during the seven-week Olympic and Paralympic period by encouraging people to work from home, Baker said: "I'm very keen to use this opportunity to record speeches remotely." He continued: "It's much better value than travelling maybe hundreds of miles to make a 10-minute speech." On top of that, you save the dry-cleaning bill – if it's all done over the internet, people will just be hurling rotten tomatoes at their own computers.

I was amused by this insight into what a transport minister does: makes speeches. So, if he's working from home, he's making speeches at home and then emailing the videos to people. I wonder if he's bought himself a little lectern? He could get a range of plastic microphones with the logos of international broadcasters stuck on them. Alternatively, he could just grab a shampoo bottle and do it in the shower. I've often suspected that endless pontificating was all a politician's life consisted of, and that the actual business of government was handled by the reviled bureaucrats, but it was surprising to hear that view confirmed by a minister.

But Michael Gove is a more senior member of the government. He doesn't just make speeches, he also comes up with "eye-catching initiatives". Whether it's sending out Bibles, buying a yacht for the Queen or letting people set up their own schools, he's got an impresario's gift for keeping us interested. He holds our attention with the £370,000 he's spending on gilded scriptures. It distracts from what's happening with unloved billions elsewhere.

* * *

The age of the weeds is finally dawning. I always knew we'd win. As I stood on the cold playing field, last to be picked for the team, I'd inwardly shake my head at the stronger, sportier boys and mutter: "Dinosaurs." When they passed me on the athletics track, leaving me wheezing in their wake, I'd cough the word "Dinosaurs" at their retreating plimsolls. As I clattered into the high-jump bar for the umpteenth time, "Dinosaurs" I'd spit at my mocking contemporaries. And when I finally got home in front of the TV, "Dinosaurs!" I'd exclaim at an episode of *The Flintstones*.

The latest research has vindicated me. My sedentary, square-eyed childhood was positively futuristic. When I resisted my parents' and teachers' efforts to make me acquire puff, I knew which way the wind was blowing – and that if it was blowing at all, I'd better stay indoors playing on my computer. Nowadays, staying indoors playing on computers is what most of us do as a job. You certainly don't meet many people at parties who earn their living playing rounders or climbing trees.

This research has been spearheaded (please excuse the atavistic language; I should say "joysticked") by Dr Grant Tomkinson, who talks about the trends it reveals like they're a bad thing. But then he is from the University of South Australia, and I reckon Australia will be where the active, outdoorsy T-rexes, who can take a lungful of air without spluttering, will make their final stand – before surrendering to the weeds' wobbling army of mobility-scootered multiscreeners, on the condition that we show them how to reboot their Wi-Fi.

"Imagine you are racing over four laps of an Olympic track," says Tomkinson, unappetisingly. "If you took the average child from 1975, transported them to today, put them against the current average child, they would beat them by almost a lap." That's in the unlikely event that the child of today would put his crisps down and agree to the contest. Tomkinson's analysis of 50 other fitness studies, involving more than 25 million children, concluded that cardiovascular fitness has fallen by 15% in a generation. I like to think I did my bit.

"If a young person is generally unfit now, then they are more likely to develop conditions like heart disease later in life," warns Tomkinson. You can tell he's a sports scientist and not an evolutionary biologist from the meaning he attaches to the word "unfit". The larger, weaker kids of today could hardly be more fit, more apt, for their crowded, carby, mechanised context. Their cardiovascular capabilities are diminishing appropriately under environmental pressures, like the vestigial wings of a flightless bird.

And our giant human brains allow us to specialise more quickly than by evolution alone. Most of us may be fatter, slower, wheezier and better at Googling than ever before, but an elite minority of sportspeople are faster and stronger than our most sun-kissed, stone-skimming, rock-climbing, fresh-air-advocating ancestors. So it's all good.

But as, over the centuries, full motor function becomes the preserve of a minority of specialist athletes and sex workers, how will all that running around and kicking of projectiles be replaced in the curriculum? We can't go on with school sport as it currently is – the kids of tomorrow won't want to look up from their tablets (in either sense) that long. What should the sports day equivalents of tomorrow consist of? Here are some ideas to ensure the metaphorical roundedness of our literally near-spherical descendants.

Takeaway Day

The term "takeaway", the ready-to-eat food which is delivered to your house by an unqualified motorcyclist, is familiar to all of us. But few know the obscure etymology of the phrase. Originally, "takeaways" were meals you had to physically go and get, and then "take away" yourself. On Takeaway Day, the whole school is bussed around to the mysterious places the takeaways come from, to see and learn about the out-of-town biryani vats and chow mein tanks, and the warehouse-sized wood-fired ovens that allow almost as great a surface area of American Hot to be cooked every day as rainforest is cut down to fuel them.

Phone Tariff Day

Childhood should be the stage of our lives when we have time for the things that the frantic realities of being an adult deny us: long summer afternoons fishing in a stream, rainy autumn Saturdays curled up with an adventure novel, or, towards the end of the school year, the chance to properly shop around for the right phone tariff. Not only will this save pupils money, the memory of the unbearable boredom of this day will mean that they won't resent being perpetually fleeced by their mobile phone providers for the rest of their lives – they'll consider it cheap at the price to avoid enduring the day again.

Privacy Day

Privacy was once a common aspiration, before, in 2013, Google futurist Vinton Cerf dismissed it as "an anomaly" and that was that. Under the combined attack of the search engine and the social network, everything about us was laid bare and soul-searching became something you could do through your web browser. But for one day of the year, pupils will be encouraged to stop sharing every aspect of their activities, hopes, dreams, fears and crushes, and keep things private for a few hours. Obviously, the urge to type will be irresistible, but they'll be given non-Wi-Fi-enabled laptops so that secrecy can be preserved for a few hours. The scheme can pay for itself by then selling this data to marketing firms.

Ingratiating Yourself With Robots Day

We can't do all this super-fast evolving on our own; we'll need ever more ingenious machinery, which will lead inexorably to the rise of a robot master race. I don't need to join the dots for you – it's obvious from TV. So a key skill our young will have to learn is how to get on with our robot masters and, if possible, conjoin with them. An inappropriate subject for a school day, you might think? Well, when the place is crawling with bitter, belligerent and laser-guided Henry hoovers, that'll be the least of our worries.

The greatest intellectual specimens of humankind will be chosen to form cyborgs: stripped of their flabby and vestigial outer bodies and installed in a Big Trak or hostess trolley – like the green scrambled egg inside a Dalek that provides the vindictive spirit with which it aims its plunger. But that can only happen after centuries of getting used to no longer being able to climb stairs.

7

A Sorry State is Nothing to Apologise For

Do you think Britain is a great country? I do, basically. It's embarrassing to admit it. And it feels un-British to admit it, except for the fact that it's embarrassing, which is a very British sensation. Embarrassment is one of our strongest emotions. Some nationalities wouldn't even count it as an emotion – it would get lost amid all the joy, hatred, love, ardour and sadness. But, in Britain, it's one of the big three, alongside scepticism and nostalgia.

I know there are a lot of things wrong with Britain, but the truth is that I quite like most of them. It's not what you'd call conventional patriotism but, in this section, I extol the virtues of sexism in the monarchy, self-loathing in the Midlands, taking pride in nuclear weapons, avoiding sunny working conditions and refusing to dance at parties. These are core British values in my book. And they are literally in my book.

* * *

Who can fail to have been impressed by the spectacle of President Obama's inauguration? I'll tell you who – the Queen. I bet she sat there watching it on an unpretentious four-by-three portable, while she sorted dog biscuits into separate Tupperware, muttering: "It's bullshit, Philip! No carriages, no horses, no crown – it just looks like a bunch of businesspeople getting in and out of cars. It's as if the Rotary Club's taken over a whole country. And the new one's not even the son of one of the previous ones, unlike last time. I thought they were coming round to our way of thinking at last."

And she'd have a point. It might have been considerably grander than a new prime minister pulling up outside Number 10 and waving but, compared to the coronation, it looked like someone signing for their security pass and being shown where to hang their mug. And that's what comes of having an elected head of state. There's always got to be some fudge between the dignity and status of the office and the politician's desire to seem humbled by the occasion.

In fact, it's one of the most startling examples of politicians' self-belief that, as they assume positions of massive power for which they have striven, to the exclusion of all other activities, for decades, they'll still back their chances of coming across as humble. Now there's an insight into the megalomaniac's mindset: "Not only can I get to be in charge of everything, I bet I can make people believe that I'm not really enjoying it, so that, thanks to reverse psychology, they'll want me to stay in power longer!"

Whereas the Queen didn't have to pretend she wasn't enjoying the coronation; from the little bits of grainy footage I've seen, it's hilariously evident. A poor, terrified slip of a girl, the fluttering eye of a storm of pageantry, hesitantly mewing her lines, while thousands of incredibly important people in fancy dress behave as if she's the Almighty made flesh. That's what I call a show.

I don't envy the Americans their political system. I envy them their success, money, inner belief that everything isn't doomed to failure, attitude to breakfast, and teeth, but not their constitution. The fact that their figurehead and political leader is the same person gives them a terrible dilemma, especially when it was George W Bush. The man's clearly a prick (he says he'll wait for the judgment of history but, if the jury's out, it's only because they're deciding between personable incompetent and evil moron) but even his political enemies were squeamish about calling him one.

They had to respect the dignity of the office and couldn't come to terms with the American people having bestowed it on someone who can't string a sentence together and would only make the world worse if he could. To completely let rip in slagging off Bush would have caused collateral damage to national prestige, not only by undermining the office of president, but more importantly, by openly admitting how far short of its meritocratic self-image America has fallen.

We in Britain have no illusions about being a classless meritocracy and it's therefore thoroughly appropriate that our head of state should be chosen by a method dominated by class and utterly and openly devoid of regard for merit. Separated from the nitty-gritty of politics and power, our monarchy can be a focus for both national pride and self-loathing, the latter being much more archetypally British than the former. A harmless little old lady dutifully going about various tasks she finds stressful seems about right for our national figurehead – neither better nor worse than we deserve.

Don't mistake me for a republican. I genuinely like this system. It means the most powerful man in the country still has to kowtow to someone (other than the president of the United States). It encourages tourism. The royal family, while nominally our betters, are in fact our captives and an interesting and profitable focus for media attention. It's as unfair as life: the royals can't escape and, if you want to become royal, you basically can't. It's a more or less functional arrangement that no one would ever have had the wit to devise deliberately.

Which is why Liberal Democrat MP Evan Harris's attempt to fiddle with it is so enervating. He wants to change the Act of Settlement whereby Catholics can't marry the sovereign and end the discrimination against female heirs to the throne. He thinks this will make the monarchy more fair. I suppose it will, in the same way that throwing some bread into the Grand Canyon will make it more a sandwich.

The monarchy is overwhelmingly, gloriously, intentionally unfair – that's the point. The defining unfairness is that you have to be a member of that family to be king or queen; fringe unfairnesses like their not being able to marry Catholics or men having priority in the line of succession are irrelevant in that context. And what's so fair about primogeniture, which Harris is not planning to touch, or the sovereign having to be Anglican, which is also apparently fine? He wants to spend parliamentary time, mid-credit crunch, on a law aimed primarily at helping Princesses Anne and Michael of Kent.

When will people get the message? If you want a fair system, have a republic, elect a president and live with some arsehole like David Cameron giving a speech every Christmas Day afternoon, bitter in the knowledge that you asked for it. Otherwise, we should stick with what we've got, rather than trying to tinker. No abdicating, no skipping Charles, no changing weird ancient laws. We get who we get because we'd rather live with the inadequacies of a random ancient structure than the inadequacies of one designed by Gordon Brown and David Cameron.

The monarchy's not perfect, but it's also not harmful, powerful or, and this is the clincher, our fault. The inevitable imperfections of anything we replaced it with would be.

* * *

Birmingham City FC's next opponent must surely feel that victory is assured – unless, of course, it's Leicester City or Wolverhampton Wanderers. For not only are these clubs located in an area where, according to a survey, most of the residents want to leave, but they also don't play in red. And red is the colour of victory, say the Germans.

This isn't just sour grapes about losing to reds in 1966, and indeed at Stalingrad, but the result of a study made by sports psychologists at the University of Munster. It found that competitors wearing red scored about 10% more than those dressed in other colours. It seems that the crimson look like they're winning, which means, more often than not, that they are.

This explains much: the size and success of the British empire, and its steady decline after the adoption of khaki; the pre-eminence of Butlins over Pontins; the one-sidedness of so many episodes of *Bargain Hunt*; why it's taking so long for communism to give up the ghost. What it doesn't explain is why a team would ever wear any colour other than red.

Maybe now they won't. But I doubt it. I don't think this study has shown us anything that we haven't long suspected. Deep down, we all know that red is the best colour – that those who take to the field in the shade of blood, fire and liberty mean business and are likely to sweep aside those emulating grass, the sky, zebras or bees. For the big red teams – Liverpool, Manchester United, Arsenal, Aldershot Town – winning is an expectation, and that usually trumps their opponents, for whom it is merely a hope.

So why don't they all wear red? "If that happened, how could we tell them apart?" you may say. Well, we'd have long since found a way if most teams weren't willing to take a 10% performance hit in aid of visual clarity. Sport's governing bodies would have stepped in and either banned red entirely, inevitably leading to players secretly wearing scarlet underwear, or developed a system of distinguishing between teams by hat shape, smell, the squeaking noise their boots make or some other non-colour-dependent factor.

Fortunately, that's not been necessary because so many clubs don't seem to want to win – or at least are so resigned to defeat that their priority is preparing an excuse rather than striving for victory. "Well, you see, we don't wear red," Birmingham City can say to themselves when their relegation is sealed at home to Arsenal in a few months' time, "so we never really had a chance."

That seems a fittingly resigned approach for a part of the country apparently so despised by its residents. This attitude was revealed in a survey conducted by Orange (I wondered what all their customer services personnel had been doing all this time) which asked people where they would choose to live if the government's promise of universal broadband access were for some reason honoured.

The question presupposes that everyone can work anywhere they can get a laptop Googling. I suppose they can, now that every job involves some variation on looking at a screen and clicking. The closest you can get to a manufacturing career nowadays is if you're the one in a Starbucks who knows how to work the panini machine. There's no man's work any more. It's all done by children in China.

But 81% of people working in the West Midlands said they'd rather do it anywhere but there, as did 70% of those in the East Midlands. Most were set on relocating to Scotland, London or, most popular of all, the West Country, which would see its population rise by 150% if the Brummies are allowed to get away from it all.

What are they trying to escape? I don't know what the Midlands was like before people put things like Wolverhampton there but I don't suppose it was ugly. It was probably nice countryside. Similarly, there's no reason to think that Devon and Cornwall, beautiful though they are, would remain so after the installation of a few Spaghetti Junctions and Bullring centres. If you want a taste of what Coventry-on-Sea could be like, take a look at Plymouth.

The problem with the Midlands is not that it's an inherently unpleasant place but that there are millions of other people there – miserable people who want to leave. 81% of them going to Cornwall is only going to give that problem a sea view, while depriving it of a proper motorway infrastructure.

Surely Midlands residents should be counting their blessings. Birmingham may be no Venice (for all its alleged canal parity) but neither is it Darfur or Luton. And there are positives: a 2009 study declared the rainy British climate, which the Midlands basks in, the ideal conditions for growing strong and healthy fingernails. That's an important part of the body – just ask any of the Wolves players' wives.

I don't think Midlanders should be downhearted about their downheartedness. Several other regions, even self-confident Yorkshire, were also found to be keen to depopulate. And a grass-is-greener attitude is far preferable to self-satisfiedly imagining oneself to be living in the best place on Earth. It reflects an engaging mix of aspiration and modesty; people living in the built-up middle indulging themselves in harmless daydreaming about moving to their vision of an idyllically quiet periphery, in the case of Scotland or the west, or a beating metropolitan heart in the case of London.

It's an example of the British "glass half empty" approach, the self-effacing "We're a bit shit, we are!" worldview that English emigrants to America mistake as "hating success". It's not that; it's a compassion for mediocrity, it's supporting your team even though they won't win and refuse to wear red. It suggests humour and integrity.

I love the "glass half empty" approach – I'm completely "glass half full" about it, which is shamingly un-British of me. But who'd want to live in a place where 100% of the population were thrilled to be there? Anywhere like that would be so insular and parochial that anyone sane would want to leave, and probably already had.

* * *

Imagine you're running an elite branch of the police, responsible for the security of the country's nuclear material and installations. Imagine you're instituting a programme of modernisation and reform so that it can cope better with the threats posed by international terrorism. Would you call the programme "New Dawn"?

Personally, I would not. If I were in the Civil Nuclear Constabulary's thousands of sensible shoes, I think I'd pick something that sounded less like the title of a post-apocalyptic sci-fi movie – something that doesn't raise the question "Over what dystopian wasteland is this 'New Dawn' breaking?", or conjure up the image of a heavy blood-red sun creeping across the ash-clogged skies of a new empire of cockroaches and scorpions.

Richard Thompson, chief constable of the nuclear constabulary, which is the country's most heavily armed police force (and that's not even counting all the plutonium it's packing), is of a different mind.

I'm not saying New Dawn isn't a catchy title but is that really a priority here? How important is it for programmes of public service reform to have exciting names? I know we live in an age when everything, from Tower Hamlets waste collection services to the branded sugar sachets of a budget hotel chain, has a tagline. Even the Kilburn High Road boasts the strap: "The closer you look, the better it gets" (which may be true for some – it all depends on how aesthetically pleasing you find the molecular structure of vomit).

I accept that tedious projects are probably made marginally more fun by giving them dramatic names. I'm all for the NHS calling its new anal hygiene initiative "Total Wipeout" if it'll get the job done in better humour. But these schemes aren't films. They don't need box office. They're not things you have to persuade people to get involved in; they're tasks that you just order people to complete.

And surely there's a public confidence issue here? It may excite those involved but it doesn't help national morale to remind us that, where nuclear material is concerned, the stakes are terrifyingly high. Just as surgeons, to lift their patients' mood, construct phrases such as "pop in, have a look round and then sew you up" to make the prospect of being eviscerated in your sleep seem less daunting, so the police could have referred to this modernisation as "just a spot of paint here and there – you know, keep everything tidy", rather than making it sound so portentous. New Dawn is the equivalent of the surgeon gripping a patient's hand and muttering, in a voice charged with emotion: "Remember, every ending is a beginning, my friend!"

Don't get me wrong, I'd have picked it ahead of "Dark Storm Descending", "Half-lives Half-lived" or "Winter's End?" but my favourite would probably have been "The Civil Nuclear Constabulary Modernisation Plan". A bit banal perhaps but, just as many people feel there are some issues that are "not a fit subject for comedy", I feel there are some places of work that are not a fit context for drama.

I was blissfully unaware of the CNC until I read that questions have been asked about security around the Sellafield product and residues store, which contains the largest declared plutonium stockpile in the world. And the answer to those questions hasn't been "It's all fine." Or at least not in a confident enough voice. Any terrorist who succeeded in breaking into the facility would be like a kid in a sweetshop, albeit one developing cancer at a futuristic speed.

The police have also been under hostile scrutiny because of their handling of the student protests over fees. I sympathise: they're in an impossible position, as there's no real national consensus on the extent to which protesting students should be beaten up. Opinions vary from "not at all" to "completely". The compromise they've reached – to let a small riot happen while hospitalising the occasional protester – is probably, like democracy, the worst option except for all of the other ones.

But there's more agreement about the extent to which Prince Charles and the Duchess of Cornwall should be beaten up. In that regard, the "small minority of troublemakers" shouting "Off with their heads!" seem to have misjudged the national mood. That their Royal Highnesses should be subjected to youthful road rage on Regent Street was described by David Cameron as "shocking and regrettable", by Metropolitan police commissioner Sir Paul Stephenson as "hugely regrettable and shocking", and by Boris Johnson as "very regrettable". It's regrettable that Johnson didn't find it shocking. The duchess, he went on to say, was "plainly alarmed". You're no oil painting yourself, Boris.

Fortunately, Charles and Camilla arrived at the Royal Variety Performance unharmed, but it's disgusting that the heir to the throne and his wife should be subjected to such an ordeal. And the fact that their car was attacked on the way only makes it worse.

The police's competence to protect what our country holds most dear is suddenly in doubt. While a New Dawn is breaking over the security of our nuclear material, the royal protection squad is considering putting the prince in a less glassy car. Maybe it could convert one of the Civil Nuclear Constabulary's old lead-lined vans.

The two things that define our sovereignty – the royal family and our nuclear technology – are under attack. In these straitened times, we may be forced to choose. In the middle ages, people feared royalty. Those born to rule were the Lord's anointed. They carried within them something of the divine, a spark of ineffable heavenly power. That's why the aristocracy were so reluctant to kill kings unless they could cast serious doubt over their right to the throne. Legitimate kings were only done away with in rare and extreme cases; for example, Richard II was starved to death and Edward II got topped. So they murdered him.

In this more secular age, we reserve our sense of mortal dread for uranium. Being a country openly in possession of nuclear technology is the radioactive jewel in our crown. Our nuclear weapons, just like our royal family, are a harmless source of national pride, but they cost a great deal more. Those missiles should be driven around London in a gold coach so that the public can have a look at what it's paying for. I suppose that's another simple pleasure that a small minority of troublemakers are spoiling.

* * *

Sometimes you don't see victory coming. It's been a long slog since the disaster of Saratoga and the humiliation of Yorktown but at last the empire has struck back. It's been tough – they've spent decades making us feel puny and irrelevant. We've relied on them for money and troops. They almost made us forget there was a time when we could launch disastrous invasions of Afghanistan without their help. But finally it seems that the American colonies' 235-year flirtation with independence is coming to an end.

Praise be: all three of the great American superheroes-of-state have fallen into British hands. The casting of British actor Henry Cavill as Superman, in *Superman: Man of Steel* (presumably the sequel to the more controversial *Stalin: A Super Man*), completes the set: Christian Bale, the British child from *Empire of the Sun* whose accent is now located about where the Lusitania sank, is the current Batman; and Surrey's own Andrew Garfield is "rebooting" the Spider-Man franchise, bringing New York's arachnoid crime fighter to a whole generation who were too young to catch the final instalment of the previous Spidey trilogy, way back in 2007. If only someone had recorded it.

But let's leave aside the fact that Hollywood is now reimagining Superman and Batman twice each for every time I descale my showerhead, and Spider-Man more often than I change my mobile phone tariff, and rejoice in having turned the tide of cultural imperialism. Stateside acclaim for *The Madness of King George*, *Mrs Brown*, *The Queen* and *The King's Speech* is all very nice but it has the patronising quality of a parent commending a precocious child on having sent up a teacher in a school play. If we were ever going to curb American self-confidence, we needed to strike at their equivalent of royalty: made-up magical people from comics.

Yet, even in the moment of conquest, I had my doubts (as Tiger Woods used to say). So I looked below the British newspapers' jingoistic headlines and read the actual articles – or, as I call them, "the small print". It turns out that Garfield was born in Los Angeles and has dual citizenship; Cavill is from Jersey, not the new one, but it still isn't part of the UK; and Bale largely grew up in Hollywood. I say "grew up", but I suppose I mean "became older". It looks, from YouTube, like he's a bit of a Peter Pan when it comes to professional conduct.

Still, they're a bit British – they're British-influenced: Cavill was in *The Tudors* and went to Stowe School; Garfield's been on Channel 4, and not just in a *Frasier* repeat; and Bale was born in Wales. He's slightly Welsh and you can't get more English than that, unless he was also a quarter Scottish with an Irish great-grandparent. So it's still something, right?

Not really, not any more. This is how Charles Gant, film editor of *Heat* magazine, explains the new global reality: "Superman,

Batman and Spider-Man might be American icons, but the primary revenue streams for these films are outside America." The important demographic, our future Asian paymasters, neither care about nor discern the difference between Britons and Americans. If Cavill's American accent's a bit shaky, they won't give a damn. We're all just impecunious round-eyes, shaking a tail feather in front of a green screen – trying to make a quick yuan to set against our astronomical debt.

The British are the new Canadians. We're not taking over American culture, we're being absorbed by it, and at the very moment when its influence is starting to wane. We're infiltrating a dying empire, like the Scots did when they took over Westminster politics.

This leaves me feeling ashamed at having enthused about British involvement in superhero movies in the first place. It's not as if I like them. It feels like rooting for Andy Murray: you can suppress misgivings that he's moody and annoying for as long as he's still in a tournament but, when he loses, the fact that you've expended emotion supporting someone you don't know, whose fortunes don't affect you, and the cut of whose jib you don't particularly like, makes the disappointment turn even sourer.

Today's Hollywood pumps out superhero stories like it once did Westerns. Not just the three superheroes of record but spoofs such as *Mystery Men* and *The Incredibles*, superhero gang shows like *The Fantastic Four* and *X-Men*, and the TV series *Heroes* and *No Ordinary Family* (which, from the trailers, looks like a non-spoof version of *The Incredibles*). It's so relentlessly two-dimensional. And I concede that there are two: the characters don't just have superpowers, they also find that strange. So, you know, bravo.

Is this the final infantilisation of entertainment? Are we the first generation of adults who, when we reached maturity, did the cinematic equivalent of giving ourselves crisps and chocolate for every meal because we never had the concentration to develop other tastes? Most of these films, however exciting their action sequences, are deeply silly.

Yet some critics make artistic claims. I quite enjoyed *Batman Begins*, but those who wax lyrical about what a disturbing character Bruce Wayne is, and claim that whichever comic it's all based on merits comparison with a proper book full of words, have lost sight of the bigger picture: it's all about a man so rich and mental he hangs around the streets at night, dressed as a bat, trying to drop on burglars. This is a daft story which, if it were true, would only be fit for a Channel 5 documentary about a disreputable Kevlar salesman exploiting billionaires with personality disorders.

I think we Brits might have been wiser to stick to playing villains. It may not get the big money but it's steady work and the villains in Hollywood superhero films are fairly similar to the heroes of British popular culture. Sherlock Holmes, Hercule Poirot, Raffles and Doctor Who all have far too many ambiguities and nuances to be Marvel comic goodies.

Some readers will refute this point by citing character ambiguities and nuances such as "obsessively pretending to be a bat every night" and "finding it unsettling to develop the powers of a spider", but we'll have to agree to differ. Just like Agree-to-Differ-Man who was bitten by a radioactive Liberal Democrat and travels the universe resolving arguments while sitting on his jet-powered fence. That's a role that only someone British could play.

* * *

The British government has submitted its list of nominees for world heritage site status to Unesco. Known as the "UK tentative list", it comprises a house (Darwin's old one in Kent), an observatory (Jodrell Bank), a bridge (the Forth), a Gibraltan cave complex, a twin monastery, some crags, various islands (St Helena and the Turks and Caicos), some areas of countryside (a boggy one and a lakey one) and a way of life (the slate industry of north Wales). Among places that narrowly missed out – presumably they were on the "extremely tentative list", the "barely a list at all" or the "few thoughts scribbled down on a scrap of paper which you must feel free to ignore" – were the former RAF station at Upper Heyford, the Great Western Railway and Blackpool.

This is an eclectic mix of . . . well, what? Buildings? I suppose a bridge is a building but the Lake District isn't. Areas? You wouldn't really call an old house or an observatory an area, would you? Places? Is the Great Western Railway a place? If so, it's a very long and thin place. The north Welsh slate industry certainly isn't, although it happens in a place. It's such an eclectic list it's difficult to find a noun that applies to everything on it other than "things". It's an eclectic list of British things. And some not-so-British things that Britain owns, such as West Indian islands and Iberian caves. But, for the purposes of Unesco, they're all sites. And often sights. Magnets for sightseers and site-seers alike.

In putting forward this mixed bag of concepts, British government experts are responding to Unesco's concern that the list of 911 world heritage sites has, as the *Guardian* put it, "become dominated by castles and cathedrals in western Europe". So they're mixing it up a bit. Admittedly, they're having another punt on Darwin's house, which has been submitted and rejected before – maybe Unesco doubts how much the building in which an important book was written retains the reflected glory of the important book, like that pub where DNA was discovered (by which I mean the site of Crick and Watson's "Eureka!" moment, not some old boozer where traces of blood led to an arrest). But they're also spicing things up with some slate manufacturing and the island where history's most famous Corsican carked it.

213

But they could go so much further. There are so many other unique and valuable expressions of our culture that should have much higher priority for "world heritage thing" status than all that tedious bricks-and-mortar, than the predictable array of pyramids and opera houses. If I may be so tentative, here's my list:

The pound

The beleaguered and ancient British currency has for too long been the plaything of politicians and speculators. Let's take politics and economics out of the equation and put its fate in the hands of heritage. Basically, people like it – they liked the shillings, pennies and farthings too, but they were abolished in the interests of reducing the nation's arithmetical agility. So let's protect it, like we protect the Tower of London, without regard to practicalities. Nobody complains about that old fortress being outdated, expensive and much less militarily useful than an aircraft carrier. The Tower is an appealing anachronism in the modern city, so why not make the pound coin the same thing for the modern pocket, nestling next to the smartphone like a Beefeater walking past Deutsche Bank?

The Aberdeen Angus Steakhouse chain

These restaurants are unique to British culture and yet they're under threat. Not for them the business model of repeat custom, these steakhouses' fortunes rely on the much tougher technique of trying to dupe everyone once. It's harder and harder for them to do, as the British tradition of culinary incompetence is eroded by pressures from abroad. When even Little Chef is recruiting Heston Blumenthal, these restaurants, now rarer than the Siberian tiger, are all that we have left of a proud heritage of serving shoe leather with Béarnaise sauce to neon-addled out-of-towners.

The Carling Black Label advertising campaign of the 1980s

Perhaps the greatest cultural achievement of the Thatcher era, the humour of this campaign, particularly the fondly remembered "very long advert where you kept thinking it was the next one and then it wasn't", not to mention "the one with the squirrel and the *Mission: Impossible* music", elevated these films above mere commerce. Most striking is the fact that they were enjoyed by millions of people who had no intention of drinking Carling Black Label, a beverage with few merits, none of which the commercials deigned to mention. Surely preservation of these works of art is worthy of some of the funding currently being monopolised by so-called "Inca treasures" which, in fact, have hardly appeared on television at all.

The Hamlet cigars advertising campaign of the 1980s

I mean, that music! The comb-over! Think about that and tell me you give a damn about the Hanging Gardens of Babylon or whatever.

The Hofmeister advertising campaign of the 1980s

This was brilliant as well. That bear must have been an alcoholic! Adverts used to be great.

Isambard Kingdom Brunel's house

It is one of the most shaming truths about our barbarous age that, while much of the great art, architecture and literature of the past may have survived, so few of the normal houses in which those works were devised have been saved for posterity. This is the house where genius lived – where Brunel worked, designed, fretted. And it's threatened with demolition to make way for a high speed rail link. Only Unesco can save it now.

The smell of cabbage at Butlins Skegness

As fragile as the Sphinx's face, as transient as the northern lights, as disconcertingly faecal as Seahenge, this irreplaceable part of our gaseous heritage is literally in danger of being blown out to sea. As Butlins struggles to modernise, introducing climbing walls and a Costa, the great bubbling pots of institutionalised holiday food have long since fallen silent. While we fetishise ancient stonework, molecules of equivalent cultural significance are discriminated against simply for being airborne.

Trident

Britain has always striven, always aspired. We're a warrior people – we have conquered vast areas of the planet and so surely it is only fitting that, in commemoration of that martial heritage, we should retain the power to wipe humanity off the face of it? The submarines are a nod to our seafaring past, while the state-of-the-art ballistic missiles are a contemporary touch of which Nelson would surely have approved.

* * *

I was shocked by an article in the *Guardian* that was incredibly down on the Queen's diamond jubilee. Really humourless and pissy. I was surprised. "If any other country were paying homage to an unelected head of state in this way, while the living standards of the majority of the population fall and schools and hospitals struggle with diminishing resources," wrote Peter Wilby, "we would call it 'the cult of the personality' and probably think about invading." What a mood-killer. The commemorative shortbread turned to ashes in my mouth and I cast aside my union flag napkin in dismay. From a man who edited the *New Statesman* for seven years, I'd expected something more fun.

Or maybe I'm the one being humourless and it was a joke? He can't really think the Queen is a cause for the international community's concern – a Kim Jong-il figure, but fortunate enough to rule over a population with a bizarre and advanced case of mass Stockholm syndrome. A people so mad they don't have to be forced into parading and cheering by the muzzles of Soviet-era weapons or the threat of starvation – we'll turn up and do it voluntarily, and even buy our own flags. The idea of a "cult of the personality" surrounding Her Majesty must surely be meant in jest as she betrays no sign of actually having a personality.

Reading on, it became clear that Wilby was properly pissed off at the prospect of royal-themed festivities, but he did have some jolly suggestions for the sort of jamboree we should be having: "a knees-up to mark the 100th anniversary of the 1884 Reform Act"; "a party, an extra bank holiday and a pageant to celebrate the 800th anniversary of Magna Carta"; and "more parties, pageantry and days off for the 100th anniversary of the Representation of the People Act 1918".

Those sound like my kinds of celebration! While we're at it, how about a big pop concert in honour of the Medical Relief Disqualification Removal Act of 1885, or a Spitfire fly-past and fireworks display when the next significant anniversary of Burke's Civil List and Secret Service Money Act comes round? With the right deployment of public cash, I'm sure we can turn millions of Britons from bunting-obsessed monarchists into hardcore parliamentary reform anoraks.

Of course, there's a risk that, if our admirably violence-free but consequently abstruse path to democracy became the focus of as much forced jollity as the waving little old lady, it could also evoke as much contrarian disdain – possibly even more, since all those historical documents, important though they are, involve a lot less in the way of gold hats, shiny uniforms and performing horses.

Personally, I don't mind the monarchy. I know a lot of people do, but I just don't. I know it's old-fashioned, illogical, pantomimic and unjust. But it's also unimportant, entertaining and, crucially, already there. I say better the devil you know. Particularly when it isn't a devil but a smiling old woman, albeit with a colossal sense of entitlement. Not entitlement, sorry. Duty. Sense of duty. Excuse me while I cut my own head off.

Seriously, though, I bet she thinks she's pretty special. I mean, how couldn't she? Everywhere she goes, there are crowds of people cheering and trying to give her flowers, and this has been going on for 60 years. If that doesn't drive you insane with a sense of your own importance, you must have been insane with self-loathing to start with. I think I'm a relatively modest-seeming person – I don't often get accused of megalomania – and yet I can sense the lurking tyrant within. "Maybe I'm the best person *ever*," I sometimes think. Christ knows what I'd be like if I'd watched millions bow and curtsy before me for several decades.

But I can live with the likelihood that the Queen has an inflated sense of her own significance. It doesn't bother me – she's canny enough to conceal it. And I like the monarchy's effect on the trappings of the British state: the fact that what is officially important isn't really, that MPs swear an oath "by almighty God that I will be faithful and bear true allegiance to Her Majesty Queen Elizabeth, her heirs and successors" rather than piously promising to defend democracy or serve their constituents. I wouldn't believe them whatever they swore, so I'd rather it was something that didn't matter. In an era when few things are what they seem and people seldom say what they really think, our constitution and oaths of allegiance are perfect – they elegantly reflect a hypocritical and duplicitous world. Our monarchy gives us constitutional irony.

The problem with national celebrations is the pressure to join in. Some people relish it – the sort who, at weddings, make it their mission to force the reluctant to dance. But some, myself included, instinctively react against it. "Don't tell me to have fun!" we want to scream. "Stop enjoying this group thing!"

That's why making our weird cartoonish monarchy the focus for a national knees-up is so cleverly inclusive: it gives the curmudgeons a role. Peter Wilby moaned that "At times like this, republicans risk being portrayed as killjoys and spoilsports." But he's wrong. It's the other way round: at times like this killjoys and spoilsports get to be portrayed as republicans. The Queen's existence means that a flabby "Bah humbug!" emotion is given a rational constitutional backbone and transformed into a credible opinion.

If freedom, democracy, creativity or culture were being celebrated, the non-joiners would have no such rationale for dissent. The royals give them their own non-joiners' campaign to join. They can pretend that this harmless family is actually a serious financial burden and a threat to democracy, that a significant reason "the living standards of the majority of the population fall and schools and hospitals struggle with diminishing resources" is this one antique constitutional anomaly.

It's no help to me, though. I'm stuck in the middle, between Charles I and Cromwell: too curmudgeonly to dance, too much of a traditionalist to ban dancing. No wonder I don't get invited to many parties.

* * *

On St George's Day 2013 the English Tourist Board, which these days is called "Visit England", formally announced a list of "101 Things to Do Before You Go Abroad". What a helpful side-effect of defeatism, I thought. It's given up flogging the dead horse of England's wintry and rain-streaked attractions and instead has come up with a handy checklist for British tourists jetting off overseas.

One hundred and one things sounded like a lot, though – but maybe it's a real idiot's guide. Not just "passport, tickets, pants, ready", but properly digging down into the detail. Travel's version of Pippa Middleton's party book. Instead of telling people they can buy food in supermarkets, it's "Remember to zip up your suitcase before carrying it out of the house" and "Do not be alarmed by the lion on your passport – it's only a drawing".

But I was wrong, of course. You probably realised that. I've been wasting your time for two paragraphs. I'm still wasting it now. You should stop staring at this page and get out there: there's a whole country to be discovered. Which is what the list was saying: 101 things that you can do in England before – in the sense "instead of" – going abroad.

I suppose this is the sort of thing Visit England is meant to do. It's showing the right sort of industry. Tourism. Which is an industry. Not industry as in chimneys. We don't have that any more. Which is a good job because it puts off tourism. The stench of sulphur dioxide is a real downer when you're on the hunt for a cream tea.

The list was carefully compiled. First, "trade and consumers" were invited "to nominate their favourite English experiences by uploading suggestions and pictures to the app", which is certainly the most instinctive way to communicate. As I'm always saying, if you're dissatisfied with something in the local area, why not upload an angry picture to your MP's app?

Then, a wealth of attractions and activities having been uploaded, an expert panel was assembled to choose the best 101. As well as the chairman of Visit England, this consisted of the publishing director of Rough Guides, a chef, four television presenters and a yeoman warder. Plus Wallace and Gromit, who were invited to choose the winner of the "Because It's Awesome" category.

The other categories are "Food and Drink", "History and Heritage", "Arts and Culture", "Wildlife and Nature" and "Health and Fitness" – they seem to be loosely based on Trivial Pursuit, which makes "Because It's Awesome" a slightly different category of category and, perhaps in recognition of that, it was judged by fictional characters rather than by live humans and Bill Oddie. After much fictional deliberation, the Plasticine national treasures made "cheese-rolling at Cooper's Hill" the winner, thereby displaying a much better understanding of the concept of brand identity than the member of Visit England's staff who reckoned "Because It's Awesome" was an apt turn of phrase with which to associate not only English tourism, but also a cheese-fixated man and his dog from Wigan who don't really exist.

To be fair, cheese-rolling is tricky to categorise. It could qualify for any of "Health and Fitness", "History and Heritage" and "Food and Drink". And who am I to say that it hasn't got a shout at "Arts and Culture", too? It says at least as much about the human condition as a pickled shark. However, what it surely cannot be described as, with all due respect to the prolific Lancastrian inventor and his mouthless dog, is "awesome". It is not awesome. It is daft. And it is old. It could have won the "Because It's Daft and Old" category now that Lady Thatcher's dead.

"Because It's Daft and Old" wouldn't be a bad slogan for Visit England. I find it a lot more aesthetically appealing than the approach they seem to be taking with this list, which is dispiritingly wholesome, energetic and young. I wouldn't contemplate doing many of their 101 things for a fee, let alone as part of a holiday. Even the "Food and Drink" section, which I was naturally drawn to, is laced with activities that seem plucky and keen, such as touring a fish market or visiting an English vineyard – ah, the smell of fish and taste of horrible wine! The rest of it is even worse: "Shop 'til you drop at Birmingham's Bullring", "Watch an open-air play", "Catch the Severn Bore", "Join a bat patrol at Cheddar Gorge", "Canoe along the Wye Valley", "Go ape in the Sherwood Pines", "Raft down an Olympic course". It's like a lost verse from "The Chicken Song".

There are altogether too many helmets on display in the pictures associated with this list. Not helmets from suits of armour in stately homes but helmets on screaming teenagers who are rafting down rapids, or on cavers, or climbers, or athletic mountain bikers. In fact mountain biking makes the list twice, which is more than scones: it's at number 88, "Mountain biking in Dalby Forest", and then later at number 97, "Learn the art of mountain biking", which suggests that the Dalby Forest excursion was a bit of a baptism of fire. What is it about situations with a vastly increased risk of severe head injury that supposedly puts people in the holiday mood?

Then again, there were plenty of daft and old attractions to appeal to the likes of me in the "History and Heritage" section. They ranged from concrete suggestions – "Lincoln Cathedral", "Tower of London", "St Michael's Mount" – to the more nebulous – "Ancient history in Northumberland", which must be a reference to the shipbuilding industry, and "Follow in Roman footsteps". I clicked the "read more" button for this last on the "101 Things" website, wondering if it was going to cop out by suggesting a trip to sunny Rome, but could get no further. A window came up that said: "Please connect with Facebook!" With an insistent exclamation mark, as if I'd been told several times before.

I suppose I have, in various ways. It's stubborn of me not to comply. But, if Visit England is honest, it should admit that the first thing it's advocating we all do before going abroad is join Facebook. Why? Because there's no point in resisting – you can't even find out the opening hours of a castle without it. Because its power and reach are vast and terrifying. Because, as Wallace and Gromit might put it, it's awesome.

* * *

Americans inclined to mock the British habit of unnecessarily saying sorry may soon be called upon to apologise as a result of research undertaken by their countrymen. A study conducted by Harvard Business School concluded that people who offer apologies for things that aren't their fault appear more trustworthy and tend to be welcomed more warmly by strangers than those who don't.

Maybe that was how our empire was won? A vanguard of diffident apologisers popped up all over the world, sweatily begging pardon for the infernal heat/malaria/monsoon/tigers, and the locals were so charmed that, before their oh-it-really-isn't-your-faults had been translated into the lovable invader's language, their raw materials had been lugged on to a gunboat which was already breasting the horizon.

The tests used by these Harvard researchers were less geopolitical and largely involved people asking to use strangers' mobile phones. For example, one was conducted at a rainswept railway station with a male actor asking to borrow people's phones, but prefacing the request with the phrase "I'm sorry about the rain!" half the time. When he didn't apologise for the weather, only 9% lent him their phone but, when he did, it rose to nearly 50%.

I am as delighted by the conclusions drawn as I am unimpressed by the anecdotal nature of the evidence. But the findings stand to reason – particularly as it's weird to ask to borrow someone's mobile without any preamble. If the control group were being asked for their phones after no more than an introductory "hello", then that alone could explain the standoffish response.

The apology is a bit of humanising chat to make it clear to the phone-owners that they're not being mugged.

Still, in picking the phrase "I'm sorry about the rain!", I think the Americans reveal that they don't really understand the superfluous apology. No one, not even someone British, could possibly be so consumed by self-loathing that they think the weather is their fault (except, I suppose, a penitent CEO of a fossil fuel conglomerate), so this apology is not credible but jokey, maybe even flirty. I wonder if the male actor was attractive? That might have elevated his post-weather-apology strike-rate.

If I wanted to borrow someone's phone in the rain, I'd apologise for bothering them or for not having a functioning phone myself, or I'd simply say sorry without attaching a reason – just a general old-world post-imperial apology for existing. That, in my view, is the necessary preface to any conversation with a stranger if one doesn't wish to come across as a horrendous egotist.

But I'm glad that this research suggests that "sorry" is a persuasive word. Because the sort of person who sets great store by studies like this is also the sort who might think saying sorry is a sign of weakness – that we should be openly brash and unashamed in order to come across as alpha-predators in the business jungle; people who think there is a key to success and that it might be firm handshakes or loud, confident socks or using as many consonants as possible in job interviews. If these people start training themselves to say "sorry", instead of "stakeholders" or "going forward", then the world can only be improved.

Life goes much more smoothly when everyone's saying sorry. It's the second most important social lubricant and, unlike the first, it doesn't damage your liver. Particularly in large conurbations, saying sorry is the best verbal accompaniment to thousands of situations: when you bump into someone, when someone bumps into you, when you walk through a door at more or less the same time as another person, when asking for something in a shop, when taking anything to the till in a shop, when telling someone they've dropped something, when someone's holding a door open for you and you're a few yards away, when you're holding a door open for someone who's a few yards away.

Basically, if any remark you make doesn't already contain a "please" or a "thank you", shove a "sorry" in for good measure. In my ideal world, whenever two people met they would both say sorry. Just to clear the air.

And I'm not just an advocate of sorry as a conversational grace note – I also believe in the rhetorical power of the apology. When I was a bad student, this was one of the few things I learned. If I could apologise in the most abject terms for failing to hand in work or not turning up to something, there was very little the nice, well-meaning academic I was serially disappointing could say other than "All right – don't do it again." If I could express exactly what was most annoying, ungrateful and unreasonable about my own behaviour before the person I'd angered, then the situation would be defused. You can't have an argument with someone who's saying exactly what you're thinking.

I remember, at some point in my childhood, my father berating my mother for saying sorry to a stranger during the insurance-details-exchanging epilogue to some minor prang she was involved in. He took the received view that saying sorry in that context was admitting liability and could have a detrimental effect on his no-claims bonus. If that's true, it's very uncivilised. In Britain, of all cultures, we surely cannot take the apology to mean anything more than a general wish that awkward moments should be avoided. Apologies should be encouraged and, in order to do so, we must divest them as far as possible of any long-term meaning.

The one thing that most discourages an apology, and is a growing phenomenon in the modern world, is calling for one. Once someone has publicly called for an apology, then it is robbed of all the disarming eloquence it has if given voluntarily. The apologiser gets no credit but instead undergoes the humiliation of being forced to submit. But that, of course, is what the people calling for such apologies very often want.

So I offer this advice to any children with irritating siblings: if you get accidentally hit by a ball, or tripped up, or otherwise injured by your brother or sister, don't say "Ow!" and leave room for a quick "sorry!" Instead, immediately shout "I demand an apology!" as a reflex. Do that, and you can be sure that, if a sorry is ever forthcoming, it'll be the sort that hurts, not the sort that makes things better.

* * *

As I write this, I can see the sun shining on the Mediterranean. Live. I'm not just looking at hotel websites, clicking from a seashell with an azure backdrop to one of those extreme close-ups of a wine glass and a napkin which all hoteliers' web designers seem inexplicably convinced will clinch custom. No, I can actually see the sea and it is a very sunny day. In short, the place where I am currently sitting is extremely nice.

Yet I am not cheerful. And you're reading the reason why: this article. I have to write this article. I have to work. I can't do holiday things. If I sit in the sun, I can't read the screen of my laptop. If I'm looking at the view, I can't be typing. I can enjoy the fact that it's pleasantly warm but – shameful fat-cat admission coming up – I'm accustomed to working in an environment maintained at a comfortable temperature whatever the prevailing weather. My working conditions are basically unaltered by the proximity of the glittering sea – and that realisation has poisoned my mood.

So when I read that a University of Leicester survey has found that those who emigrate to southern European climes tend to be less happy than those who don't, I was as unsurprised as a Mancunian seeing there's rain forecast for tomorrow. Unless he's relocated to Ibiza and opened a bar. Dr David Bartram, who led the research, found that those who'd made the sunseeking move rated their happiness, on average, at 7.3 out of 10, compared to 7.5 for those who stuck it out in drizzlier latitudes.

This makes perfect sense to me as I stare across sun-dappled olive trees and then wrench my eyes back to Microsoft Word. It was easier to concentrate when my screen was only competing with the wallpaper for my attention. Working here is more annoying than working at work, and I imagine that's what most sunseeking British emigrants immediately find. Added to which, these were already people discontented enough with their lot to change countries in the first place. And, in rich areas like western Europe at least, discontent has as much to do with who you are as what's happening to you.

People who relocate to sunnier places than Britain, who aspire to live the poolside dream, remind me of that guy who has Christmas every day. Have you heard of him? There may be more than one such person, but I remember seeing a particular bloke profiled on the local news. I think he was a dustman – his daily work was certainly over by lunchtime – so he could return home to his festively decorated house by 1pm sharp and eat a full Christmas dinner to the accompaniment of carols and Cliff Richard No 1s. Every afternoon he had a snooze in a cracker hat.

This lifestyle seemed to make him happy – but then he was, to put the most positive spin on it, an extremely odd man. Most people would know that, however much fun Christmas can be, that sort of jollity can't be sustained and any attempt to do so would drive you mad.

A more seductive illusion is that, if you enjoy spending time in the pub, you might also enjoy owning and running one. It is remarkable the number of people who believe that drinking alcohol involves skills which are transferable to selling it – that, if a crossword or a quiz makes a few pints even more fun, then doing the books of a marginal business and changing the fuse on a glass washer must be an absolute scream.

This is the mindset of the sunseeking emigrant – they've realised that they derive immense pleasure from their annual fortnight of basking and so have reasoned that, by living where that happened, they'll multiply their joy 26-fold. Just like me this morning when I smugly set up my laptop on the balcony, they've massively overestimated the importance of where they are, and ignored that of what they're doing. The main joy of a holiday – certainly the sunseeker's holiday – is relaxing, snoozing, eating and drinking somewhere comfortable. You don't need a passport to access those activities – just ask Mr Seven-Christmases-a-Week.

So it's inevitable that, once permanently settled in holiday-land and getting on with selling insurance, doing data entry, microwaving 50 frozen paellas, dealing with an oligarch's septic tank or web-designing with a view of strangers guzzling ice cream, a certain glumness can set in. You'd start to think about the things you miss.

Top of the list, for this group, must be looking forward to a holiday. That was surely a favourite pastime before they permanently moved poolside and tried to get a phone contract. What's going to replace that sanity-giving ray of hope? Are they to look forward to coming back to Britain to visit relatives? Or to joining the National Trust and joyously tramping round castles in low cloud? Or to going somewhere even hotter? Or on a refreshing polar expedition, away from the accursed smell of sun cream?

Suddenly, a nice day is no excuse to knock off early and go to the pub – this is when business is conducted. And it's no cause for self-satisfiedly looking at the weather in Spain to see if it's worse – you're already in Spain, so you'd better hope it's raining in Cornwall or you won't sell enough Carling this season to pay the lawyer who's trying to retrospectively legalise the existence of your villa.

Excuse me if I sound like John Major, but what about drinkable tea, John Lewis, terrible Radio 4 plays, decent pavements, cats that don't look like they're at death's door, sarcasm, immanent social awkwardness, seeing your breath in winter, that grey look leafless trees get at dusk, and frost? Maybe if you're the type to be drawn permanently to the Med, most of that list was always lost on you – but then, if you were brought up in Britain and none of that strikes even a faint chord, you must find it hard to appreciate things for what they are. You'd probably hate pasta if you were Italian, long lunches if you were French and bovine victimisation if you were Spanish.

Some of us are fundamentally dissatisfied. If you move abroad to address that, you risk shattering the comforting illusion that you'd be happy if only you lived somewhere sunny.

8

Some Things Change and Some Things Stay the Same – and That's One of the Things That Stays the Same

This is the "Baby or bathwater?" section. The key thing in judging change is working out which is being thrown away. And I'm probably not the best judge. One of the first things I ever wrote in a newspaper – in the Guardian *in the spring of 2006, long before I was given a regular column anywhere – included this:*

> It's very difficult to argue against the rhetoric of change. Change is so often presented either as progress or as inevitable (though not very often as both) and the implication is that people who don't like something that's changing are losers, lacking the flexibility of mind to cope with the next stage of human evolution. It's very difficult to say: "I don't like this change and, even if you're right that it's inevitable, you're not going to get me to pretend I do."

I must admit I find it reassuring to note that, even when I was only 31, I was already a massive curmudgeon. But, if I was right and it is difficult to say "I don't like this change . . .", then the following section is a feast of such difficulties overcome. I say it about the name of Staines, the consequences of the first world war, the use of language, fashion and snakes. Having said that, I'm not entirely reactionary when it comes to apostrophes, sharing weapons with the French, Christmas cards, sexism in football and nocturnal jogging. So I haven't quite dressed up a bucket of bathwater in a sailor suit and named it David Junior.

* * *

The key to conservatism is knowing what to conserve: what we're rightly treasuring and what's turning us into Gollum; what's an antique tapestry and what's a snot-streaked security blanket. Some would fight for the three-pin plug; others say that we lost everything that mattered when KitKats changed their wrappers. Some feel a tradition of public service broadcasting is worth hanging on to; others that being an attractive environment for rapacious financial practices is crucial to our way of life. Personally, I don't think things have been the same since Consignia changed its name to Royal Mail.

Many take pride in our martial traditions. We don't see ourselves as a violent people, going around the world kicking the crap out of everyone. So much so that, when we have, instead of pissing off gracefully like the Vikings with a tip of a horned helmet and a "Thank you for the rape, ma'am", we've hung around, setting up schools and churches in which to teach people how much better off they are without all that crap we kicked out of them. Our self-image is of a strong but gentle people who, when violence regrettably breaks out, do what is necessary: contact the Americans.

Consequently, many conservatives, whether Tory or not, dislike our new military agreements with France. We're going to be sharing nuclear research, aircraft carriers and air-to-air refuelling. And this with a country which is famously – and I know I'll get some stick for saying this but, let's face it, it's a fact – riddled with clap. It's called "the French disease" – is that a coincidence? Are you going to tell me that "French bread" is a coincidence? Because I've been there and baguettes are EVERYWHERE. And they call it *la maladie anglaise*, which means they're insulting as well as syphilitic.

But David Cameron isn't that sort of conservative. He's delighted with the deal because, by sharing services with France, we can conserve both our military capability and more of our money. Not all of his backbenchers agree: Bernard Jenkin MP said the Americans would "cut us off" from their technology if they felt we were sharing intelligence "too freely" with a country that has "a long track record of duplicity".

Like all opponents of the deal, he's hedging round his real concern. He hates that it'll mean we won't be able to invade France any more. That's what our armed forces were basically set up to do, isn't it? True, we've found other uses for them – peacekeeping, colonial expansion, defending ourselves against Germany – but that's not what they're primarily for.

I don't really think lots of Eurosceptic Tories actually want to attack France, but they want to be able to. It gets them out of bed in the morning – the thought that, if all else fails, we could fling ourselves at the Normandy coast, get it out of our system, like a 48-year-old man screwing his secretary and joining a band. They'll miss that sense of possibility and, indeed, of mercy – of restraint demonstrated every day that, once again, this great nation chooses not to nuke France.

It's like Manchester United and Chelsea, in some dystopian future when they've become footballing irrelevancies, sharing a goalie. "Would Sir Alex Ferguson have stood for this?" their supporters will say, just as military conservatives now ask: "Would Sir Winston Churchill?"

The answer is: "Yes, he would." In June 1940, Churchill proposed not just a military accord but a complete merger of the French and British states. The official offer from the British coalition government read as follows: "France and Great Britain shall no longer be two nations, but one Franco-British Union. The constitution of the Union will provide for joint organs of defence, foreign, financial and economic policies." There's a coalition that's thinking about a big society.

The French turned us down, though, with one minister saying that it's "better to be a Nazi province" than a British dominion.

I hope Canada and Australia don't feel like that. To me, the episode shows that Churchill, who was no radical, better prioritised what to conserve than the Petainist-dominated French cabinet, than appeasers like Baldwin and Halifax, than the *Daily Mail* at the time, than Spelthorne Business Forum today.

I should clarify that Spelthorne Business Forum aren't apologists for Hitler. They're the group who are proposing that Staines should change its name to Staines-on-Thames to distance itself from Ali G. You might question why they care. Well, Staines comes under the aegis of Spelthorne borough council – it's basically in Spelthorne, which makes me wonder whether a quicker solution to their problem might be to refer to their home as Spelthorne, not Staines.

There are several things wrong with this campaign. First, it's unnecessary. As a comic phenomenon, Ali G peaked several years ago. Staines is surely through the worst that those associations can bring.

Second, they've missed the joke that Sacha Baron Cohen was making by locating Ali G in Staines. He's not saying that it's "an urban wasteland off the end of the M25", as Alex Tribick, chair of the forum, laments with apparent ignorance of the shape of the M25. Baron Cohen is saying it's precisely the unremarkable satellite town it is. Ali G's citing of "Da West Staines Massiv" perfectly encapsulates how his clumsy "gangsta" image belies his middle-class suburban background. He is making the character ridiculous, not the place.

Third, it smacks of snobbery. It reminds me of the petition by some residents to change the name of the tube station near me, Kilburn, to Mapesbury. They just wanted it to sound posher. That's not an admirable desire. By all means, aspire to a pleasant, safe, leafy area, but it's not going to become one by calling it Darlingford or stop being one because its name's Grottibotts.

Property prices form an unofficial tax on this vanity: if you want to live somewhere that sounds swanky, do so in the knowledge that you've been overcharged for your dwelling. And it should be an honour for Staines to be associated with a classic comic creation – it puts it up there with Neasden, Peckham and Torquay.

This is badly prioritised conservatism, a willingness to jeopardise a place's identity to conserve its reputation or a few locals' view of its reputation. Incidentally, Churchill had no truck with these experiments in civic cosmetics, impishly writing to the Foreign Office: "You should note, by the way, the bad luck which always pursues peoples who change the names of their cities. Fortune is rightly malignant to those who break with the traditions and customs of the past."

* * *

I find myself in the unprecedented position of agreeing with a French designer. Philippe Starck, who invented that fancy juicer which looks like it's been regarding this earth with envious eyes only to discover on arrival that we're much bigger than it thought, has brought out a range of clothes that he insists are "not fashion".

An anti-fashion French designer! "It produces energy, material, waste and gives birth to a system of consumption and over-consumption that has no future," he says. Bravo! It's a strange thing to hear from a man who's made a fortune designing faddish and weird-looking furniture, but that's fine – I'd still welcome an anti-drugs quote from a junkie. Starck describes his new clothes as "non-photogenic" and has designed them to be long-lasting.

As someone who hates fashion, and resents all the money, fun and attention people get out of it, I find this tremendously promising. Starck may just be the right man to make rejection of fashion fashionable. I look forward to an eco-friendly future where everyone wears drab and similar clothes until they wear out, just like I do. Obviously I don't do it out of environmental conscience; it's laziness and the fear that, if I try to demonstrate taste, I'll be exposed as a twat.

But however puny my motives, I am basically right not to buy expensive yet flimsy new togs all the time. Replacing things that aren't broken causes a lot of environmental damage. I, for one, am keen to find a way of stopping the planet flooding, boiling, freezing, baking or imploding for some reason to do with leaving things on standby, without having to sacrifice electric light, TV or beer. If everything from London Fashion Week to Claire's Accessories has to go, I say it's a price worth paying.

It's easy for me to say, though. I'm not sacrificing anything. On the contrary, I'll make a net sartorial gain when everyone else is dragged down to my got-dressed-from-a-skip-in-the-dark level. I don't derive my sense of individualism from what I wear. Only if those who stand to lose financially or emotionally from a rejection of fashion altruistically adopt Starck's approach will his remarks amount to anything more than a zeitgeisty rejection of the zeitgeist.

Sacrificing our rights and freedoms, or the use of them, for the greater good is much called for these days. There's pressure to recycle, pay higher taxes, not travel on planes, avoid products manufactured by enslaved children, stop borrowing money we can't pay back, stop lending money to people who won't pay it back, and abstain from tuna. And psychologically we couldn't be worse prepared.

For decades our society has trumpeted liberty and its use, choice, self-expression, global travel and all forms of spending as inalienable rights. But only as the environment and economy teeter are we gradually becoming aware that with the power such liberties give us comes the responsibility to deal with the consequences.

What a horrific realisation. I hate it. I was perfectly happy living in my London flat, talking to my friends and ignoring my neighbours, earning my money, spending it on my stuff, going on my holidays, telling my accountant to minimise my tax liability, writing my opinions in my newspaper. And then suddenly, in all sorts of frightening ways, it becomes clear I'm living in a society.

No wonder we kick against it. A national newspaper recently ran a campaign against wheelie bins called, without any irony that I can detect, "Not in My Front Yard". Maybe, as a thin-lipped, judgmental liberal, I'm missing the self-knowing humour behind their selfish rage, but to me it seems that these NIMFYs are just railing against society's attempts to restrain the disastrous exercise of their liberties.

Councils issue wheelie bins to make collection and recycling more efficient and effective. They're better than normal bins – they've got wheels and can be emptied mechanically. Because they're bigger, they can be collected fortnightly. Because collections can be fortnightly, recycling collections can be slotted in without doubling the refuse budget. I'm sure the NIMFYs would hate me for saying this, which is why I'm doing it, but it's good, simple, common sense. The bins might not look lovely, but there are more important considerations in play here.

But any self-sacrifice feels to us westerners like tyranny. We're not ready for it. Our evolution into apex individualists has superbly attuned us to injustices against us while atrophying our awareness of the vastly greater number that work in our favour. It's not our fault, it's just how we were raised.

Our fear of being encroached upon has made us forget that there are few freedoms that can be fully exercised without impinging on someone else's. The freedom to stab has long since been subordinated to the freedom not to be stabbed. But we still have the freedom not to recycle and to borrow or lend money recklessly, regardless of others' freedom to live on a habitable planet and in a functional economy. We've hugely prioritised our rights over our duties because it's only the former that tyrants try to take away.

But it can make us ridiculous. Explaining why mid-terrace residents had no option but to keep unsightly wheelie bins in front of their houses, a Chester resident said: "Otherwise they would have to walk three bins all the way down the street, round the corner and into the backyard. Imagine doing that with three bins? It's just crazy."

I can almost hear the Oxfam advert: "This is Andrea. Every week she has to walk three bins all the way down the street, round the corner and into the backyard. It's either that or people will see her bins. It's crazy, but you can help."

What's crazy is that, in the face of environmental disaster, when councils are at last prioritising recycling in a way most scientists would describe as "much, much, much, much, much too slowly", people are moaning about ugly bins rather than grasping a fairly simple opportunity to do their bit. So you have to keep the bins in front of your house? Well, keep the bins in front of your house then, you moaning bastard.

* * *

Only three days into 2010 and the analysis of 2009 was already well advanced . . .

Susie Dent, dictionary cornerstone of *Countdown*'s revamped cathedral, has come up with her annual list of the new words that have entered common usage. Compiled for the *Oxford English Dictionary*, it provides an excellent opportunity to reinforce the conclusions we've already come to about the year that's just finished.

2009, 12 months of being broke and online, has thrown up exactly the kind of new term you'd expect: "staycation", "tweetup", "bossnapping" and "unfriend" are all set to lose their red wavy underlining in the Microsoft Words (or should that be Microsofts Word?) of Christmas Yet to Come. I'm only surprised that "duck island" hasn't entered the language as a new expression for a hysterical-consensus-inducing irrelevance. Maybe people are still using "Sachsgate".

I get uncomfortable around these heartwarming celebrations of words. It smacks of the view that some words, almost in isolation from their meaning, are fun and interesting because they roll round the tongue or have lots of syllables. "Ooh, 'perforation', that's a good word, isn't it?" "I do love the word 'drizzle' – it really makes you think of drizzle!" Does it? That may be because you speak English.

It reminds me of teachers at school who, undoubtedly with the best motives, would criticise the use of words such as "nice" and "good" because they were boring. "Boring, are they? That's rich, considering how tedious this whole schooling experience is proving," I used to think as I glumly flicked through my mini-thesaurus. They're not boring words, any more than potatoes and bread are boring foods. If you start describing everything as "rambunctious" or "celestial", you end up with sentences like meals in expensive ethnic restaurants – all flavoursome sharing plates and no bloody chips. Slagging people off for saying "nice" and "good" is what leads to their resorting to "awesome".

There's a lot of this nerdy wordiness about. Jaunty anthologies of archaic or quirky phrases are piled high around bookshop tills – the perfect gift for a diabetic, recovering-alcoholic cousin who you think can read. People collect words as decorative objects, like Victorian kitchenalia – attractive curios which they have no intention of using. In those standardised list-interviews beloved of newspapers at the moment (for understandable, labour-saving reasons), a common question, between "Have you ever said 'I love you' and not meant it?" and "When did you last bleed a radiator?" is: "What's your favourite word?" It seems wilfully inane, taunting the interviewee to say "tumour" or "rape".

The most dispiriting new word to be coined in 2009 is, in my opinion, "simples". It's not a new expression for people with learning difficulties, but a line from a TV advert. In a way, I should be relieved to see any evidence of television's continued cultural penetration, but instead I'm irritated.

For those unaware of comparethemarket.com's TV campaign, let me explain that it features a fictional website called comparethemeerkat.com, whose Russian-accented meerkat proprietor is supposedly disconcerted by the number of hits his site is getting from car insurance customers with no interest in his unspecified meerkat-based services. Presumably these surfers also have Russian accents and voice-activated web-browsers, as that's the only way I can imagine the confusion arising. On a keyboard, it's very unlikely that you'd mistype "market" as "meerkat". "Makret" would be much more likely. But please don't let me undermine this joyous piece of comic invention with my bleak logic.

Anyway, at the end of his explanation of the confusion, the meerkat says "Simples!" to mean, I assume, "It's simple", and now people have started saying that in real life. It beats memorising cracker jokes, I suppose, and provides a wonderful opportunity for the advertising creatives involved to give each other some awards.

I think that's what annoys me most about it. My experience of working in advertising – usually doing voiceovers – is that, while everyone's keen on making the ads funny, they're keener on selling something and, as my job has made me bitterly aware, it's hard enough to be funny when that's all you're trying to be.

Hence commercials that attempt humour rarely succeed, and it's particularly galling for professional comedians when they do.

To have achieved the double of both promoting their product and amusing people – albeit only people with a fair amount of parrot in their DNA who probably also pepper their conversation with "Should have gone to Specsavers!" and "I bet he drinks Carling Black Label!" – makes me boiling green with envious rage.

The truth is that I instinctively resent novelty in language. I know it's important and gives English its all-conquering strength – I'm not arguing for the approach taken with French, which has been as weakened in the name of its purity as a home-schooled child. But when language changes, slang becomes correct, mispunctuation is overlooked and American spellings adopted, I feel that I'm a mug for having learned all the old rules to start with. If those who misuse the apostrophe are not adversely judged for it, then why did I waste so much time listening in class?

I realise that's not the most persuasive way of expressing the stickler's point of view. I should have said that correctness in language is vital to avoid unintentional ambiguity. But it usually isn't. No one ever accidentally bought more potatoes than planned because they were told to buy less rather than fewer. Of all the times I've typed "Hopefully see you then" in an email, no one has ever subsequently complained that, when they saw me, I didn't seem hopeful. We sticklers say we fear confusion of meaning, but it's the feeling that we've learned and obeyed a set of rules that doesn't matter that really spooks us.

In the end, though, the rules do matter; it's just that obeying them doesn't. They need to be there to create a tension between conservatism and innovation. If the innovation continued unchecked, unmonitored by Susie Dent, then the language would fragment into thousands of mutually incomprehensible dialects. The stickler-advocated rules of spelling, grammar and punctuation slow the speed of change and allow the language to remain united. They're as important to the continued strength of English as the internet's power to coin new usages. I only wish that were the real reason I cling to them.

* * *

Michael Gove has made a startling attempt, in advance of the centenary of the outbreak of the first world war, to redefine the conclusions the nation has painstakingly come to about the conflict. After glancingly conceding that "the war was, of course, an unspeakable tragedy", he went on to dispute many of the ways in which it has conventionally been deemed tragic.

He condemned the widely held view that the prosecution of the war was "a series of catastrophic mistakes perpetrated by an out-of-touch elite" as the misrepresentation and myth-making of "dramas such as *Oh! What a Lovely War, The Monocled Mutineer* and *Blackadder*" and "left-wing academics" such as Sir Richard Evans, regius professor of history at Cambridge. In fact, he denounced Sir Richard's views as "more reflective of the attitude of an undergraduate cynic playing to the gallery in a Cambridge Footlights revue rather than a sober academic contributing to a proper historical debate". A dismissive comparison indeed coming from a man who thinks *Blackadder* is a drama.

Evans himself, Tony Robinson from Blackadder and Tristram Hunt from Labour all returned fire, and even Margaret Macmillan, a historian praised by Gove, responded coolly, saying: "You take your fans where you get them, I guess . . . but he is mistaking myths for rival interpretations of history." Meanwhile, a fellow Tory member of the government said that "Michael should get back in his box".

Gove's arguments are all over the place. He makes a reasonable case for Britain's decision to go to war being an acceptable response to German aggression, but establishing the justness of the war is hardly a refutation of those who claim it was incompetently waged. His only response to them is to cite the "new light" that Professor Gary Sheffield of Wolverhampton University has cast on Field Marshal Haig, revealing him to be "a patriotic leader grappling honestly with the new complexities of industrial warfare" – as I recall, it wasn't Haig's patriotism or honesty that was the problem – and the fact that military historian William Philpott has "recast [the Battle of the Somme] as a precursor of allied victory". Well, it's certainly a precursor in the sense that it happened first.

But Gove's main point – and he's far too intelligent not to know that it's just naked trouble-making – is that the lefties who question Britain's conduct display "an unhappy compulsion . . . to denigrate virtues such as patriotism, honour and courage". So, by criticising the British generals, you do down the private soldiers. By emphasising the uncontrollable slaughter, you deride honour and courage. That's the "ambiguous attitude to this country" displayed by *Blackadder Goes Forth*, he's saying. Those pinkos at the BBC have ruined everything again, turning glorious and honourable victory into snide and spiteful disparagement of righteous authority. So argues our secretary of state for education. To hear him, you'd think the Germans had won.

Fortunately, Gove's senior aides are working on a remake of *Blackadder* that is more respectful to his take on what he calls "our nation's story".

A British first world war dugout, July 1918. Captain Goveadder enters. Private Baldrick is cowering under a bunk bed.

Goveadder   What are you doing under there, Baldrick?

Baldrick   Taking comfort from the fact that this is a just war, sir.

Goveadder I hope the discordant note of irony I thought I detected in that remark was merely an illusion brought about by the constant shellfire.

Baldrick Oh yes, sir! Anyway, I have a cunning plan to avoid dying in this war.

Goveadder Oh dear, Baldrick, why would you want that? What an unhappy compulsion you have to denigrate patriotism, honour and courage. I sense you're a Labour voter.

Baldrick The franchise has yet to be extended to the likes of me, sir.

Goveadder I didn't know you were a woman!

Baldrick I'm not, sir. Many working-class men still don't have the vote, which is why this war is such a splendid and rare opportunity, not yet afforded in the ballot box, for us lot to root for the western liberal order.

Goveadder Careful, private!

Baldrick Stop reading irony into things, sir! And you still haven't heard my cunning survival plan.

Goveadder Go on then, and you'd better make it establishmentarian.

Baldrick It's to obey the generals' orders and all will be well because they know best, sir.

General Melchett enters.

Goveadder Speak of the devil.

Melchett	At every christening! Quite right, Goveadder. Make the godparents denounce him and all his works, that's what I say. We're a God-fearing lot, we British. Just look at our island story – God-fearing for centuries till the lefties briefly ruined it. Such a shame.
Goveadder	Damn those future lefties, sir. It's almost enough to make you hope we lose the war so they won't be able to abuse the freedom and democracy we're all definitely consciously fighting for.
Baldrick	That's certainly what I'm definitely consciously fighting for! And to suggest otherwise is exactly the same as saying it's funny and trivial that I'll probably die.
Melchett	Unlike the Germans – they're definitely consciously fighting for expansionist militarism in the same vast numbers that we're definitely consciously fighting for freedom and loveliness.
Goveadder	Never before in human history have ethical and national divides coincided so uncannily.
Melchett	Yes, it's as unprecedented as the horrific industrialised nature of the seemingly endless slaughter we're currently trapped in.
Goveadder	That sounds a bit cynical, sir. I never had you down as one of those Cambridge Footlights types.
Melchett	Oh yes! Back in the 90s, I made a great hit with a sketch questioning the beneficial effects of European colonisation of Africa, and another about a vicar who couldn't stop breaking wind, both of which I'm incredibly ashamed of now, of course.

Baldrick farts. They all laugh.

Melchett   Now, this regiment goes over the top tomorrow and there's every chance you'll both get shot. I'm sorry about that.

Goveadder   If so, sir, I'm sure any concerns I have that my colossal personal sacrifice has achieved nothing will be assuaged by the thought that future academics will re-evaluate this supposed "waste" as being a vital component of the western powers' ultimate attritional victory.

Baldrick   Speaking for myself, I shall be thinking of our great ally, who's as liberal as he is western, the tsar of Russia.

Goveadder   Should you not be thinking of our own king and emperor, George V, personification of near democracy?

Baldrick   I would do, sir, but he and the tsar look so alike, and I'll have more in common with the tsar.

Melchett   Why's that, private?

Baldrick   'Cos he's just got shot as well.

* * *

The world needs snakes more than it needs apostrophes. That's something I never thought I'd see myself type. To be fair, I only saw my hands type it, as I was looking out of my face at the time. But I'm afraid I think my brain might be behind it. My heart certainly isn't.

With all my heart, I hate snakes. They're clearly evil. I'm not the first person to have had that reaction. Whoever wrote

Genesis agrees with me, and some people think that's God. It's no accident that Adam and Eve were tempted disastrously to test out their free will by a serpent rather than a kitten. Whoever it was, he, He, she or She knew about narrative.

We tend to find small furry mammals cute and reptiles repulsive, but lay much more significance on the former than the latter. Cruelty to animals is despised largely because of our sense that anyone who could inflict unnecessary pain on something as adorable as a bunny must be perverted. But to follow that logic, anyone who doesn't spontaneously recoil at a snake, scorpion or spider must have similar problems with their mental wiring.

It's not fear of the predator. We're quite keen on mammalian killers such as lions and bears and it's experience, rather than repulsion, that dissuades us from petting them. And few would seriously argue that the animals that induce the cute reflex are morally superior to sharks or crocodiles. Cats are clearly psychos. But, for some reason, I'm keener on one of them curled up on my knee than, say, a viper – even one that's been de-fanged and trained to doze off to the opening credits of *The One Show*.

Apostrophes, however, I love with all my heart. I support the correctly used apostrophe with that kind of fierce emotional investment in an irrelevance that most people reserve for football. I know punctuation rules well, derive a lamentably high percentage of my self-esteem from that knowledge and feel, again with my heart, not my brain, that I'm a higher form of life than people who have either forgotten those rules or never been taught them.

So my heart should be warmed by a week in which (a) steps have been taken to preserve the habitat of the apostrophe by setting up an "Academy of English" to preserve correct linguistic usage, and (b) scientists have warned of a sharp global decline in snake numbers. This is where my brain steps in to ruin its fun.

Apparently we need snakes. They don't just hiss, bite and hamper maverick archaeologists. They're important in all sorts of ecosystems and they predate on rodents in agricultural areas. While I'd much rather come across a mouse than a snake, I'm not sure I wouldn't prefer the snake to 2,000 mice, particularly if I'm trying to grow a supper that isn't mouse.

Meanwhile, there's no counterbalancing evidence that correctly applied apostrophes keep comma numbers down, or that the grocer's ones encourage pesky hyphens. Misuse or omission of the apostrophe seldom confuses meaning and its extinction would do no real harm and is probably inevitable.

The Queen's English Society (to which my knee-jerk response is: "No, she isn't. Doesn't everyone say she's mainly German?") takes a different view. It's decided that English needs an academy so that it can compete with less successful languages such as French and Italian. "We do desperately need some form of moderating body to set an accepted standard of good English," it says, while the academy's founder, Martin Estinel, a 71-year-old who claims still to use the word "gay" to mean "happy", declares: "At the moment, anything goes . . . Let's have a body to sit in judgment."

Obviously this is absolute horseshit. By what authority would they sit in judgment? Where is their evidence that manacling our language to past usage is at all helpful or necessary? It would only stand in the way of the all-conquering self-diversification that has made English the global lingua franca, and allowed "lingua franca" to become an English phrase, while the French kick impotently against "le weekend". Fortunately, people won't take a blind bit of notice of this self-appointed academy and will continue, quite rightly, to use words exactly as they find convenient.

But what most annoys about the scheme is that it completely misses the point of linguistic pedantry. It's no fun prissily adhering to grammatical rules if it's mandatory. This academy wishes to turn something I have chosen to do – an attitude by which I define myself – into something I'm forced to do, along with everyone else. That's like making everyone support Manchester United. It's the blandly didactic product of priggish, literal, two-dimensional thinking. They should be saving snakes, not the fifth syllable of "deteriorate", which isn't going to keep vermin under control in any paddy fields.

As with so many terrifying problems, the challenges of biodiversity are only being addressed with real creativity by the Chinese. Their current craze for dyeing the hair of pet dogs to make them look like other animals has already had some startling results. I've seen pictures of a retriever very convincingly got up as a tiger and some small furry dogs who would make uncanny giant pandas for the zoo of a miniature village.

Suddenly the solution to the snake crisis is obvious: heavily made-up dachshunds. I'm sure, given time, we could breed them even longer and thinner and with shorter, more vestigial legs. Not only would they happily kill rats and mice, but they are also non-venomous, don't constrict and can be house-trained. For years, the absurdity of the shapes and sizes that dogs can be bred into – little pugs who can only breathe upside down or massive-eared spaniels that wee when anyone sneezes – looked like a cruel Crufts-induced fad, but it turns out it's an environmental lifeline.

Many are worried by the crisis induced by falling bee numbers. On the face of it, this seems like too big a challenge for a canine solution, but remember that dogs can be trained. I'm sure it's not stretching the ingenuity of breeders too far to envisage, within the decade, the emergence of some form of black-and-yellow-dyed miniature scottie–chihuahua cross that can be taught to hang-glide. We may end up with a dog-eat-dog world but, with this kind of lateral thinking, it's not just death that will lose its sting.

* * *

The first printed Christmas cards, I'm told, were manufactured in 1848 and were the brainchild of Sir Henry Cole. "Brainchild" is an odd word. You hear it a lot in explanatory voiceovers and I suppose I was trying to join in, but I don't really like it. I'm not keen on the idea that my brain could have a child. Would it be made of brain – a child, made of grey brain, like a squelchy zombie? As metaphors for inspiration go, I prefer the lightbulb.

Bad, dangerous or evil concepts are never called brainchildren. Our imagined ideas playground doesn't contain bullies or failures. Nasty little scrotes like Eugenics and Nuclear Weapons aren't allowed free rein to give sensitive Sliced Bread a wedgie or steal runny-nosed Roll-on Roll-off Ferries' lunch money. And severely disabled brainchildren, like Aromatherapy and The Amstrad Emailer, are never let out to play or laugh like a healthy little brainboy or girl.

Calling the product of an organ its "child" is a massive load of steaming bowelchildren. It relegates an actual child to a "wombchild". And how should I think of my urine and semen? Are they respectively bladder and testicle children, or non-identical penis twins? Anyway inventions don't spring from the brain fully formed. Just ask Trevor Baylis – it also takes a lot of artery, dermis and eye children.

So the printed Christmas card is the proud cerebral progeny of Henry Cole, later Sir Henry Cole, later the late Sir Henry Cole, formerly "Who the hell's he?", a civil servant, inventor and museum co-founder (the V&A is the brainbastard of Sir Henry and some other eminent Victorians whose minds got knocked up during an ideas orgy). Three surviving multipurpose festive messages from his original print run were auctioned at Sotheby's in New York in the run-up to Christmas 2010. Apparently their Christmas cheer was still discernible, like the bubbles in those bottles of champagne that have spent a century in the rusting hull of a sunken U-boat.

It's natural to think of Sir Henry as an admirable fellow for having established this most respectable of Christmas customs. It's natural, but it's a mistake. Bear in mind that, before printed Christmas cards existed, seasonal messages were written individually and in longhand. Before Sir Henry's brain started to gestate, that was the tradition. His idea was to industrialise it.

He mechanised the exchange of greetings so that more greetings could be exchanged more quickly between more people. He considered the previous rate of greeting-exchange to be tediously slow and resolved to speed it up. This way, he presumably reasoned, people can show how much they care with much less effort. It's carefree caring: now your heartfelt solicitude can reach dozens of people at once. The man must have thought he was actually manufacturing love.

How he would have adored the e-card! In a second, you can deliver seasonal cheer to everyone you know and thousands you don't. By clicking a mouse, each of us can demonstrate more warmth and concern for our fellow man in an instant than Gandhi could in his whole life.

It's not that I hate Christmas cards. I just think Cole's reasoning is perverse. He's confronted with a system in which people are accustomed to exchanging small numbers of personal greetings and decides it should be superseded by one in which, while they're able to send many more messages, each one, as an inevitable consequence, means much less. I don't see what's been gained other than another bloody thing for everyone to buy. I suppose I don't really get commerce.

I don't send Christmas cards. My parents do and slavishly keep a record of whom they've sent to and received from. They're mortified if they receive from someone to whom they've not sent – desperately rushing to make the last post with their reciprocation – and put black marks against the names of those who don't return their greetings: two years missed and you're off the list. The whole process is designed to avoid any net gain or loss of goodwill. This seems strange. For me, every card I get is in the plus column. I have successfully extorted Christmas cheer from a world into which I have injected none. Take that, my accountants and Sky broadband! I'm accepting your best regards of the season and enjoying them alone.

My only defence for this "Bah! Humbug!" attitude is that a modern-day Scrooge wouldn't say "Bah! Humbug!" He'd say: "Make this Christmas special with a Scrooge and Marley loan." Christmas is no longer the interruption in trading that he so resented, it's the time of year when businesses expect to sell most stuff. That's a trend that Sir Henry spotted and the Ghost of Christmas Yet to Come didn't.

Santa knows I'm not the first person to say this, but the problem with the mass-produced goodwill of the modern Christmas, where we're constantly wished happiness by carrier bags, receipts, coffee cups and TV channel idents, is that it can feel like a denial of all the things we're fed up or angry about. Charities exhort us to "think of those less fortunate than ourselves", while corporations rub our noses in goodies only affordable by those more fortunate. We're expected to endure stressful family gatherings and gruelling catering tribulations and count ourselves lucky in the process.

This involves a lot of rage suppression, which can be dangerous. After all, this is the nation of the Cat Bin Lady, where fury lurks in the most surprising places. As festive decorations were being put up in the quiet Hertfordshire town of Hoddesdon one recent Yuletide, the residents discovered, on viewing the footage from their newly installed CCTV cameras, that the vandalism with which their street had been plagued was committed not by teenage hoodies, but by the 63-year-old co-ordinator of their neighbourhood watch scheme, a Mrs Jennifer Bibby.

She'd been hurling flour and eggs at people's cars. One of the neighbours summed the situation up with breathtaking, stultifying exactitude: "She should be stopping behaviour like this happening rather than committing antisocial crimes herself." Although another way of looking at it is that she was doing both. She's a one-woman "big society".

Mrs Bibby didn't give much of an explanation for her actions, saying: "I admitted it to the police and put my hands up and said, 'I'm sorry.' The flour was unprovoked, but it was the build-up of a number of years of provocation." As apologies go, that's as bland and nonsensical as a Christmas card from Yo! Sushi.

* * *

In January 2010, Sky football pundits Andy Gray and Richard Keys saw their careers collapse around them when evidence came out of sexist behaviour that would make Henry VIII blush.

"The game's gone mad," says Richard Keys.
    "I know. Women just don't understand the offside rule."
    "Course they don't, Andy."
    "Napoleon."
    "Napoleon, sorry."
    "It's to do with wombs, probably."
    "The offside rule?"
    "No, not understanding it."
    "Thank God for that."
    "A female linesman – it's lunacy. But nobody seems to realise, Rich– I mean, Napoleon."
    "Apart from us, *mon empereur*. It's madness."
    "OK, we're on air in 30 seconds. Are you going to take the hat off?"
    "The general's hat? Don't see why."
    "I won't either then. Why should I? It's PC gone mad. Twenty seconds."

"Have you ever met one who understood it?"

"No, they just wave the flag at random, like a cheerleader. Ten seconds."

"I think I will take the hat off, actually."

"Me too."

Let's leave aside the avalanche of subsequent revelations and go back to the initial leaked recording, because nothing more clearly reveals the bizarre mental world that football commentators Andy Gray and Richard Keys have been inhabiting. They're Napoleon, and the rest of us are too insane to realise. They knew they had to keep this knowledge a secret or the lunatics would turn on them, and so it has proved.

A few apologists defended their first remarks as merely humorous. Former England women's cricket captain Rachael Heyhoe Flint said: "These were tongue-in-cheek comments and we are blowing something enormously out of proportion here." But when you listen to that recording, it's not tongue in cheek at all. Their criticisms of female assistant referee Sian Massey are marked, as Gabby Logan wrote in *The Times*, with a "total lack of laughter".

I find that fascinating. These men weren't making sexist jokes or taking the piss. They seem genuinely to believe that women can't understand the offside rule. Not just women who don't like football or only watch the occasional match; not just scatter-brained sculptresses or isolated Pacific island tribeswomen; not just Katie Price or the Queen; but women who have worked their entire careers to get a job in football, been fully trained as referees and officiated in hundreds of matches. They think even those women can't understand the offside rule.

It seems reasonable to conclude that these broadcasters are implying that women are, at the very least, slightly less intelligent than men. But possibly only slightly: maybe they reckon that the offside rule is the most complex and difficult concept known to, well, man. They may think women can do anything else men can do – right up to rocket science, brain surgery and transubstantiation – but that female intelligence cuts off just before that most elusive and nuanced of human ideas, the offside rule. If that's the case, Keys and Gray are a bit sexist, but their main mental health problem is believing a slightly tricky rule from an incredibly straightforward game – a notion on the level of buying hotels in Monopoly – is like existentialism, string theory, the double helix, long division and backing-up-Nokia-phone-contacts-on-an-Apple-computer all rolled into one.

But it may be that they've got a better sense of proportion about the trickiness of offside, yet still consider it to be beyond any woman's intellectual grasp. If that's the case, they must spend most of their lives looking around in horrified bewilderment. They think women are imbeciles and yet there women are, walking around, wearing clothes, holding down jobs, being allowed to vote – driving around in cars, for God's sake! Gray and Keys must be terrified.

Could chimps be taught the offside rule? Or dolphins? That octopus seemed to know a lot about football. How basic an organism do Andy and Richard consider the female of their species to be? And why has Andy had sex with so many of them? Sarah Palin must be even more horrifying to them than she is to the rest of us: they're not worried that, if she became president, she'd destroy the world out of evil, inflexible rightwing rage, but just because the red button looked like a Smartie.

Is that why they've forged careers in football, the last bastion of male dominance? The moron women – the shaggable zombies, the lipstick-wearing Borg – hadn't yet broken into that citadel. It was safe. But now, with the sight of a woman on the touchline, randomly waving a flag or not waving a flag (and occasionally doing it at the right time by pure luck, the jammy bitch), they know that the Matrix's machines have entered Zion.

These men have so completely misapprehended the nature of humanity that they should be pitied. Poor, stupid Richard Keys – he probably doesn't even understand how funny it is that he said: "Did you hear charming Karren Brady this morning complaining about sexism? Yeah, do me a favour, love." But it's hard to pity people who have built massively successful careers in spite of mirthless arrogance, a towering sense of entitlement and disdain for a world they're convinced has got everything wrong. So I don't.

And these guys aren't alone. Football is full of Napoleons. Croatian FA president Vlatko Markovic is a good example. In 2010, he said: "While I'm a president of the Croatian Football Federation, there will be no homosexuals playing in the national team", adding: "Luckily, only normal people play football." Yeah, normal people like Paul Gascoigne, Wayne Rooney, Gordon Ramsay, George Best and Craig Bellamy. What normal people.

It's certainly true that very few professional footballers admit to the "abnormality" of being gay. Maybe it's fancying men that messes with the brain's offside-understanding lobe? But surely that would make lesbian refs OK?

The worst thing about the footballing Napoleon complex is that it's so possessive of a game that shouldn't, and ultimately can't, be possessed. The human urge to kick a ball around and attempt to get it into a goal, and the urge to watch other people doing that, are innocent and harmless pleasures. How come they're so often marred by tedious bastards – from Andy Gray to Roman Abramovich to Sepp Blatter – trying to own the fun? They want to be able to take their balls away if we don't play with them in the way they like. When they can't, they start whining.

So, yes, Andy and Richard, the game's gone mad. Enjoy St Helena. I hope it's St Helena, not Elba.

* * *

"Do you want to tell that to Her Majesty Queen Noor?" thundered the estate manager to the head gardener. Or at least she did according to the now ex-head gardener, Amanda Hill, who has brought a constructive dismissal case against her former employers. Allegedly this remark was the response to Mrs Hill explaining that, for compelling climatic reasons, she was unable to accede to her boss Queen Noor of Jordan's demand that she grow mangoes and avocados in the Berkshire countryside.

"Can't is not a word for princes," as Elizabeth I said (or at least did in *Blackadder*). If this story is true, then it's inspiring that Queen Noor, an educated woman who must surely have a reasonable grasp of the flora of the home counties, has sufficient belief in the power of royalty to ask for the impossible. That's what command is all about – exhorting people to superhuman efforts, making them believe that, with royal favour, anything can be done. This is the spirit of Agincourt, the bravado of Canute, the self-belief that allowed Henry VIII to cock a snook at the Pope. Alternatively, she may have thought there was a greenhouse.

Queen Noor's regal hauteur compares favourably with our own royal family's beleaguered self-esteem. When the Duke of York went to India to represent his mother on the occasion of the diamond jubilee, he was criticised for flying first class. This made me feel sorry for him. Maybe we just shouldn't have princes at all – it's not exactly the most modern of systems. Personally, I'm fine with it but I can see the arguments against. But if we're going to have them, we can't really make them fly economy, can we? If we're having a constitutional monarchy, we've got to accept that the royals will be on one side of the barrier accepting flowers and smiling while the rest of us are on the other, presenting them and waving flags. That system doesn't really work if these arbitrarily appointed guests of honour have to travel to the event by bus and then queue with everyone else to meet themselves.

Even the Queen (EIIR, not Noor) faces problems. Her diamond jubilee pageant underwent a funding crisis, with the organiser Lord Salisbury complaining that "the lack of generosity from British firms has given me a huge amount of unnecessary work". Do you want to tell that to Her Majesty Queen Elizabeth? Come on, man, stop moaning! Pull your finger out before she chops your head off! You've only got to organise a boat show, not make the Aberdeenshire loam bring forth pineapples. Sadly though, he clearly has no fear of his sovereign's wrath.

Maybe she should take a leaf out of Ray O'Rourke's book. He's the multimillionaire construction boss who wants to demolish his Essex mansion and build an identical one in its place. Or more or less identical, anyway. Obviously it'll be a lot more horrible and have a home cinema. The council won't let him – it seems "can't" is still a word for captains of industry. For now. But he's appealing. Which is deeply unappealing.

But that's only because he's a businessman. What seems unpleasantly vulgar in a tycoon is appropriately headstrong in a king. Getting massive portraits painted of yourself, wearing enormous gold accessories, employing staff in funny uniforms, being driven around in horse-drawn carriages – these are the preserves of the most and least pukka: of Charles II and Mr T, of Louis XIV and Richard Branson, of the Queen of Jordan and Jordan. When Henry IV of France built the Grande Gallerie of the Louvre in 1607, it was the longest corridor in the world and he reputedly used it to hold indoor fox hunts. People thought that was classy as hell but, in modern terms, it might as well have been a revolving rooftop bowling alley lined with tropical fish tanks.

When commoners do these things it seems pretentious and presumptuous. But what does being royal really mean? It just refers to families who have kept up the pretence and continued to presume for centuries. William the Conqueror took England by force and most of his descendants have subsequently held their nerve: royalty is a confidence trick, and that requires confidence. You can't keep that show on the road with humility; you do it by claiming to be anointed by the Almighty, by asserting that you can cure scrofula, by branding rivals as traitors and usurpers when in truth they're just competitors, by demanding loyalty with the intensity of an organised criminal, by expecting home-grown mangoes in Berkshire.

The Queen needs to get back to basics. She's talked the talk of service so long that she's started to believe it. Most of her ancestors would not approve. "I serve" may be what the Prince of Wales's motto means but the monarch's translates as "God and my right". If she wants to keep her right, she may have to assert it more forcefully. Napoleon Bonaparte knew a thing or two about claiming royal status, having styled himself an emperor. He was amazed that, on the night the Tuileries palace was finally stormed, Louis XVI taken into custody and his guards slaughtered, the king didn't make more of a show of resistance: "If Louis XVI had mounted his horse, the victory would have been his," he said.

For our monarch, though, the answer may lie in dogs rather than horses. I was heartened to read of an occasion in 2011 when, according to "a royal insider", the Queen "quite simply . . . went bonkers". This was when she discovered that the food that her beloved corgis were being given wasn't fresh but had been frozen and reheated. "That's more like it, ma'am," I thought. "Going mental because the dogs have been given, not dog food – that would be unimaginable – but normal human-quality food that's been in the freezer." That's exactly the sort of thing you can imagine George V or Mariah Carey doing.

Royal protocol is nothing but a massive rider, dignified by centuries. Bowing and curtsying is only a historical version of a bowl of M&Ms with the brown ones removed. Both rock stars and royals are treated with the sort of weird reverence that, if not rigidly maintained, will quickly turn to contempt. Stop demanding impossible mangoes for one second, and you'll end up shopping in Iceland with everyone else – and it won't just be for the dog.

* * *

There are lean times ahead for Britain's high streets: Weight Watchers is opening a chain of shops. And, if you hated that joke, take comfort from the fact that its days are numbered. As obesity rather than thinness becomes established as the west's poverty signifier, lean-equals-broke will have no resonance in the shiny, sweaty, globulous and wheezing future.

The rich thincats of the decades to come will pay good money to remain skinny, and the aspirant plump to become so, which is presumably why Weight Watchers thinks it's on to a winner with these new "Lifestyle Centres", which will provide one-to-one weight-loss consultations and "express weigh-ins" and in general will, as spokesman Chris Stirk puts it, "offer a more personalised and flexible service for busy people like working mums and office workers who can pop in when they have time".

You can see the way they're styling themselves: it's weight loss for today's busy, connected, results-orientated fat person. It's for the fatty on the move, wobbling dynamically from one meeting to the next: they've only got time to hop on those scales and get a pep talk from a dietician before whizzing off to their next appointment, executive muumuu billowing in their wake. If they haven't had time for lunch (unlikely but possible), they might get one of the centres' "grab and go" meals, such as their 243-calorie prawn mayonnaise sandwich, which would probably leave you hungry, but that's OK because, on a British high street, there's bound to be a KFC next door.

But will this catch on? Won't people be embarrassed to be seen wandering into a high-street weight-loss centre, however much it adopts the rhetoric of business class? Going there is still an admission that you're worried about your weight, of lack of confidence. In normal-sized people this might betray poor self-esteem; in the skinny, it looks anorexic; and, even in the demonstrably obese, it would be a sign that they're not as proud of "who they are" as we're all supposed to be nowadays. Getting help with weight loss is a brave confession of weakness and need – but few are comfortable displaying those traits publicly. That's why so many dirty-video stores went out of business because of the internet, while Waterstones limps on. There aren't many of us who'd be happy to stride openly from the sex shop to the Lifestyle Centre, proclaiming to the world: "Yeah, I'm a fat guy who wanks – deal with it."

A survey into women's attitudes to exercise conducted for mental health charity Mind suggests this sort of embarrassment might be a problem for the centres. More than half of those questioned said they were too self-conscious to exercise in public. Fears of unforgiving Lycra, "wobbly bits", sweating or going red, lead them to try to get fit, if they try at all, very early in the morning or late at night. So that's why everyone you see jogging looks intimidatingly fit! The flabby do their running under cover of darkness.

It's easy to understand their feelings. Watching a fat or unfit person jog evokes two main responses. First, it's funny – in the way a pratfall is funny. It's a physical misfortune that's happening to somebody else. The sweaty, panting discomfort, the glazed-over expression of dread, the pink-and-cerise-pocked face, the hilariously slow rate of progress that has nevertheless proved so exhausting, the thought of the cakes and ale that went before – you want to laugh. And the runner knows you want to laugh.

Worse still is the other simultaneous response: sympathy, empathy, even pity. Most of us have been there or think, if we broke into a run, we'd soon find ourselves there. But those feelings are seldom welcomed, any more than it is soothing when you bump your head for someone to say: "Ooh, that must have hurt!" On some deep evolutionary level, we reject this pity – maybe we sense that it leads gradually but inevitably to people concluding that we may be surplus to the tribe's requirements.

Our aversion to sympathy for quite trivial misfortunes is laid bare when you watch someone narrowly miss a train or bus. Almost everyone, in the moment it becomes clear they're not going to catch it, tries to make it look like they didn't really want to. "It's fine, I was just kind of jogging anyway – I'd rather get the next one" is what they're desperate to convey, in the face of all the evidence to the contrary. Even those who go the other way and express annoyance usually do it in a slightly performed way: they are portraying an annoyed person, but concealing their true desire, which, more than to have caught the train or bus, is now for the ground to swallow them up. It's very rare to see annoyance unselfconsciously or unashamedly expressed in those moments – I certainly can't do it myself.

As a species, we seem much more comfortable with implausible shows of empty pride than unremarkable admissions of weakness. This may explain the existence of the Heart Attack Grill in Las Vegas, which offers free meals to anyone weighing over 25 stone and where a woman recently suffered a cardiac arrest while eating one of their "double bypass burgers". She was also drinking a margarita and smoking a cigarette, but was being abstemious compared to the establishment's previous heart-attack victim, a man tucking into a "triple bypass burger" two months earlier. Presumably one of the things such customers are trying to say is: "We know what we're doing – we're going into this with our eyes open. We're unafraid, we're not running away from anything, and that's not just because we'd immediately be drenched in sweat if we tried."

We humans have a deeply conservative instinct that we should know our place: paupers should stay in hovels and kings on thrones. Gyms should be full of fit people exercising, diners full of fat ones eating. Everyone just being and no one trying. It's the trying, the aspiration, that people find threatening – trying to get a better job, move somewhere nicer, lose weight. And that's why those who are doing it feel vulnerable.

Can Weight Watchers outlets thrive on the high street? I hope so, but I doubt it. More than they're ashamed of overeating or buying pornography or missing a train, people are ashamed of wanting to change themselves. They fear they can't and that others will resent the attempt. That's why fat people exercise by night.

When I wrote this column in April 2012, only one Weight Watchers Lifestyle Centre was open. That's one of the things that's stayed the same.

Horrible, Horrible Progress

We're far too near the end of this book for me to retain an open mind. I think I might feel guilty about expressing hatred for the internet if there were any chance that it would thereby be stopped. I might pause to consider its blessings and possibilities if its fate were genuinely in my hands. But, for some reason, it's not – so I reckon I can let rip in slagging it off, safe in the knowledge that it won't make a blind bit of difference.

The truth is that modern technology is amazing. The machines most of us use every day are like magic. If I'd seen an iPad as a child, it would have been like an episode of The Box of Delights *had come to life.*

But the people who sell us those machines are getting rich, so I see no reason for them also to get praised. And let's not forget all the havoc these advances are wreaking. In this section, I slag off automatic arse-wipers, cameraphones, snazzy weather maps, online comment sections and internet dating. It also contains the secret of eternal life.

* * *

Dare you compromise on sphincteral cleanliness? According to Toto, a Japanese sanitaryware company, that's what most Britons have been doing for years. But that's all set to change with the opening of Toto's first UK shop selling, among other luxury bathroom fittings, loos that clean the shit off your arse for you.

The British market has hitherto proved resistant to such products, perhaps because they're expensive or perhaps because we're nervous of entrusting a vital orifice to the tender mercies of an array of electric squirters, deodorisers and driers. We imagine such contraptions having a dial of settings that, under cover of ominous music, could be covertly turned up to "Dangerous" by a sinister gloved hand. None of us wants to meet our maker, pants round ankles, *Schott's Original Miscellany* clutched in agony, the victim of a lethal hygienic bombardment.

Toto's UK general manager, Jill Player-Bishop, doubts this: "People tend to think Britons don't want to experiment but they do," she claims. I agree, but this isn't about discovering DNA or being open-minded about suburban sex games. Is bottom-wiping really a field of activity where experimentation is helpful?

Who knows why Toto thinks the time is ripe to relieve the British of a grim but levelling chore. Maybe it consulted the Duchess of York, who promised to whisper in a royal ear in exchange for a hot bath and somewhere indoors to sit. A futuristic loo, she might suggest to Prince Andrew, is an excellent way of staying "whiter than white" all over. At the very least, it would save having to employ the most euphemistically job-titled of all his footmen (the one he hopes never shakes hands with the toothpaste guy).

Or maybe it's the British reputation for being repressed that convinced the company that we'd want to live in denial of a bodily function. On Toto's American website, the descriptions of its range of "Washlets" (the fixtures that actually deal with the dirty), with their coy references to "comfort" and "cleansing" rather than poo and bottoms, seem aimed at customers who wish to renounce the entire alimentary canal. As soon as medical science permits, they'll have their anuses sewn up and will subsist on hourly nutrient injections.

This prudery aside, the website seems to have been designed for cultures yet to discover the double entendre: the cheapest washlet is described as "entry-level", and they also sell a "Guinevere Self-Rimming Lavatory – Single Hole" which, bizarrely enough, is a sink. This is the sort of copy that could attract an intellectual property suit from the writers of *Carry On at Your Convenience*.

I'm sure a state-of-the-art washlet works better than Andrex once you get used to the sensation of a machine lapping away from below – although if, *Matrix*-style, the machines subsequently turn on us, we're going to be seriously short of moral high ground. So why not embrace the future or, rather, sit on its face? After a long lecture on gum health from my dentist, I now use a machine to clean my teeth. Why not banish the loo roll to the social history museum, alongside the fax, the mangle and the reusable French letter?

Because there's no going back, that's why. It's what my ex-flatmate calls "a valve decision" – one you can put off making but cannot reverse, much like egestion. He ably demonstrated the advantages of delaying such choices by refusing to watch the French Open tennis on an HD channel, on the basis that, if he got used to HD, the non-HD coverage would start to look shoddy. Take that, early adopters! I shall not eat your Turkish delight!

If you get used to a new technology, you start to need it. Within weeks, the prospect of wiping my arse with a paper-covered hand would seem like having to spend a day birthing calves. People say of their dishwasher: "I genuinely don't know how I lived without it." If that's true, they need to consult a doctor about the memory lapses they're suffering. What they mean is: "I have come to despise my former existence and now have an addict's need of the money that provides the equipment to save me from a return to it." Although that would be an odd remark to make socially.

"You'll never look back!" they say to those without dishwashers – or iPhones, satnavs or Sky+ – trying to lure others into their hell of technology-dependence. Resist such valve decisions, I say, for the simple contentment of not knowing what you're missing is irreplaceable once lost.

If the world plunges into a new dark age on our watch, it'll be hard enough to keep chipper without electricity, the sensation of a full stomach and a third of the UK above sea level. We don't want to compound that grief by feeling bereft without the robot that used to ease our bums into freshness with a tepid spritz and a mist of cologne. Any luxurious pleasure it may give now will be dwarfed by the misery of its loss and what that represents, in the event of a penurious future.

Which is why I've always been very careful when buying wine. When I was a student, everyone bought the cheapest bottle – the £3 red. But then, at some point, a mixture of shame and a sense of entitlement, or the prospect of a dinner party at which the origin of each brought bottle will be impossible to conceal, makes you spend a bit more, go for the £5. This does not merely equate to an extra cost of £2, but to £2 multiplied by the number of bottles of wine you will buy for the rest of your life. It's another valve decision – go up a notch in wine price and your palate won't let you go back. This means that if you get poorer in the future, you will just have to – and I hesitate to use such an offensive phrase – drink less wine.

I'm sounding like a miser – or as if I take a "glass half empty" attitude to a ludicrous conclusion, where the joy of any purchase is pre-emptively counteracted by the fear of future dismay at not being able to repeat it. Maybe I should buy a top-of-the-range washlet to prove I can be optimistic? Or would people just think that was typically anal?

* * *

At the high points of my childhood – holidays, birthdays, picnics, Christmas – my father took photographs. This took the shine off many of the high points. Watching my dad take a photo is exquisitely frustrating. Until about 1995, he still had the camera he'd been given for his 21st birthday. This was quite an expensive item in its day. Clearly capable of "proper" photography, it should've made light work of capturing my mum, my brother and me in front of a castle or behind a Knickerbocker Glory.

But the ice cream would usually have melted by the time the snap was taken because the camera had dozens of dials and buttons to adjust. My father was uncomfortable doing this unobserved and would make everyone pose with the appropriate grins before he started to grapple with the settings. Just when you thought he was ready and he'd put the camera to his eye – just when you really believed you were about to get your life back and actually enjoy the leisure experience he was attempting to immortalise – he'd remember there was one more knob to fiddle with and start studying the machine again while asking "How far am I?" to which my mother would, in an exhausted monotone, invariably reply: "Ten feet."

These photos are a bizarre historical document. These were a people, future archaeologists will think, who spent their whole lives in weary celebration. Their dwellings were permanently festooned with greenery and tinsel, their children expected to spend hours digging aimlessly by the sea, using flimsy tools, in a state of near nakedness. And their diet consisted almost entirely of ice cream, turkey and plum pudding. I hadn't realised, until I looked through a few of the annual pictures of our Christmas pudding being set alight, that my father was engaged in an ambitious time-lapse photography project to illustrate the human ageing process. I can watch myself grow tall, speccy, spotty, then plump, then wrinkled, while the Christmas pudding, for all its engulfing flames, is unchanging.

Photographs happen very differently now. As someone off the telly, I'm acutely conscious that everyone is carrying a phone and every phone has a camera. If there's any truth in that whole photographs-stealing-your-soul thing, then much of my soul is divided between hundreds of images of me grinning inanely next to strangers. And what most of those soul-shards are thinking is: "This is even slower than my dad! Why does no one know how to work their own cameraphone?" And those are the nice people who ask. There's always the risk of running into someone who thinks that a shot of me picking my nose on the tube will make a perfect desktop backdrop to share with their Facebook friends.

The England football team learned this to their cost when a snap taken of them a few hours after being knocked out of the 2010 World Cup leaked into the public domain via defender Ledley King's BlackBerry. In the *Daily Mail*, it was accompanied by the headline: "Cigars, drinks, feet up . . . you'd think this bunch of flops had won the World Cup."

Whoever wrote that has an extremely tame idea of what a World Cup winners' party might be like. There is one cigar on show and one foot on a table. Maybe cigars do conjure up notions of victory – although I doubt Churchill abstained during Gallipoli – but I don't think a foot on a table and a lager is much of a celebratory binge.

The picture shows some men sitting in chairs chatting, and that's exactly what I'd imagine the England team would be doing soon after losing a match. Are they supposed to be crying, tearing their hair out or whipping themselves? Grief isn't usually physically noticeable, still less disappointment – neither precludes smiling. If you took a picture at most wakes, you'd see people laughing at jokes, eating and drinking – and they've lost a lot more than a football match. The absence of self-harm and ululation doesn't mean people are callously unmoved any more than its presence guarantees that they care.

It's not just a problem for people in the public eye; intrusive images are everywhere. Google Street View had to apologise to a mother when one of its camera cars accidentally photographed her naked child. And the BBC has been criticised for its lingering shots of Wimbledon crowd members canoodling. The corporation says it only uses such pictures to conjure up the atmosphere of a relaxed and romantic setting, but the poor man who was filmed nibbling his girlfriend's ear is still going to feel stupid. Particularly if he's also got a wife.

And there are the thousands of people walking trepidatiously into job interviews in the knowledge of all the compromising pictures of them at student parties that, thanks to some overzealous Facebook acquaintance, are freely Googleable. The internet and the cameraphone are fighting a devastating pincer movement against privacy.

I don't know how scared to be. On the one hand, it all feels like a terrifying advance in surveillance, as if the CCTV cameras, like Triffids, are now moving towards and among us. On the other, if millions and then billions of photos are being taken every day, maybe any individual one will lose its force.

Our attitudes to photography are stuck in the past: instinctively, we assume both that "the camera never lies" and that all photos are imbued with significance and care, just like the ones my dad takes. Tabloid newspapers still make hay out of putting a snap of a celebrity looking tired and wrinkly next to a glossy publicity shot. They wouldn't do that if it didn't still shock and fascinate some readers.

But if we maintain our current levels of casual cameraphone photography, maybe a more accurate cumulative truth about humanity will emerge. We won't fall for the airbrushed glamour shots any more because there'll be so much evidence showing what these people, what all people, really look like on an average

Tuesday. We'll realise that the camera can lie, but that 10 million cameras are unlikely to.

And we might also realise that a snap of someone smiling despite having lost a football match, looking tired despite being a millionaire pop star or throwing up at a party despite wanting to be an accountant, doesn't actually mean that much.

* * *

On the occasion of an accurately predicted cold snap in 2010 . . .

Weather forecasters must be breathing a sigh of relief this weekend and congratulating themselves as they watch it billow out in front of them. They successfully forecast a big weather event. There'll be no hostile headlines. No one asking what we're paying these wastrels for and why we don't go back to consulting chicken gizzards. They could still be in trouble with their long-term predictions – perhaps they've promised a humid Christmas or barbecue spring – but they told us we were going to freeze our arses off last week and we did.

Maybe this cold snap was a cinch for them. Maybe the big stuff is easier to spot than fiddly yet crucial details like whether it will start raining in Harrogate before or after it gets dark. It's been 23 years since they last missed a hurricane and I can almost feel the frustration of any meteorologist stumbling across this article at reading another mention of it. "You miss one hurricane and you never hear the end of it! What about all the drizzle that we got right? If Michael Fish has never self-harmed, it's no thanks to the media."

The media are pretty tough on the Met Office. It isn't helped by its association with the BBC. The thought of being able, even tangentially, to blame bad weather on the BBC is enough to make some tabloid editors have an erotic accident. When it rains in August, but the Met Office has said there was a 70% chance it would be a dry month, or we have an icy February when it's said a mild winter is more likely than not, the press denounces it as incompetent with the vehemence of a boy who has rolled a one in Snakes & Ladders and is screaming at his mother: "YOU told me it probably WOULDN'T be a one!"

Newspapers seem to imply that they don't think the Met Office is trying its best to work out what the weather's going to be like; that this organisation, established and funded with the sole aim of working out what the weather's going to be like, might have let working out what the weather's going to be like slip down its "Things to Do" list, below such items as "Have huge boozy lunch at taxpayers' expense"; "Book summer holiday a long way from Britain (where it's going to piss down despite our assurances to the contrary)"; and "Meet BBC execs in champagne bar for lots of cocaine and a giggle at some child porn."

Contrastingly, I'm convinced that weather forecasters are genuinely trying their hardest to forecast the weather but quite often get it wrong for the simple reason that it's impossible to know for sure. Letting that fact slip from the public's consciousness is where they're at fault. I think they should start every bulletin with it: "Good evening. Please remember that it is impossible to know for sure what the weather's going to be like. Nevertheless . . ."

Maybe they thought that, like the rules of *Countdown*, it went without saying these days. They decided they could save time by dispensing with all the coulds and mays. It was a mistake and their George Lucas-like enthusiasm for snazzy computer graphics has made the situation worse.

When I was a child, TV forecasters stood in front of solid, non-virtual maps on to which they stuck little symbols denoting the type of weather they considered most likely to occur in that region. But at one point in the bulletin, they'd cut away from the man and his maps to "the satellite picture". This was a grainy photograph of the UK and its environs, taken from space, showing the cloud cover at a particular time. This was fact. The stickers were speculation but the satellite picture showed weather that had definitely happened.

The snazzy graphics have destroyed this demarcation. Satellite-style footage of what the weather has definitely been like slides seamlessly into projections of what the forecasters reckon it's going to be like. Well, a seam is needed – or a lighting change or a klaxon – something to herald the point at which we enter the realm of educated guessing.

Instead, they present what they think will probably happen as fact and do little to differentiate forecasts where they estimate the likelihood of the predicted events coming true at 90% from those where it's much lower.

Forecast and reality look the same; and this comes straight after the news, in which viewers rightly expect the distinction between truth and speculation to be rigorously drawn. It's no wonder that we sometimes feel, when weather forecasts turn out to be inaccurate, that we've been lied to.

Forecasters would do well to adopt Peter Snow's phrase about election night swingometer extrapolations: "Remember, this is just a bit of fun." No one ever watched that and thought it was the result. Not in Britain anyway; after the US election of 2000, Fox News's bit of prediction fun got horribly out of hand. That organisation had the influence to make its forecast come true. Sadly, the same cannot be said for Michael Fish.

* * *

On Valentine's Day, as usual, I received several heartfelt anonymous messages. "You're not funny, you cock," "Why are you such a smug shit?", "Just seen you on a repeat of *Mock the Week*, I wish you would die." That sort of thing.

But then I get that every day – all comedians do (apart from the funny non-smug ones who are already dead). In fact, everybody does; that's one of the joys of the internet age. On 14 February everyone used to look forward to the possibility that someone would share their passionate feelings incognito, and now it happens all the time. As soon as you have a Facebook wall, a Twitter feed or simply a name that someone can type, Anonymous Missives Inc is open for business. And it's not only people who are the targets of strangers' ardour – restaurants, bars, hotels, books, movies and DVDs are all the objects of feelings so strong that those holding them are embarrassed to reveal their identity.

I'm sure embarrassment is what it is. Like love, hate is something that makes us go red in the face. It's safer expressed covertly lest it be rejected. If the local cafe knew it was *you* who found the service unfriendly or the muffins overpriced, it would make you feel vulnerable. This way, you get to call the manageress a wart-faced crone without it getting personal. Anonymity, like a secret ballot, is a guarantee of sincerity.

There was certainly nothing insincere about the 30 negative reviews of The Good Life restaurant in Shrewsbury that were posted online in autumn 2011. They came from the heart. In fact, they came from the same heart: all 30 were written, under different names, by Ms Helen Griffiths, a marketing manager from Salford. But she wasn't managing the marketing for The Good Life – this wasn't an elaborate exercise in reverse psychology. Ostensible offence at "cold and unattentive" staff and "hairs in my quiche" hid Ms Griffiths's real dislike: the vegetarian restaurant's owner, Joanna Langfield. Griffiths was angrier than even tofu can make you, because Langfield is the ex-partner of Griffiths's husband and, last August, became involved in some legal dispute with him.

The online review dispute, in contrast, was deemed illegal. Ms Griffiths, after being given a police caution for harassment, had to publish an apology for the aspersions she'd cast, carefully picking them out of the house hummus and admitting that she'd "never actually visited or eaten at the restaurant". This was the end of a long battle for Joanna Langfield to restore The Good Life's good name in the face of a hate barrage that had caused a 25% slump in the restaurant's profits.

One can readily see Langfield's problem. When a restaurant owner approaches a website to ask for some negative reviews to be removed, saying they're biased, the claim is going to be viewed with scepticism – in the unlikely event that the website has any staff to view it at all. Online reviews, either anonymous or with no verifiable name, customarily go up unchallenged. We assume that the wisdom of crowds will ensure that a fair impression is given overall – that the uncensored self-expression of hundreds of millions will tend towards the truth. Half the time it just regresses to the mean.

And the rest of the time it goes the other way: overeffusive, hysterical praise. So often you'll read a review that couldn't be bettered if the hotelier, restaurateur, musician, bar owner or author had written it themselves. In the notorious case of the description on Amazon of Orlando Figes's *The Whisperers – Private Life in Stalin's Russia* as "Beautifully written . . . leaves the reader awed, humbled yet uplifted . . . a gift to us all," it's because he had. But he was even-handed enough to cast his eye over rival works of Russian history, anonymously describing *Molotov's Magic Lantern* by Rachel Polonsky as "the sort of book that makes you wonder why it was ever published" and Robert Service's history of communism as "an awful book"; and, while sucking on the sourest grapes of all, to write of Kate Summerscale's *The Suspicions of Mr Whicher*, which beat *The Whisperers* to the Samuel Johnson Prize: "Oh dear, what on earth were the judges thinking when they gave this book the Samuel Johnson Prize?"

Figes was unmasked in 2010 and apologised unreservedly for having been caught. But let's imagine for a moment that Figes isn't just a foolish man whose sense of proportion and decency got lost in a research trip to the interminable steppe and give him the benefit of that imagined doubt: perhaps he was trying to teach the internet a valuable historiographical lesson about the limited value of unattributed sources. If you don't know who's written something, you can't know why it was written and so you can't trust it. It might genuinely be a fan of Russian history rightly panning some sloppy research, or a quiche expert correctly informing potential customers that, if there's human hair in it, it isn't vegetarian any more. But, if so, why won't they give their names? If they remain anonymous, there's a decent chance it's an envious historian or the wife of the owner's ex.

When you read a bit of graffiti that says something like "Blair is a liar", you don't take it as fact. You may, independently, have concluded that it *is* fact. But you don't think that the graffiti has provided that information. It is merely evidence that someone, when in possession of a spray can, wished to assert their belief in the millionaire former premier's mendacity. It is unsubstantiated, anonymous opinion. We understand that instinctively. We need to start routinely applying those instincts to the web.

Some argue that anonymous online commenting should be restricted, that websites shouldn't allow it – they should make you put your name to your words. But that would lead to annoying cries of "Censorship!" and would inhibit the web traffic by which news agencies hope to increase their imperceptible online advertising revenues to a noticeable pittance.

Instead, we should merely heed Figes's warning. If you read a review, an opinion, a description or a fact and you don't know who wrote it, then it's no more reliable than if it were sprayed on a railway bridge. We should always assume the worst so that all those who wish to convince – whether vegetarian gastronomes or lovelorn suitors – have an incentive to identify themselves.

* * *

In October 2012, it became horrifyingly clear that even superheroes can't resist the advance of technology . . .

Those of us who worry about the old media have had a fraught week – and we're used to stress. The last few days have been up there with those anxious months in the 1480s when the bottom fell out of illuminated manuscripts. They've seen the demise of Ceefax, probably the most recent of all the old media, a brand spanking new old medium, hardly conceived before it was careering towards obsolescence. Useful, if clunky – like a seatbelt, but it didn't save lives – this valiant example of British innovation will be sadly missed and reminds us that not everything that came out of the BBC in the 1970s is tinged with rape.

Worse than that, the most powerful journalist in the world has quit. It has emerged that Clark Kent, aka Superman, is to leave his reporting job in the forthcoming issue of the comic. Initially I assumed he was protesting against all the nasty commenters on the *Daily Planet* website: the thousands calling him an arsehole without having paid for the paper, or complaining that he only got to save the world because of his posh upbringing on Krypton. But apparently not: as well as his other powers, Superman is super-thick-skinned and embraces the internet age. He's off to work in new media and, according to Scott Lobdell, the writer of the series, is "likely to start the next Huffington Post".

Presumably Kent originally chose to work in the print media in order to be at the beating heart of news, so he'd find out about impending world crises and sport before his fellow citizens and would consequently be best placed to save their lives. But, as the under-resourced *Daily Planet* came increasingly to rely on stories cobbled together from Twitter, the giving out of free DVDs and endless pages of comment, Kent's disillusionment must have grown. The last straw was a disagreement with proprietor Morgan Edge over his preference for celebrity gossip over hard news. Apparently they'd also just given some comedian a column.

Superman will be all right, of course. If his internet start-up founders, he could reboot his career on *Dancing with the Stars*. But, in an era of crumbling institutions, where will the fictional heroes they once sheltered end up? What hovels will they fashion for themselves in the entrepreneurial rubble?

Jimmy Olsen becomes a pap

The *Daily Planet*'s keen young photojournalist has long since noticed which way the technological wind is blowing and gone freelance. With his digital camera and close working relationship with Superman, he can sell pictures of world disasters to the highest bidder. "No sooner has Superman heard that there's a bus about to fall off a suspension bridge than we're there: Superman rescues the bus while I see if I can get up-the-skirt shots of the flustered passengers. People really lose their sense of modesty when they think they're about to die. I can have the shots online before Mr S has repaired the bridge with his laser eyes."

Dr Watson sets up a reflexology clinic

Disillusioned with the NHS, Watson has been searching out a better way to spend his time during Holmes's frequent cocaine binges. "Medicine is a mug's game," is his diagnosis. "People resent what you earn and sue if you accidentally kill them. Worse than that, you're constantly having to meet diseased people and deal with the insoluble problem of their mortality. Far better to earn my crust sympathising with affluent malingerers. After all, alternative medicine does a hell of a lot of good for those who don't happen to be ill. Also, in my Harley Street clinic, I get to meet the kind of rich person who's likely to be involved in an interesting murder."

Mr Chips says goodbye early

In the latest reimagining of the tale of Mr Chipping, the noble and dogged public schoolmaster who inspired generations of schoolboys with his principles and erudition, Chips leaves Brookfield in disgust when the prime minister, an old Brookfieldian, slashes spending on libraries and the arts. "You can't spend your life worrying about whether or not children know Latin," he concludes. "You've got to follow your dream!" In this case, a gay dance reimagining of the *Satyricon* which he's staging above a pub in Wandsworth.

Rumpole of the Bailey makes sideways move into corporate law

With legal aid now capped at the bus fare for a trainee solicitor to come and explain how to plead guilty, Rumpole desperately needed a more remunerative outlet for his legal knowledge. Inspired by an old university friend who makes an excellent living concocting legal challenges to anything nasty that gets printed about Jeffrey Archer, Horace decided he'd had enough of criminal law and is now doing a roaring trade defending chemical conglomerates against class actions from the various poor people they've maimed.

Inspector Morse takes the plunge into app design

In ITV's latest remake, following the success of *Lewis, Endeavour, Morse at School, Morsel* (the Inspector's Infant Cases), *Space Morse* and *What If Morse Was in the Sweeney But He Wasn't Regan He Was Still Morse?*, comes *Morse Code*, a brand-new quality drama in which Morse didn't die but just went into hiding and had plastic surgery to look like Robson Green. Increasingly disillusioned with the police force post-Hillsborough, Morse does an IT course, moves to the Isle of Skye and tries to make a living designing cryptic-crossword- and real-ale-based smartphone apps.

Mary Poppins works in PR
Preferring to leave the tedium of caring for other people's children to those who are trying to obtain residency rights, the former magical nanny is forging a very successful career since founding Practically Perfect PR. "There are two types of PR company," she explains. "Those who tell people about events, movies, shows and products that are already very popular and don't really need PR, and those who fail to tell them about those that aren't and do. The trick is to be in the former camp."

Jeeves is now an accountancy whiz
The news that Bertie Wooster has enrolled at film school so horrifies Jeeves that he puts his days in service behind him. Far from a revolutionary, though, he finds another way of shoring up the status quo by optimising the tax arrangements of his former employer and other members of the Drones. So brilliant is the ex-valet's interpretation of tax law that the British taxpayer accidentally ends up owing Bertie the entire GDP of China.

* * *

The flaw in dating websites' business model has come into focus. They seek to make money out of loneliness and sexual frustration but their services threaten the existence of those very feelings. It's not the same as selling food or porn, which satisfied customers return to buy more of. If a dating website has any properly satisfied customers, it'll never hear from them again.

You may think that's unlikely to be a pressing problem. Perhaps you're of the view that internet dating is the last resort of the socially dysfunctional or irredeemably unattractive – that signing up for a dating website is just the final hopeless gesture you make before resigning yourself to dying alone. On a singleton's "to do" list, it's one place above "Bequeath all my money to a cats' home".

If so, you're railing against the tide of general chat. Everyone's saying how internet dating is the future – the technological solution to busy, modern, disconnected urban life. "There's no shame in it," people declare – which obviously implies there's *some* shame in it or they wouldn't have brought up the concept of shame. Nobody ever bothered to point out that there's no shame in eating soup or going for a walk. But nevertheless, it could genuinely mean that there's now less shame in it (unless it's an S&M dating site, in which case there's exactly the amount of shame that you're into). And, anecdotally, I've heard online dating can be a great way for professional men on the rebound to have one-off sex with women seeking long-term relationships.

Whatever your view of the efficacy of the phenomenon, many of the dating websites themselves seem to think that simply introducing the single to the single doesn't constitute a viable commercial plan. There have to be lies to entice people in. A recent edition of *Panorama* exposed a number of ploys that sites have been using to prey on the horny and alone. For example, there's "pseudo profiling", which a former employee of Global Personals explained thus: "We'd steal someone's identity through, say, MySpace or something. We'd take someone from a totally different country – Spain or wherever. We'd take the person's photos online and we'd start knocking out messages. It was all fake."

So, behind many online dating profiles, there's just a stranger dishonestly typing bullshit to attract the desperate. On top of that, the websites are generating pseudo profiles. How unfair of these companies to ensnare with their corporate lies lonely people who are quietly trying to lie each other into bed. Customers should be able to assume that the falsehoods they're reading contain at least a kernel of truth: their correspondents are sincerely looking for sex or company, and are willing to endure sex to get company, or endure company to get sex.

If I sound cynical about dating, it's because I've never really understood it. But then I was never introduced to it properly. At a formative age, nobody ever told me that it was something you were supposed to do if you fancied a girl: that you should invite her on some sort of prearranged social encounter and, in so doing, irretrievably and unilaterally betray your feelings. Obviously I'd seen dating depicted in films and stories – but the same could be said for dragons and talking badgers.

"How can two people who don't really know each other very well possibly spend all that time having dinner with a candle in between them, or walking round a museum, or even going to the theatre, which admittedly is mainly sitting in silence but with all sorts of intervals and snack- and programme-buying gaps, not to mention the drink afterwards, while in denial of a huge, mortifying subtext of mutual judgment?" I thought, not in exactly those words. I didn't really believe that, post the era of widespread ballroom dancing, such a formal and artificial way of piloting a relationship was what anyone actually did.

It's quite an odd concept to a shy teenager, and so I think it warranted a full explanation. I wish someone had said to me: "Honestly, this genuinely happens. Ask her to the cinema or something. It won't necessarily work out, but posterity will judge your actions to have been perfectly reasonable." I might have had a go then. I was an obedient adolescent and underwent all sorts of odd and awkward situations – piano lessons, university interviews, French exchanges – because I was reliably informed it was part of the unavoidable ordeal of growing up.

But the only relationship advice I can remember being given was that I should "be myself" – a disastrous suggestion that, for many years, meant "silently infatuated". "Being myself" was never going to encompass saying: "There's a rather nice little Italian restaurant I've been meaning to try – perhaps I could pick you up at 7.30?" Just typing that has made me feel slightly sick, but there's no doubting the logic that, if you want someone to go out with you, asking them out is not an insane first step. But, like with algebra, the logic needs to be pointed out for all but the most gifted.

For my generation, a proper grounding in dating chutzpah, like the teaching of English grammar, had been removed from the curriculum. A lot of men my age went into the world thinking that the only way you got a girlfriend was to find a way of copping off with someone at a party. And the level of drunkenness often required by both individuals in order to make that happen can impair judgment of mutual compatibility. I'm not saying I approve of arranged marriage, but it sometimes works better than getting hammered, having a cry, drinking through it, throwing up and then returning to the party's chaotic closing minutes saying to yourself: "Right, who's left?" Which is why I usually stopped at the throwing-up stage.

Had online dating existed when I was growing up, it might have been harder for me to treat such interactions like the mythical unicorn. I might have learned sooner about how to converse on random subjects with a subtext of wanting to be found attractive – or "flirtation", as I believe it's known by non-robots. I think that would have done me good, even if the person I was exchanging lies with was just an employee of the website. With dates, as with piano lessons, there's not much point turning up unless you've practised.

* * *

Scientists may have discovered a way of reversing the ageing process, according to recent research. It's not certain, though. You probably guessed that from the way I introduced the topic. If a definite way of reversing ageing, if the elixir of life itself, had been announced, I wouldn't need to make direct reference to it. It would be the main news story for months, barring further Yewtree revelations, and I'd be able to bring it up more informally. "So this elixir of life we've been hearing about . . .", I might have written. "Quaking as we now are at the terrifying prospect of immortality, spare a thought for the undertakers!" or: "I can't see property prices sliding any time soon now people won't necessarily ever perish."

So don't get too excited. I'm not about to inform you of something you actually need to know, when what you expected was a few sarky paragraphs on the Lib Dems to doze off over. The research is very vague and small scale and inconclusive and difficult to understand. A sample of only 10 men underwent this anti-ageing treatment, which isn't very many – although it is very menny. In fact, it's only nine more than the sample group for Spider-Man (10 more if you don't count fictional people), and no one's saying it's reasonable to infer from that study (I think of it as a study) that, if you get bitten by a spider, you'll be able to walk up walls. No one's claiming that. It's simply too early to draw any firm conclusions.

Anyway, in this study it was found that, after five years, the telomeres of the treatment group were, on average, 10% longer, whereas those of the control group were 3% shorter. "The telomeres of the treatment group" is not, I should point out, the title of a fantasy novel but a series of science words which can be used to convey meaning. Specifically, telomeres are stretches of DNA that protect our genetic code. Got that? I expect you can pretty much imagine exactly how that all works.

Well, I can't. To be honest, I was just parroting an incomprehensible snippet from an article written by someone who had probably uncomprehendingly cut and pasted the phrase straight from somewhere else. And you can now pass it on to other people. "Telomeres are just stretches of DNA that protect our genetic code," you can say and I doubt you'll get questioned any further. Let's just all pass that phrase around and it'll work just as well as genuinely understanding anything.

That's what social conversation is based on, anyway: the good-humoured exchange of vaguely recognisable noises. Let's not get too deeply into the concepts they represent – after all, it's difficult to hear in this clattery room with that music on. Let's just repeat them to each other: "telomeres", "five-iron", "twerking", "laburnum", "DNA", "CIA", "RNB", "R & LI", "two over for the round", "prune at this time of year", "shoffice", "sashimi". "Telomeres? We've got a hedge of them at the back!" "Oh yes, just off the M4 isn't it? Horrible loos."

If you insist on understanding telomeres better, it might help to hear that, according to Fergus Walsh writing on the BBC website, they're "often compared to the tips on shoelaces as they stop chromosomes from fraying and unravelling and keep the code stable". It's a comforting explanation as it creates the illusion of understanding a complex piece of biology out of the fact that most people understand shoelaces.

The key thing to know about telomeres is it's better if they're longer. Unless it isn't. But it probably is. Having short telomeres seems to be an indicator of being generally screwed: cancer and heart disease and dementia are all abrading away at your poor genetic laces like a microscopic version of whatever it is that makes shoes get cancer. Whereas the long-telomered man walks tall, in securely fastened footwear. They reckon. Probably. Although Dr Lynne Cox, lecturer in biochemistry at Oxford, strikes a note of caution when she says: "Globally increasing telomere length in cancer-prone mice actually predisposes to more aggressive cancers." Good point, well made. Might be worth taking a wedge to this difficult lie. Yes, absolutely nose-to-tail on a Friday at about six. But then it's been a wet year and now they've gone absolutely crazy all over the trellis.

"But what is the treatment?" you must be asking by now. "You may as well tell us what the treatment is – we've stuck with you this long. What is it that lengthened the telomeres of 10 men in a way that might make them live longer and feel younger, or might make them as aggressive-cancer-prone as a mouse, or might make no difference either way? What is the secret?" I'll tell you: it's regular exercise, sensible eating and a less stressful life.

It's a bit of an anticlimax, isn't it? It helps to have a bit of a rest now and again. It helps to have a bit of a walk now and again. It helps to eat your greens. On the face of it, the only interesting thing about this blindingly obvious conclusion is with what meticulous scientific tentativeness and by what a bafflingly circuitous route it's been drawn.

Worse than that, having thought about it a little more, I realise that it's offensively out of step with our culture. Having a rest, taking a stroll, eating carefully: I've never heard anything so geriatric. They might as well have said that the secret to youthful-looking skin is smoking a pipe and wearing a cardigan. How do they recommend we all maintain a teenager's sex drive into middle age? Wearing slippers? Do those little tartan trolleys help to reduce cellulite? Our civilisation is far too image-obsessed to accept, even for a second, that mortality-acknowledging prudence can possibly be the way forward.

Age, like beauty, is in the eye of the beholder. If you want to cheat death, you must first cheat those eyes. You must race around on a motorbike between bungee-jumping engagements, pausing occasionally for massive bouts of cosmetic surgery. You must impersonate youth, spend your money while you do it and let the length of your telomeres go hang – it's your socio-economic duty. Never mind how you feel. Ask any exhausted, starving, coked-up supermodel whether she feels young and she'll tell you: it doesn't matter – it's about how you look.

* * *

You may be surprised to hear that, when writing this sort of thing, I try, if at all possible, to avoid venturing opinions. If at all possible, I hasten to repeat (which is another of my writing techniques). I realise my job necessitates a certain amount of opinion-venturing – it's a good day for me if I get through a thousand words conceding only one or two. But, if I can avoid any more, I will.

This wasn't always the case. When I started writing for the *Observer*, I sprayed my views around with the innocent joy of a toddler who's yet to contemplate the possibility of not being loved, and as if they came from a source as bottomless as the water table. But I soon realised that I was simultaneously using up a finite resource and randomly annoying articulate interest groups more effectively than a Home Counties fracker. And mine is not the sort of gas that keeps anyone warm.

I don't think I have particularly weird or extreme opinions – on good days, I reckon I come across as pretty reasonable. And that's the key to the problem: I seem reasonable and most people think of themselves as reasonable. Before I opine, they would probably presume I was in agreement with them. But, if I open my mouth, they may find otherwise. Every time I say something I think, a new swath of well-disposed readers have their assumption or hope that I thought as they did swept away.

Lots of people – maybe most people – are broad-minded enough not to dismiss someone just because he or she has said one thing with which they disagree. But, as an attitude to life, I wouldn't say that approach was on the rise in the current climate. To the many raised and furious voices of the internet, straying from their view of whatever thing they're monomaniacally obsessed with is heresy. In that context, agreeing to differ about a medium-sized issue counts as quite a sophisticated approach to life. A bit permissive, even. It smacks of the impure.

I'm not the only one to have noticed this. Most politicians definitely have. Their jobs are ostensibly even more about the purveying of opinions than columnists', but these days they obsessively save their views for special occasions. Rather than risk alienating anyone at all, the current strategy for political success is to be serially photographed in mundane settings – pubs, cafes, high streets, etc – in the hope of seeming reasonable, and then issue bland statements saying you're concerned about something concerning. Clues about what they really reckon are barely more forthcoming than they are from the Queen – and much less so than from Prince Charles.

So I was surprised, and heartened, by two opinions that were recently voiced by people who didn't really need to. One was Richard Dawkins, who's already very much on record with one personal opinion, so I thought he was really spoiling us when he apparently said, at the Cheltenham Science Festival, that fairytales and believing in Father Christmas were bad for children. For those of us who seek to take the mickey out of him, this could hardly have been more fun if we'd scripted it. "There is a God!" I thought.

But, according to Dawkins, I was wrong. The next day, he killed the joy as usual, condemning the media for twisting his words. "I did not, and will not, condemn fairytales," he insisted. He accepted he'd said that it was "rather pernicious to inculcate into a child a view of the world which includes supernaturalism", but then clarified: "The question is whether fairy stories actually do that and I'm now thinking they probably don't." Smashing.

Just when the poor media think they've winkled a genuine opinion out of someone, it disappears like so much fairy dust.

However, the other opinion was even more surprising. It came from Royal Mail and it concerned fish stocks. The Mail is issuing a 10-stamp set depicting various species of fish. Five of the stamps are marked "SUSTAINABLE" – the herring, red gurnard, dab, pouting and Cornish sardine – and the other five "THREATENED" – the spiny dogfish, wolffish, sturgeon, conger eel and the (presumably now not so) common skate.

"Where's the opinion here?" you may ask. "Aren't these just informative facts?" It depends on your definition of a fact. One definition might be: "something that may be asserted on BBC News without their having to balance it out by giving broadcasting room to someone who will assert the contrary". By that definition, of course, it isn't a fact that the MMR jab has no link to autism, so I suspect that what the Royal Mail is implying is perfectly true. But the National Federation of Fishermen's Organisations considers it arguable at best. And thinks it an argument Royal Mail should have kept out of.

I'm glad, but also amazed, that it didn't. It's been privatised – it has no obligation to the public good, and will gain nothing by changing people's fish-eating habits. And it's not as if, had the fish stamps not all been marked "SUSTAINABLE" or "THREATENED", anyone would have called for Royal Mail to "get off the bloody fence" about the sustainability of fish stocks. Try as I might, I find it difficult to avoid the conclusion that someone took this inevitably divisive decision purely because they thought it was a good thing to do. Bravo.

It's obviously also a worrying development. Now a precedent has been set that stamps can express an opinion, who's to say that future views will be so noble, or expressed for such (as far as I can tell) unimpeachable motives? Will there be advertising on stamps? Or, more plausibly, and also more insidiously, will they become the equivalent of those newspaper reports that are generated by a press release about a corporation-sponsored survey? Maybe a manufacturer of Red Gurnard Bites has yet to emerge from behind this initiative?

Even if the views remain sincere, that doesn't mean they'll stay apolitical. If you make your living from commercial fishing, I suspect you'd say that Rubicon has already been crossed. Who will be editorially responsible for the stamps' content? A journalist? A regulator? A respected intellectual like Richard Dawkins?

That would make for a cheery Christmas issue: a painting of some children sledging with "SUSTAINABLE" written across it; a choir of angels marked "A PERNICIOUS LIE"; and a jolly Santa captioned "A LIE – BUT PROBABLY NOT PERNICIOUS". I'm not going to tell you what I think about that.

APPENDIX

The Future – A Retrospective

The *Observer* is always at the cutting edge of journalism and, at the end of every year, instead of all the tedious retrospectives on the previous 12 months that you read in lesser newspapers, it publishes an article looking back on the *next* 12 months – which, I'm sure you'll agree, is much more constructive. It falls to me, each year, to write it.

This is a difficult task, as you can imagine, and I must admit I have been guilty of one or two inaccuracies: some of the events I reported did not occur when I expected them to. And have still not occurred. But, in an infinite universe, it can only be a matter of time.

To which end, I thought it might be useful if I included some of them here so that you can be prepared.

Boris loses it at the Cenotaph

Prime Minister Boris Johnson would surely have caused outrage at 2017's Remembrance Service, when he got the giggles during the minute's silence, if his laughter hadn't proved so infectious. His Majesty the King, in his weekly vodcast, commented: "In the end we all just pissed ourselves. It was a really good way of seeing the funny side of war." Johnson later apologised, saying that: "Something about how old some of the veterans were just set me off and that was that."

Murder of the Chuckle Brothers

As the controller of BBC1 put it: "I asked Richard Curtis, 'What could Comic Relief do that would involve both the Chuckle Brothers and Frankie Boyle?' and this is what he came up with. As soon as I heard it, it seemed so obvious – the sort of thing we should have done years ago. Barry and Paul were thrilled to be involved in Frankie's edgier brand of comedy, and Frankie jumped at the chance to show his charitable nature, as well as, of course, to murder the Chuckle Brothers."

Richard Curtis described it as the toughest thing he's ever had to organise: "Getting those guys together, at the same time, in the same room, with a chainsaw – I mean, it was like co-ordinating Band Aid. And, obviously, it was a nightmare for the legal team. But, fortunately, the Chuckle Brothers were really up for it, Frankie had a window in his touring schedule, and it made an unforgettable piece of television."

Gordon Brown and John Major embark on world tour

In October 2016, it was announced that Britain's two most successful caretaker prime ministers are going to cash in on the new global phenomenon of "mediocrity chic" brought on by the success of Susan Boyle. In what is described as "an eclectic mix of glum fiscal satire, Morris dancing and cricket anecdotes", they'll be taking in over 100 countries, playing venues of up to 100 seats. Asked whether it was SuBo's success that gave them the courage to put the show together, Brown said: "It was actually her idea."

James Bond to commit suicide in next film

Bond purists were outraged by the news that the suave, womanising, superspy hero will finally lose the will to live at the end of the next movie, *Die and Live Death Is Golden Casino Gun Depression* (working title). Unconfirmed reports suggest that, in the film, the suicide is prompted by M "complaining about Bond's moaning". Daniel Craig has said he's excited by the challenge and that the new film will be "classic 007", except with the main character "teetering on the brink of an abyss of despair".

The England football team's triumph

Coming in the aftermath of their pitiful 2018 World Cup exit – the irony of both losing all of their group matches and testing positive for performance-enhancing drugs was particularly bitter – the England team's brave and emotional journey to the final of *Celebrity Team Masterchef* against the *Eggheads* was a thrilling testament to the redemptive power of sport. The whole nation was willing Wayne Rooney's ricotta and walnut soufflé to rise but ultimately it was CJ de Mooi's failure to prepare any dish that didn't, in the words of judge John Torode, "taste very strongly of his fingers" that gave the soccer stars the edge.

Esther Rantzen launches campaign to grant British citizenship to retired Oompa-Loompas

Rejecting claims that this was a cynical attempt to steal a march on Joanna Lumley, Rantzen said: "It's obscene that this proud chocolate-making people are given no recognition for their efforts." She particularly focused on the plight of the Oompa-Loompas of Bourneville, who work 14-hour days and are then expected to sleep in dormitories above the factory floor in an ill-ventilated atmosphere thick with nougat vapour.

"The effects of 'toffee-lung', 'cracknell shin' and 'vibration white chocolate finger' on the Oompa-Loompa communities of the Midlands have to be seen to be believed," Rantzen claimed. A spokesman for Cadbury's said: "If they could get the chocolate to stick to the Curly Wurlys properly, maybe they'd deserve the minimum wage."

Shock WikiLeaks revelations

The debate over transparency and freedom of information intensified in 2019 when WikiLeaks published details of what everyone in the world would be getting for Christmas.

"Secrets are used to control people," said Julian Assange via Skype from his Mars-bound prison rocket. "Wrapping paper is one of the most oppressive inventions in human history. As for the Christmas cracker, it is a highly dangerous form of violent concealment. In order to satisfy the human need to discover what is kept hidden, one must actually trigger an explosion. Hence al-Qaida."

Toby Young to be given own hospital

In the run-up to the 2015 election, the coalition scheme to give reclusive writer Toby Young the life of his dreams at the taxpayers' expense continued apace despite Prince Charles's comment that he thought "that was what *we* were for". A new hospital is to be set up within walking distance of Young's west London home which is to focus on, as the columnist put it, "the sort of ailments that people like me get".

"We made our commitment to Toby Young very clear before the election," said health secretary Jeremy Hunt. "This is just the second of the thousands of things we hope to do for him. He's great."

Call the Midwife remake trumps original show

The BBC was at the heart of a media storm in 2020 when it emerged that executives had accidentally commissioned a remake of the BBC1 hit *Call the Midwife* before the original show had actually been axed.

The head of drama announced the commission as "the latest in a long line of vibrant and robust reimaginings of much loved classics that the public holds so dear", adding later that her remarks had been taken out of context as they were "just what I say about everything anyway".

With the disdainful headline "You Couldn't Remake It Up" splashed across the *Daily Mail*, it was a difficult first day in the office for incoming chairman of the BBC Trust, David Beckham, particularly when it transpired that the mistaken commission was precipitated by a *Mail* editorial inaccurately citing *Midwife*'s cancellation in a list of "Recent Outrages".

As a result of the confusion, the original show has now moved to Sky.

Murdochs launch new Miliband

The disgraced media dynasty, currently believed to be hiding out with the 47 surviving children of Colonel Gaddafi in a fortified compound in the Liberian desert, made an ambitious comeback bid in 2019 by announcing that they'd genetically engineered a new Miliband. They claim to have used DNA harvested from Ed and David's hotel rooms during the 2002 Labour party conference. Six-month-old Rupert Miliband is being brought up in an oxygen tent to speed growth, is to be tutored by Glenn Beck and Niall Ferguson, and has also been fitted with laser cannon. He's expected to be launched on to the British political scene in 2030 at an event to be hosted by Tony Blair and a robotised reimagining of Baroness Thatcher.

China steals Radio 4

Britain was left reeling by the theft of the BBC's flagship speech radio station by communist China. "They came for us by night!" a stunned John Humphrys told news cameras as he stared into the abyss left by the ripping out of the ground of London's Broadcasting House. It was carried off by a fleet of Chinook helicopters and was last seen heading east over the North Sea. Everything is believed to have been taken, apart from Humphrys and Nicholas Parsons, who was mysteriously abandoned on an oil rig. The BBC has dragged its feet over the issue of fetching him.

Appendix

Sir Cliff Richard wins *The X Factor*

Throughout 2018's competition, the nation had taken octogenarian Glaswegian country singer Tavish McAndover to its heart, despite the fact that his name sounded fictional. Scorning the cover versions that most acts rely on, McAndover wowed crowds with heartfelt ballads such as "It's Hard to Dance Sexy When You've Got a Metal Hip", "I Remember When Tennis Balls Were White But I'm Not Being Racist", and "I Know E4 Isn't Aimed at Me But That's What My Sky Box Is Stuck On". But the nation was astounded when, seconds after winning the public vote, McAndover appeared to rip away his face to reveal Sir Cliff cleaning off the remains of prosthetic makeup. The Peter Pan of pop duly walked away with his fourth Christmas No 1 and a furious Simon Cowell's £1m record contract. The *Mirror's* TV critic captured the national mood: "It's difficult to know which of those annoying people to side with. It's like Israel and Palestine all over again."

Israel and Palestine all over again

An end was twice called to the Arab–Israeli conflict in 2017. The first agreement, signed in March, was abandoned on the advice of Tony Blair, who was concerned that, without such tensions, the region would be "like Frasier after Niles and Daphne got together". It was six months before diplomats realised that this wasn't as good an analogy as it had initially seemed and a second peace was signed.

Peter Ebdon accidentally shot in Vladimir Putin assassination attempt

When a small bald man, famed for his insane drive and frightening monomania in pursuit of his goals, was found floating dead in the Baltic, Chechen separatists were quick to claim responsibility, not realising that, instead of Russia's latterday tsar, they'd taken the life of one of snooker's favourite sons. World snooker was thrown into chaos by the news, plans for a ranking tournament in Vladivostok were shelved and John Virgo broke down on *The One Show*, muttering "He was so beautiful" over and over again.

Duchess of Cornwall rap leads to calls for charity to be stopped

The month of inexpensive programming surrounding the BBC's Children in Need night was marred in 2016 by a segment in which the Duchess of Cornwall was forced tearfully to improvise a rap about declining literacy rates. "Why!? Why is this happening? How is this helping anybody?" the Duchess was repeatedly heard to ask as she inexpertly struggled for rhymes, robotically egged on by a glassy-eyed Tess Daly, who was later to take her own life. In a public apology for the broadcast, the director general said: "It becomes clear that the explanation or excuse 'it's for charity' has its limits. After seeing that, no one will ever want to help needy children ever again."

Shakespeare suspected of touching teens

As Operation Yewtree had its remit further extended in 2015 and acquired the services of 400 historians, yet more shameful allegations about Britain's show business past emerged, including the suggestion, inferred from the stated age of Juliet in *Romeo and Juliet*, that William Shakespeare may once have touched a teen's boob. The consequent fury at the Bard's betrayal of public trust led to a flurry of questions: should he have his knighthood posthumously removed? Who forgot to give him a knighthood? Can he be given one posthumously? Is Shakespeare too talented to be retrospectively shamed? This led to a *Guardian* editorial calling for a formula to be devised that would balance a dead public figure's alleged abuses with their artistic achievements and then tell us whether or not we have to take all their statues down: "Jimmy Savile's talents as a performer frankly wouldn't excuse him so much as a cheeky knee squeeze. The likes of Shakespeare, Beethoven or JK Rowling can have done whatever the hell they liked."

The Real Full Monty fetches £2.3m at Sotheby's

In a sale of film memorabilia, the no clothes the cast of hit Britcom *The Full Monty* wore at the film's climax were the star attraction. There was some controversy when the winning bidder said he thought he was buying the clothes the metal-workers had discarded earlier in the scene. "I'd wanted to get my hands on Robert Carlyle's pants," complained the anonymous millionaire. A Sotheby's spokesman clarified: "This lot isn't the clothes they weren't wearing at the end – this is the no clothes they were." Asked if it was a bit "emperor's new clothes", he said that "couldn't be further from the truth. That emperor was a nude man claiming to be wearing clothes. The absence of clothes in this lot isn't something we're denying – it's something we're celebrating. This is a chance to buy not only a unique, and easily storable, piece of film history, but also a share in the very concept of nudity."

Reading tourist board sues actress Emilia Fox

"Reading, gardening and butterflies." That was the answer that an article on the BBC News website quoted Emilia Fox as giving to the question: "Tell me three things that you like." The Reading tourist board seized on this rare vote of confidence with a high-profile campaign heavily focusing on the popular actress. It was only when the hoardings were up, the local TV commercial shot and the adverts placed in magazines that a videotape of the original interview, which Fox had given nearly three years earlier, emerged. The head of the tourist board explained his horror:

"She said 'reading' to rhyme with 'weeding'. The capital letter was only there because it was the start of a sentence. Or what passes for a sentence these days – there was no verb." He explained his decision to take legal action: "It's negligence, pure and simple. She knew there could have been transcripts. She could so easily have said 'Gardening, reading and butterflies' and there would have been no confusion."

Schadenfreude bounce in economy follows Hammond driving ban

The 200-point rise in the FTSE 100 share index on the day that Richard Hammond was banned from driving gave economic theorists a lot to think about. "People just loved that story – it was the perfect misfortune for that public figure to undergo and the schadenfreude seriously lifted the public mood for several hours, which added billions to stock prices . . . Markets are emotional places and we can't underestimate the importance of this sort of boost at difficult times like these," said a leading analyst from HSBC. The government was quick to see the potential of this insight and over the next few weeks Cheryl Cole suffered an outbreak of Bell's palsy, Seb Coe dramatically succumbed to male pattern baldness and Eamonn Holmes got stuck for several hours in the doorway of a branch of Greggs.

Duke and Duchess of Cambridge sex tape goes viral

"I don't see why the NSA should have the monopoly on surveillance #hypocrisy," tweeted teenager Obadiah Jenkins (those old names really are coming round again!) from his prison cell.

The self-styled "nerd and wanker" was convicted of several breaches of the European convention on human rights, as well as a violation of French airspace, for filming an intimate royal moment using his Google Android parcel-taped to a remote-controlled helicopter. Jenkins had been holidaying with his parents, Kylie and Han, at a caravan site only a mile from the chateau where the duke and duchess were the honoured guests of a social-climbing Russian kleptocrat.

Royal watchers were appalled by what Obadiah referred to as "the ultimate in royal watching #doingit", but perhaps the most upsetting consequence was a distressed yet perceptibly aroused Nicholas Witchell attempting to describe the footage on the *10 O'Clock News*.

James Bond revealed as Time Lord in new film

"I don't think we're really changing anything," said a spokesperson for Eon Productions. "Just making explicit what has long been heavily implied. There are lots of vampire films where they're too cool to use the word 'vampire', but it's clear from all the blood-sucking. Similarly, I think the fact that Bond's face keeps changing and he's apparently holding down the same extremely physical job after more than half a century makes it pretty obvious that he's a time traveller who can regenerate.

"We just never see his Tardis because, most nights, he's pulled. But it's been evident from the start. For the avoidance of doubt: we don't envisage a royalty payment to the BBC."

Gang of cyclists trap a lorry and eat the driver

"It was like something out of *Blue Planet*," a traumatised witness said afterwards, "when all the orcas gang up on one humpback whale."

His wife disagreed: "I think it was more like the Ewok bit from *Return of the Jedi* – where they attack the imperial walkers. It showed incredibly innovative use of bicycling technology. Except then they ate him, which the Ewoks didn't do. I was really rooting for them until they ate him."

The couple had been stuck in slow-moving traffic on London's North Circular Road when dozens of cyclists sliced through the gridlock and surrounded an Eddie Stobart truck.

"I think they wanted a Stobart," another onlooker said. "They passed an M&S lorry and an Ocado van and left them both alone."

Most of the cannibal riders were subsequently arrested but remained unrepentant. "We only ate one of them," they said in a statement. "They've killed loads of us and it barely makes the news but we eat just one of them and suddenly that's more interesting than Syria or Tulisa's new tattoo!"

Al-Qaida win the Turner Prize

"Quite simply, they shouldn't have been allowed to enter," spluttered Brian Sewell when the controversial decision was announced. His evening was only made worse with the news that, in the absence of anyone from the organisation itself, the notorious terrorists had nominated him to receive the award on their behalf.

When the radical Islamist group expressed their intention to try for the award, eyebrows were raised – and they headed even further towards the art community's hairlines when the al-Qaida entry actually arrived.

"I think we'd all assumed it would be a video of a beheading or something," said one of the judges. "So when we were confronted with an adorable watercolour of some gambolling New Forest ponies on a summer's day, we were taken aback. And of course the very incongruity made a profound statement."

Valentine's Day to relaunch as Christmas 2

With the spring came news that, after years of intense and secret negotiation with the world's various Christian denominations, Google had finally managed to secure the global rights to Christmas.

In an impish masterstroke, the corporate giant made the announcement on 1 April, with the result that humanity's consternation was mitigated by most people assuming it was a joke. But not since Disney acquired *Star Wars* has a franchise been exploited with such fearless celerity as, over the summer, the search engine bought Valentine's Day and announced plans to revamp it as a sequel to the midwinter knees-up.

"What has Santa been doing since Boxing Day?" said a Google spokesman. "The answer is obvious: giving dating tips and making sex toys. We're going to get him back out on his sleigh spreading a romantic vibe with loads of click-through opportunities to local florists and restaurants. I am in love with this idea."

Corruption suspected as Cardiff branch of Café Rouge comes third in international restaurant awards

"The whole team was thrilled," said Gareth Jones, the manager of the popular branch of the French-style restaurant chain. "But then the wind was rather taken out of our sails when Antony Worrall Thompson started comparing us to al-Qaida. I mean, what's that about? They're extremist murderers and we're an affordable brasserie!"

Mr Jones, a practising Muslim, was unmollified by Worrall Thompson's hasty backtracking: "I only meant that they were similar in terms of being the extremely surprising recipients of awards," the chef explained at a launch event for his new range of spoons.

"It's not like we won," said an exasperated Jones. "We came third. And this is a bloody good branch of Café Rouge – just ask anyone."

ACKNOWLEDGMENTS

I'd like to thank:

My editor, Laura Hassan, for being consistently encouraging and wise (assuming that it is wise to be encouraging).

Robert Yates and Ursula Kenny at the *Observer* for editing my column and, in the case of Robert, asking me to write for the paper in the first place.

Luke Bird, Anna Pallai, Kate McQuaid, John Grindrod and Julian Loose at Faber & Faber.

Sara Montgomery and Lindsay Davies at Guardian Books.

My agents, Michele Milburn and Ivan Mulcahy.

Toby Davies, Tom Hilton, Jonathan Dryden Taylor and my brother Daniel Mitchell for reading many of these columns and excising countless pieces of crap.

Robert Hudson for tremendous help on many occasions, particularly in the early days before I really knew how to write things I wasn't going to read out myself.

And my wife, Victoria Coren Mitchell, whose ideas, advice and jokes have hugely improved many of these columns and are the least of the blessings she has brought to my life.

POST-CREDIT SEQUENCE

This bit is supposed to send you on your way with a warm feeling. A good warm feeling, that is – like after a glass of brandy, not a lapse in bladder control. The fact that too many of the former can lead to the latter's onset is not the least of the mysteries of the human condition.

I'm not sure mentioning the dehumanising effects of alcohol is striking the right tone. Sorry.

Yes, so imagine a sort of engaging blooper reel of me writing things on my computer and then for some reason bursting out in uncontrollable tearful laughter. Not at my own jokes, I hasten to add – that would be awful. But perhaps at some typo. Maybe I've written "boobs" instead of "the euro" or something similarly saucy and incongruous and I lose it because I'm just a regular guy, yeah?

And then the boom comes into shot and a couple of guys in headsets appear, and an arty woman with pens in her hair holding a clipboard, and we all have a good old giggle together, before they hurry off and I try and type "the euro" again, and this time it comes out as "fart" or "gurgle" or "cake" or "George Orwell". Cue more hilarity and a charming insight into the "process", which, when all's said and done, is just a hell of a lot of fun.

Unfortunately, since this is a book, there isn't the facility for showing video clips, so, as I say, you'll just have to imagine all that. Unless you're reading on a Kindle or something, in which case God knows. I dare say you can click on most of the words and buy stuff. I should have mentioned *Peep Show* more. That brandy paragraph was probably co-sponsored by Courvoisier and Tena Lady.

The other problem, of course, is that this book was written alone so there are no techie colleagues to slap me on the back when I start to smirk. Any blooper giggling occurs unobserved, which is lucky because sitting in a room laughing on your own is, in fiction at least, a sign of unhinged villainy – and, in real life, suggests that social services have dropped the ball as usual.

A friend of mine once lived next door to a woman who just sort of screeched and giggled and yelled for no reason all the time, which was obviously very sad but, much more relevantly, extremely annoying. And the council did nothing, of course. And then her collection of columns was published to sniffy reviews, despite a cover quote of fairly unspecific, but nevertheless genuine, goodwill from a comedian. Not all of this paragraph is true.

Last impressions count – that's the point. I remember the end credits of *Cry Freedom* listing all the people the apartheid regime had covertly murdered, and that certainly made it a difficult film to call shit. Although, in fact, it also wasn't shit and perhaps the list would have seemed wrong if it had been. You've got to get it tonally right. Liam Neeson getting the giggles about some squeaky jackboots would not have helped the credits of *Schindler's List* and, conversely, a list of the abuses of the British Raj was, in the final edit, cut from the closing titles of *Carry On Up the Khyber*.

I'm pretty sure I didn't get this tonally right. I must have overthought it.

LIST OF COLUMNS

a list of *"101 Things to Do Before You Go Abroad"* appeared as "Discover white-knuckle England with this handy holiday guide . . .", on 28 April 2013

p. 223 *Americans inclined to mock the British habit of unnecessarily saying sorry . . .* appeared as "There's no need to apologise for the sorry state of Britain. But I'm sorry", on 27 October 2013

p. 226 *As I write this, I can see the sun shining on the Mediterranean* appeared as "Now is the summer of my discontent: it's just too sunny to write this column", on 27 April 2014

p. 232 *The key to conservatism is knowing what to conserve* appeared as "Churchill could teach conservatives a thing or two and not just about France", on 7 November 2010

p. 235 *I find myself in the unprecedented position of agreeing with a French designer* appeared as "Spare me that rubbish about your 'rights'", on 21 June 2009

p. 238 *Susie Dent, dictionary cornerstone of* Countdown's *revamped cathedral . . .* appeared as "Only a poltroon despises pedantry", on 3 January 2010

p. 242 *Michael Gove has made a startling attempt, in advance of the centenary of the outbreak of the first world war . . .* appeared as "'Goveadder': the education secretary meets his fate in the trenches", on 12 January 2014

p. 246 *The world needs snakes more than it needs apostrophes* appeared as "Snakes are evil, but save your venom for the self-appointed language police", on 13 June 2010

p. 250 *The first printed Christmas cards . . . were the brainchild of Sir Henry Cole* appeared as "Christmas cards allow us to say much less to a greater number of people", on 12 December 2010

p. 253 *"The game's gone mad," says Richard Keys* appeared as "Andy Gray and Richard Keys have met their Waterloo. I'm glad", on 30 January 2011

p. 257 *"Do you want to tell that to Her Majesty Queen Noor?"* appeared as "Royals have the right to be picky . . . so let them eat mangoes in Berkshire", on 6 May 2012

p. 260 *There are lean times ahead for Britain's high streets* appeared as "An appetite for self-improvement is more embarrassing than overeating", on 29 April 2012

INDEX

(the initials DM refer to David Mitchell)